D0661514

Discover
London

Experience the best of London

This edition written and researched by

**Steve Fallon,
Emilie Filou, Damian Harper, Vesna Maric**

Discover London

The West End (p47)

The very heart of London, and where your London adventure will begin.

Don't Miss Westminster Abbey, British Museum, Buckingham Palace, Houses of Parliament

The City (p95)

Almost two millennia of history plus many of London's must-see sights in just one square mile.

Don't Miss Tower of London, St Paul's Cathedral

The South Bank (p119)

The roll-call of sights straddling the River Thames includes the London Eye, Shakespeare's Globe Theatre and the Millennium Bridge.

Don't Miss Tate Modern

Kensington & Hyde Park (p141)

Three world-class museums and the largest of the royal parks in a well-heeled district.

Don't Miss Victoria & Albert Museum

Clerkenwell, Hoxton & Spitalfields (p165)

Great food and an even better night out in what has rapidly become one of London's trendiest neighbourhoods.

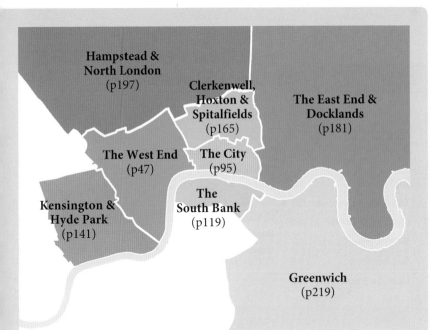

Hampstead &
North London
(p197)

Clerkenwell,
Hoxton &
Spitalfields
(p165)

The East End &
Docklands
(p181)

The West End
(p47)

The City
(p95)

Kensington &
Hyde Park
(p141)

The
South Bank
(p119)

Greenwich
(p219)

The East End & Docklands (p181)

This ethnically diverse district stood to gain the most from the Olympic Games and it certainly did.

Hampstead & North London (p197)

Wild expanses of heath, bustling markets and Camden and Islington after dark guarantee a glorious day and night out.

Don't Miss British Library

Greenwich (p219)

The home of world time is steeped in the maritime history that brought wealth and fame to London.

Don't Miss Royal Observatory & Greenwich Park

Contents

Plan Your Trip · Discover London

In Focus | Survival Guide

This Is London

What can be said about London that hasn't been said so many times before? That the weighty resonance of its name suggests history and might? That it is the premier city in Europe in terms of size, population and per-capita wealth? That its opportunities for entertainment by day and by night go on and on and on?

London is all these things and much, much more. Not only is it home to such familiar landmarks as Big Ben, St Paul's Cathedral, Tower Bridge, the London Eye and the River Thames, it also boasts some of the greatest museums and art galleries anywhere and more parkland than any other world capital. And it's an amazingly tolerant place for its size, its people pretty much unshockable. 'As long as you don't scare the horses, mate, you'll be all right,' as they say here.

The capital of Britain is very multicultural. A third of all Londoners are foreign born, representing 270 different nationalities. And most get along fairly well together. What unites them and visitors is the English language, for this is both the tongue's birthplace and its epicentre.

For many of us a visit to London is something of a homecoming. London is where Portia first told Shylock that 'The quality of mercy is not strained/It droppeth as the gentle rain from heaven' in Shakespeare's *The Merchant of Venice;* where Charles Dickens penned the poignant words 'It is a far, far better thing that I do, than I have ever done' for Sydney Carton in *A Tale of Two Cities;* where the women in TS Eliot's *The Love Song of J Alfred Prufrock* in 'the evenings, mornings, afternoons... measured out life with coffee spoons'.

London is at once a gritty and a savant city. It exhilarates and stimulates but it can irritate too; this is a city that offers different things to different people and in abundance. Breathe deeply in this world-class city and you will have ingested enough history, culture, sleaze, joys and disappointments to last half a lifetime.

> 66
>
> London is at once a gritty and a savant city
>
> 99

Changing of the Guard (p59), Buckingham Palace
PHOTOGRAPHER: MARK THOMAS/GETTY IMAGES ©

London

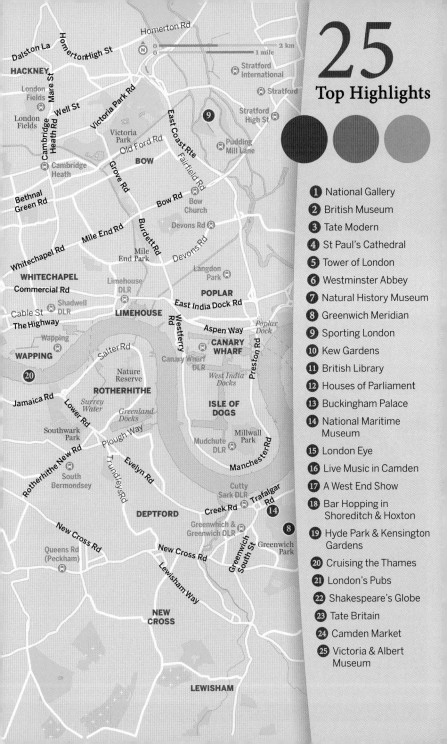

25

Top Highlights

Dalston La
Homerton Rd
Homerton High St
HACKNEY
London Fields
Mare St
Well St
London Fields
Cambridge Heath Rd
Victoria Park Rd
East Coast Rte
Stratford International
Stratford
Stratford High St
Victoria Park
Old Ford Rd
Pudding Mill Lane
Cambridge Heath
BOW
Grove Rd
Fairfield Rd
Bethnal Green Rd
Bow Rd
Bow Church
Mile End Rd
Burdett Rd
Devons Rd
Whitechapel Rd
Mile End Park
Devons Rd
Langdon Park
WHITECHAPEL
Commercial Rd
Limehouse DLR
POPLAR
East India Dock Rd
Shadwell DLR
LIMEHOUSE
Westferry Rd
Aspen Way
Poplar Dock
Cable St
The Highway
Wapping
Salter Rd
CANARY WHARF
Canary Wharf DLR
Preston Rd
WAPPING
Nature Reserve
West India Docks
ROTHERHITHE
Jamaica Rd
Lower Rd
Surrey Water
Greenland Docks
ISLE OF DOGS
Southwark Park
Plough Way
Rotherhithe New Rd
Trundleys Rd
Evelyn Rd
Mudchute DLR
Millwall Park
Manchester Rd
South Bermondsey
Cutty Sark DLR
Trafalgar Rd
New Cross Rd
DEPTFORD
Creek Rd
Greenwich & Greenwich DLR
Queens Rd (Peckham)
New Cross Rd
Greenwich South St
Greenwich Park
Lewisham Way
NEW CROSS
LEWISHAM

2 km
1 mile

1 National Gallery
2 British Museum
3 Tate Modern
4 St Paul's Cathedral
5 Tower of London
6 Westminster Abbey
7 Natural History Museum
8 Greenwich Meridian
9 Sporting London
10 Kew Gardens
11 British Library
12 Houses of Parliament
13 Buckingham Palace
14 National Maritime Museum
15 London Eye
16 Live Music in Camden
17 A West End Show
18 Bar Hopping in Shoreditch & Hoxton
19 Hyde Park & Kensington Gardens
20 Cruising the Thames
21 London's Pubs
22 Shakespeare's Globe
23 Tate Britain
24 Camden Market
25 Victoria & Albert Museum

25 London's Top Highlights

National Gallery (p71)

This superlative collection of pre-1900 art in the heart of London is one of the world's largest and a roll-call of some of the world's most outstanding artistic compositions. With highlights including works by Leonardo da Vinci, Michelangelo, Gainsborough, Constable, Turner, Monet, Renoir and Van Gogh, it's a bravura performance and one not to be missed. On-site restaurants and cafes are also quite good, rounding out a terrific experience and putting the icing on an already eye-catching cake.

1

❷ British Museum (p54)

With more than 5.5 million visitors passing through its doors annually, the British Museum in literary Bloomsbury is London's most popular tourist attraction. It's a vast and hallowed collection of artefacts, art and age-old antiquities reaching back seven millennia; you could spend a lifetime here and still make daily discoveries. Failing that, join everyone else on the highlights (or more frequent eyeOpener) tours for a precis of the museum's top treasures.

Tate Modern (p124)

An international favourite, this modern and contemporary art collection enjoys a triumphant position right on the River Thames. Housed in the former Bankside Power Station, the Tate Modern is a vigorous statement of modernity, architectural renewal and accessibility for art lovers of all denominations. The permanent collection is free, but make sure you enter down the ramp into the Turbine Hall, where the gallery's standout temporary exhibitions push the conceptual envelope and satisfy more cerebral art-hunters.

The Best...
Modern Architecture

30 ST MARY AXE
Colloquially dubbed 'the Gherkin', this is the city's most iconic modern edifice. (p109)

SHARD
A crystalline spike over London Bridge. (p133)

LLOYD'S OF LONDON
Richard Rogers' inside-out London masterpiece. (p109)

LONDON EYE
Unsurprisingly visible from many remote parts of town. (p128)

MILLENNIUM BRIDGE
At night, Norman Foster's creation becomes a 'blade of light'. (p129)

The Best...
Royal Sights

TOWER OF LONDON
Royal residence, mint, zoo, armoury, prison, medieval execution site and home to the Crown Jewels. (p101)

BUCKINGHAM PALACE
The Queen Mother of all London's royal palaces, with lovely gardens and the Changing of the Guard. (p58)

WINDSOR CASTLE
The Queen's preferred residence and where she spends most of her time is open to visitors year-round. (p240)

HAMPTON COURT PALACE
Tudor palace with beautiful grounds, on the River Thames. (p236)

KENSINGTON PALACE
Princess Diana's erstwhile home and now that of her son, William, and his family, this stately palace is the highlight of Kensington Gardens. (p155)

CULTURA TRAVEL/LAURIE CASTELLI/GETTY IMAGES ©

St Paul's Cathedral (p104)

4

Wren's 300-year-old masterpiece became a striking symbol of London's dogged resilience during the Blitz of WWII, when Firewatch volunteers fought to extinguish hundreds of incendiary devices threatening to consume it. Today, the City landmark is as rewarding inside as it is sublime on the outside. Climb the marvellous dome for superb views of London and explore the cathedral's astonishing interior and crypt.

JOHN HAY/GETTY IMAGES ©

Tower of London (p100)

5

Few parts of London are as steeped in history, or as impregnated with legend and superstition, as this fortress. The tower is not only an architectural odyssey – there's a diamond here almost as big as the Ritz, free tours run by magnificently attired 'Beefeater' guards, and a dazzling array of armour and weaponry. Get here early and count on spending at least a couple of hours (and probably more) to see it properly.

Westminster Abbey (p52)

Fans of medieval ecclesiastical architecture will be in seventh heaven at this abbey and hallowed place of coronation. Almost every nook and cranny has a story to tell, but few places are as beautiful or well preserved as the Henry VII Chapel. There's also England's oldest door, Poet's Corner, the Coronation Chair, 14th-century cloisters and the burial places of 17 monarchs.

Natural History Museum (p158)

With its thunderous animatronic Tyrannosaurus rex, towering skeleton of Diplodocus (a mascot named 'Dippy'), magical Wildlife Garden, outstanding Darwin Centre and architecture straight from a Gothic fairy tale, this museum is a work of great imagination. Kids are the target audience but, when you look around, adults are equally mesmerised. Popular sleepovers in the museum have young ones snoozing alongside the dinosaurs; summer brings a tent filled with butterflies on the east lawn, while in winter a glittering ice rink on the same spot swarms with skaters.

Greenwich Meridian (p224)

The highlight of a day out in Greenwich is a visit to the Royal Observatory. It's an oddly satisfying feeling, placing yourself on the Greenwich meridian, knowing that everyone on earth is setting their watches in relation to where you are standing. Add to that the neighbouring cluster of classical buildings and the surrounding Greenwich Park and the result is a fascinating excursion from central London.

The Best...
Art Galleries

TATE MODERN
A breathtaking collection of modern and contemporary art in a power station on the South Bank. (p124)

NATIONAL GALLERY
Stupendous collection of some 2300 pre-20th-century paintings housed in fabulous premises in the heart of London. (p71)

TATE BRITAIN
Works by JMW Turner are the standout pieces in this excellent museum of British art. (p75)

NATIONAL PORTRAIT GALLERY
Celebrated British people (often creatively captured by equally famous artists) from the past 500 years. (p69)

COURTAULD GALLERY
Home to London's largest and best collection of Impressionist art. (p78)

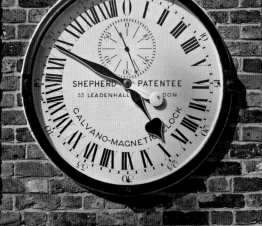

Sporting London (p187)

The eye-catching, state-of-the-art facilities in the Queen Elizabeth Olympic Park – the stunning Aquatics Centre, the cutting-edge Velodrome – encapsulate the sporting zeitgeist, but there's much more, from watching first-round matches at Wimbledon, cheering runners at the London Marathon or hopping on a Barclays bike. You may not land tickets to the FA Cup Final at Wembley Stadium or front-row seats for the men's 100m finals at Olympic Stadium, but there are plenty of ways to enjoy sport in London. London Marathon (p40)

The Best...
Restaurants

PROVIDORES & TAPA ROOM
Fusion food at its absolute best. (p85)

GORDON RAMSAY
Three Michelin stars and a celebrity chef – say no more. (p160)

NEWMAN STREET TAVERN
The ultimate London gastropub with excellent seafood and service. (p81)

TOWPATH
Seasonal Mediterranean specialities with Regent's Canal as a backdrop. (p211)

VIAJANTE
Inventive gastronomy in an unexpected East End setting (p191)

Kew Gardens (p160)

Where else in London can you size up an 18th-century 10-storey Chinese pagoda and a Japanese gateway in one of the world's most outstanding botanical collections? Kew Gardens is beloved for its 19th-century palm house, Victorian glass-houses, conservatories, tree canopy walkway, architectural follies and mind-boggling plant varieties. You'll need a day to do it justice, and you could find yourself heading back for more.

British Library (p202)

The British Library is the nation's principal copyright library: it stocks one copy of every British and Irish publica-tion. But for visitors, the highlight of a visit is the Sir John Ritblat Gallery where the library keeps its (and the British Museum's) most precious and high-profile documents. The collection spans almost three millennia of history and contains manuscripts, religious texts, maps, music scores, autographs, diaries and more.

JOHNNIE PAKINGTON/GETTY IMAGES ©

12

Houses of Parliament (p60)

There's nothing more London than the sublime view of Big Ben (now officially named Elizabeth Tower but let's not be pedantic) and the Houses of Parliament from the River Thames, especially when the sun is shining on its neo-Gothic facade. What is also called the Palace of Westminster can be explored on guided tours, but visitors can also watch debates in both the elected House of Commons and the appointed House of Lords.

13

Buckingham Palace (p58)

Paying to snoop around a section of the Queen's lodgings may seem a bit, well, intrusive but for royalists it's a superlative highlight. That the hoi polloi can breach this imperious, blue-blooded bastion is remarkable enough and there's nowhere else quite like it in town. The royal household is only open for two months (late July to late September), but get your ticket from Buckingham Palace, have it stamped, and you are allowed repeat visits.

MAX ALEXANDER/GETTY IMAGES ©

National Maritime Museum (p232)

This shipshape museum is not just a first-rate lesson in seamanship and England's rich maritime traditions, but also an occasion to come to Greenwich and soak up its riverine charms. The museum is an inspiring flick through the brine-soaked pages of English history, and kids are well catered for, with ample hands-on stuff to keep young salty sea dogs occupied.

14

The Best...
Theatre

NATIONAL THEATRE
Cutting-edge theatrical productions in a choice of three halls. (p138)

SHAKESPEARE'S GLOBE
For the authentic open-air Elizabethan effect. (p136)

ROYAL COURT THEATRE
Constantly innovative and inspirationally driven theatre in Sloane Sq. (p162)

The Best...
Views

SHARD
You aren't going to get any higher than floor 72 anywhere in London but it will cost you. (p133)

ST PAUL'S CATHEDRAL
Climb up into London's largest ecclesiastical dome for awe-inspiring views of town. (p104)

LONDON EYE
Gently rotating, tip-top views of London – but choose a fair-weather day. (p128)

DUCK & WAFFLE
This restaurant and bar on the 40th floor of Heron Tower in the City offers stunning views both day and night. (p115)

GREENWICH PARK
Clamber up to the statue of General Wolfe for superlative views over the park and centre. (p224)

London Eye (p128)

You may have eyed up London from altitude as you descended into Heathrow, but your pilot won't have lingered over the supreme views that extend in every direction from London's great riverside Ferris wheel. The queues can move as slowly as the Eye rotates (though there are ways to fast-track your way on), but that makes it even more rewarding once you've lifted off and London unfurls beneath you. If you've got only a few days in the capital, make this your first stop and you can at least say you've seen *all* the sights.

(ABOVE) EURASIA PRESS/GETTY IMAGES ©; (LEFT) STUART STEVENSON PHOTOGRAPHY/GETTY IMAGES ©

Live Music in Camden (p213)

16

London's South Bank and the West End have a monopoly on quality classical music performances, but if you want music with more bite and attitude, head for Camden. The edgy North London neighbourhood has traditionally nurtured a plethora of indie and rock bands through its grungy galaxy of clubs and live music venues. Big-ticket names also play here so whatever your taste, you should find a band to fit your musical persuasion.

Savages perform at the Electric Ballroom

A West End Show (p88)

17

A trip to London is incomplete without seeing a West End show. Whether it's world-class drama or smash-hit musicals, you'll find it in this glitzy theatreland. There's always something new drawing accolades from critics and an enthusiastic public alike, alongside the filler of long-run hits. Watch Hollywood stars keep it real, or discover something more experimental on the fringe in the world's most famous concentration of theatres.

Bar Hopping in Shoreditch & Hoxton (p176)

Thread your way from bar to bar through hip Shoreditch for a taste of the neighbourhood's trendy watering holes. Many also serve pretty decent food, so you can build an entire night's entertainment in boozers without breaking stride to find a restaurant. Many bars only shut up in the early hours at weekends, while a bevy of cutting-edge clubs adds to the late-night buzz. Cargo (p177) in Shoreditch

The Best...
Live Music

PROUD CAMDEN
Leading North London bar with foot-stomping live music and a superb terrace. (p217)

ROYAL ALBERT HALL
The UK's most iconic concert venue for both pop and classical music and home to the Proms. (p161)

606 CLUB
Get into the subterranean swing of things at this atmospheric, world-famous jazz club. (p162)

ROYAL FESTIVAL HALL
Smashing acoustics and an excellent program of music across the aural spectrum. (p139)

Hyde Park (p151) & Kensington Gardens (p154)

19

London's urban parkland is *the* place to see locals at ease and in their element. Hyde Park alone ranges across a mighty 142 hectares; throw in Kensington Gardens at 111 hectares and you have even more room to roam and everything you could want: a central London setting, a royal palace, extravagant Victorian monuments, boating, open-air concerts, an art gallery, magnificent trees, and a tasteful memorial fountain to the late Princess Diana. Hyde Park (p151)

The Best...
Parks & Gardens

ST JAMES'S PARK
Feast on sublime views in London's smallest but most attractive royal park. (p63)

VICTORIA PARK
The East End's bucolic playground is a riot of colour in every sense, recently restored and tidied up. (p187)

HAMPSTEAD HEATH
Woods, hills, meadows and top scenic views, all rolled into one sublime sprawl. (p208)

HYDE PARK
Grand gardens, lovely lawns, a head-turning number and variety of trees and inviting expanses of greenery. (p151)

KEW GARDENS
A botanist's paradise, huge gardens and a great day out with the kids. (p160)

26

(20) Cruising the Thames (p286)

Cleaving the British capital into north and south and pumping through a riveting panorama of both urban and bucolic backdrops, London's 215-mile-long tidal river begs for your attention. For such a great maritime city, it's no surprise that many of London's most iconic sights lie dotted along the riverbank. A cruise along the River Thames is a chance to see the city's riverine magnificence unfold before you at a relaxed pace.

IMAGE SOURCE/GETTY IMAGES ©

 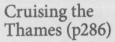

London's Pubs (p116)

London without pubs would be like Paris *sans* cafes or New York shorn of its bars. Pub culture is part of London's DNA, and pubs are the place to be if you want to see locals in their hops-infused element. Longer hours have only cemented the pub's reputation as the cornerstone for a great night out. Mix your ale-drinking with history in one of London's older pubs, starting with magnificent Ye Olde Cheshire Cheese (p117).

Shakespeare's Globe (p136)

Few London experiences can beat a Bard's-eye view of the stage. It's even fun to get a ticket to stand (Elizabethan style) as one of the all-weather 'groundlings' in the open-air yard in front of the stage, taking whatever the London skies deliver. But if you want a comfortable perspective on Shakespeare, pay a bit extra and get one of the seats in the galleries. If you've a soft spot for Shakespeare, architecture and the English climate, you'll have an absolute ball.

Tate Britain (p75)

Founded in 1897, the venerable Tate Britain contains a definitive collection of British art from the 16th to the late 20th centuries. The star of the show at Tate Britain is JMW Turner, with some 300 of his oil paintings and 30,000 sketches and drawings bequeathed to the nation. There are also seminal works by such artists as Constable, Gainsborough and Reynolds, as well as more modern artists like Lucian Freud, Francis Bacon and Tracey Emin.

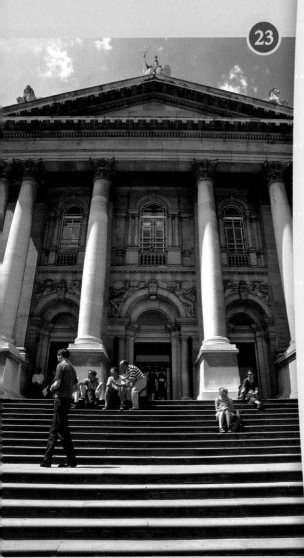

23

The Best...
Historic Pubs

JERUSALEM TAVERN
Tiny but delightful, with original beers from a Norfolk brewery. (p176)

PRINCESS LOUISE
Beautifully decorated and perfect for settling in all evening. (p88)

LAMB & FLAG
Just about everyone's West End favourite and tiny so expect a scrum. (p87)

EDINBORO CASTLE
Boasting a huge beer garden in Primrose Hill, this is the perfect place for long summer evenings. (p214)

GOLDEN HEART
A great local pub where you can mix with both hipsters and drinkers. (p178)

Camden Market (p208)

A foray into trendy North London is a crucial part of the London experience. Camden's market – actually four markets in one great mix – may be a hectic and tourist-oriented attraction, but snacking on the go from the international food stalls is a great way to enjoy browsing the merchandise. Camden's dining scene, throbbing nightlife and well-seasoned pub culture is well known to night owls citywide.

The Best...
Shops

LONDON SILVER VAULTS
The world's largest collection of silver – from cutlery to jewellery – and all for sale. (p117)

HARRODS
Garish, stylish, kitschy yet perennially popular department store. (p163)

JOHN SANDOE BOOKS
A treasure trove of literary gems and excellent staff recommendations. (p163)

SISTER RAY
A top independent music shop that has an everchanging collection of vinyl and CDs. (p92)

STANFORD'S
The place to go for all you travel needs – from guidebooks and maps to travel literature and phrase books. (p93)

24

25

Victoria & Albert Museum (p146)

You could spend your entire trip in this museum alone and still be astonished by its variety and depth. The world's leading collection of decorative arts has something for everyone, from imposing 19th-century architecture to antique Chinese ceramics, Islamic textiles, a beautiful collection of jewellery and such modern design classics as the revolutionary Sony Walkman.

Top Days in
London

The West End & the South Bank

On your first day plunge into the heart of the West End for some of London's top sights. This itinerary also spans the River Thames to the South Bank, taking in Westminster Abbey, Buckingham Palace, Trafalgar Square, the Houses of Parliament and the London Eye.

DAY 1

1 Westminster Abbey (p52)

Begin at Westminster Abbey to steep yourself in British history back to 1066.

WESTMINSTER ABBEY ➊ BUCKINGHAM PALACE

🏃 Cross the road to Storey's Gate and walk west along Birdcage Walk.

2 Buckingham Palace (p58)

Peer through the gates, go on a tour of the interior (summer only) or catch the Changing of the Guard at 11.15am.

BUCKINGHAM PALACE ➊ INN THE PARK

🏃 Stroll through lovely St James's Park to the northeast corner.

3 Lunch at Inn the Park (p83)

Set on the lake in St James's Park; a particularly fine place in the warmer months.

INN THE PARK ➊ TRAFALGAR SQUARE

🏃 Walk past the ICA and under Admiralty Arch to Trafalgar Square.

4 Trafalgar Square (p67)

Visit London's epicentre (all distances measured from here), and explore the National Gallery (p71).

TRAFALGAR SQUARE ➊ HOUSES OF PARLIAMENT

🏃 Walk down Whitehall.

5 Houses of Parliament (p60)

Dominating the east side of Parliament Sq is the Palace of Westminster, with Big Ben.

HOUSES OF PARLIAMENT ➊ LONDON EYE

🏃 Cross Westminster Bridge.

6 London Eye (p128)

Hop on a 'flight' on the London Eye. Pre-book tickets online or grab a fast-track ticket to shorten wait times.

LONDON EYE ➊ SKYLON

🏃 Walk 100m north to the Royal Festival Hall.

7 Dinner at Skylon (p135)

Just steps away atop the Royal Festival Hall is this fine restaurant, grill and bar. To tie up the day, consider a concert in one of the hall's three venues or a play at the National Theatre (p138) next door.

Trafalgar Square (p67), National Gallery (p71) and
St Martin-in-the-Fields church (p70)

Ancient Heritage to Funky Art

Your second day has more top sights in store – once again on either side of the Thames. You'll visit the British Museum in Bloomsbury, climb the dome of St Paul's Cathedral, explore the Tower of London and admire contemporary art at the Tate Modern.

① British Museum (p54)

Begin with a visit to the British Museum and ensure you tick off the highlights, including the Rosetta Stone, the Egyptian mummies and the Parthenon Marbles.

BRITISH MUSEUM ➲ ST PAUL'S CATHEDRAL
Take the Central Line from Holborn or Tottenham Court Rd to St Paul's.

② Lunch at St Paul's Cathedral (p116)

Enjoy lunch at the Restaurant at St Paul's before exploring the cathedral above. Don't miss climbing the dome for its astounding views of London, but save plenty of time for visiting the fascinating crypt.

ST PAUL'S CATHEDRAL ➲ TOWER OF LONDON
Hop on bus 15 from St Paul's Cathedral to the Tower of London.

③ Tower of London (p100)

The millennium of history contained within the Tower of London, including the Crown Jewels, Traitors' Gate, the White Tower and its armour collection and the all-important resident ravens, deserves at least a couple of hours to fully explore.

TOWER OF LONDON ➲ TOWER BRIDGE
Walk along Tower Bridge Approach from the Tower of London to Tower Bridge.

④ Tower Bridge (p106)

Cross the Thames via elegant Tower Bridge, popping into the exhibition en route. Check the Tower Bridge website for the bridge lift times if you want to see it open and close.

TOWER BRIDGE ➲ SHAKESPEARE'S GLOBE
Walk west along the river or hop on bus RV1 from the Tower Bridge/City Hall stop to the stop on Southwark Bridge Rd.

⑤ Shakespeare's Globe (p136)

Admire the Globe theatre from the outside or pop in to join a tour of this fascinatingly replica of an Elizabethan playhouse. If you're visiting from April to October, try to attend a matinee or evening performance at the Globe; the new indoor Sam Wanamaker Playhouse is open year-round.

SHAKESPEARE'S GLOBE ➲ OXO TOWER RESTAURANT & BRASSERIE
Keep walking west; about 500m past the Tate Modern you'll find Oxo Tower.

⑥ Dinner at the Oxo Tower Restaurant & Brasserie (p135)

Stop for an evening meal at this restaurant on the 8th floor of London's most iconic tower, which rewards you with excellent food and jaw-dropping views.

OXO TOWER RESTAURANT & BRASSERIE ➲ TATE MODERN
Backtrack 500m to the Tate Modern.

⑦ Tate Modern (p124)

Round out the day at this one-time power station, now a powerhouse to modern and contemporary art. It's open late on Fridays and Saturdays (on other days, you'll have to pop in before dinner). Make sure you experience the Turbine Hall for the latest art installations and avail yourself of the panoramic views from the Tate Modern Restaurant on Level 6.

Millennium Bridge (p129) and Tate Modern (p124)
PHOTOGRAPHER: ALAN COPSON/GETTY IMAGES ©

Kensington Museums, Knightsbridge Shopping & the West End

Passing through some of London's most attractive and well-heeled neighbour-hoods, this route takes in three of the city's best museums and a world-famous department store before delivering you to the bright lights of the West End.

DAY
3

① Kensington (p150)

Start your day in South Kensington, home to several of the best museums in the city: the Victoria & Albert Museum (p146), the Natural History Museum (p158) and the Science Museum (p150).

SOUTH KENSINGTON ➡ KENSINGTON GARDENS & HYDE PARK

🏃 Walk north along Exhibition Rd to Kensington Gardens.

② Kensington Gardens & Hyde Park (p151)

Follow the museums with an exploration of Kensington Gardens (p154) and Hyde Park (p151). Make sure you take a look at the Albert Memorial (p155) and the Royal Albert Hall (p155), take a peek inside Kensington Palace (p155) and stroll along the Serpentine (p154).

KENSINGTON GARDENS & HYDE PARK ➡ ZUMA

🏃 Stroll through Hyde Park to Zuma, tucked away in Raphael St between Knightsbridge and Brompton Rd.

③ Lunch at Zuma (p159)

Dine on tremendous Japanese food in attractive and stylish surrounds at this signature Knightsbridge restaurant. With more than 40 types of sake at the bar, drinkers will find themselves in capable hands.

ZUMA ➡ HARRODS

🏃 Cross Brompton Rd to reach Harrods.

④ Harrods (p163)

A visit to Harrods is both fun and fascinating, even if you don't plan to buy anything.

Pop into chic Harvey Nichols (p163) for some more glamorous displays and window-shop your way down exclusive Sloane St.

KNIGHTSBRIDGE ➡ PICCADILLY CIRCUS

🚇 Take the Piccadilly Line three stops from Knightsbridge station to Piccadilly Circus.

⑤ Piccadilly Circus (p67)

Jump off the tube at this busy roundabout to have a look at the famous Eros statue and then wander around bohemian Soho (p66) and aromatic Chinatown (p67).

PICCADILLY CIRCUS ➡ BAR SHU

🏃 Walk up Shaftesbury Ave and turn right onto Frith St and Bar Shu.

⑥ Dinner at Bar Shu (p83)

For the most authentic Szechuan food in town, head for Bar Shu, where the decor is stylish and the spicy portions substantial.

BAR SHU ➡ OPIUM

🏃 Cross Shaftesbury Ave to Gerrard Pl and turn left into Gerrard St. Look for the jade-coloured door just west of Macclesfield St.

⑦ Drinks at Opium (p86)

Ease further into the evening with drinks at this super-stylish Chinatown speakeasy with a stunning cocktail menu.

Natural History Museum (p158)

Greenwich to Camden

You don't want to neglect sights farther afield, and this itinerary makes a big dent in what's on offer. Lovely Greenwich has a whole raft of stately sights; then you'll explore ancient churches, the East End, trendy Shoreditch, and Camden to develop a feel for Londoners' London.

① Greenwich (p219)

Start the day in riverside Greenwich and make sure you visit Greenwich Park and the Royal Observatory (p224), checking out the National Maritime Museum (p232), delightful Queen's House and the renovated Cutty Sark (p226) clipper ship. Greenwich Market always turns up surprises.

GREENWICH ➲ THE CITY
🚎 Take the DLR from Cutty Sark station to Bank.

② The City (p95)

The area of the City not far from Bank station contains a host of historic churches built by Christopher Wren, including St Stephen Walbrook (p111) and St Mary-le-Bow (p111). Afterwards, walk to the Monument (p107) for excellent views of the City.

MONUMENT ➲ TAYYABS
Ⓔ Take the District Line from Monument station to Whitechapel station then walk west along Whitechapel Rd to Tayyabs on Fieldgate St.

③ Lunch at Tayyabs (p190)

Dip into the multicultural East End with lunch at this classic Punjabi restaurant. After your meal, wander around Whitechapel, soaking up its atmosphere and visiting the local sights including the Whitechapel Gallery (p186) and the Whitechapel Bell Foundry (p186).

TAYYABS ➲ SPITALFIELDS
🏃 Walk north from Whitechapel Rd up Osborn St and Brick Lane to Spitalfields.

④ Explore Spitalfields (p171)

Wander along Brick Lane (p174) and explore absorbing Georgian Spitalfields before browsing through Spitalfields Market (p179). The best days for the market are Thursday, Friday and Sunday.

SPITALFIELDS ➲ SHOREDITCH
🏃 Walk from Spitalfields Market along Commercial St and cross over to Great Eastern St.

⑤ Have a drink in Shoreditch (p176)

Sample the edgy, creative and offbeat Shoreditch/Hoxton atmosphere by dropping in on a local bar. Check out Book Club (p176), a standout bar in an old Victorian warehouse, or the Queen of Hoxton (p177).

SHOREDITCH ➲ CAMDEN
Ⓔ Jump on a Northern Line tube from Old St station to Camden Town.

⑥ Dinner in Camden (p209)

Conclude the day in North London by browsing the stalls of Camden Market (p208) – if still open – and dining at the excellent Market (p209) before turning to the riveting choice of local bars, pubs and live music venues in this invigorating neighbourhood.

Camden Lock Market (p208)
PHOTOGRAPHER: LATITUDESTOCK/GETTY IMAGES ©

Month by Month

January

🎇 New Year's Celebration

On 31 December, the famous countdown to midnight to Big Ben is met with terrific fireworks from the London Eye and massive crowds in Trafalgar Sq.

👁 London Art Fair

Over 100 major galleries participate in this contemporary art fair (www.londonartfair.co.uk), now one of the largest in Europe, with thematic exhibitions, special events and the best emerging artists.

February

🎇 Chinese New Year

In late January or early February, Chinatown fizzes, crackles and pops in this colourful street festival, which includes the *sine qua non* lion dance.

March

🏃 Head of the River Race

Some 400 crews take part in this colourful annual boat race (www.horr.co.uk) held over a 7km course on the Thames, from Mortlake to Putney.

🎇 St Patrick's Day Parade & Festival

Top Irish festival in London, held on the Sunday closest to 17 March, with a spectacular parade through central London and festivities in Trafalgar Sq.

April

🏃 London Marathon

Some 35,000 runners – most doing it for charity – pound through London in one of the world's biggest road races (www.virginmoneylondonmarathon.com), heading from Greenwich Park to the Mall.

🏃 Oxford & Cambridge Boat Race

Crowds line the banks of the Thames for the UK's two most famous universities going oar-to-oar from Putney to Mortlake; check the website (www.theboatrace.org) for exact date.

May

👁 Chelsea Flower Show

The world's most renowned horticultural event (www.rhs.org.uk/chelsea) attracts the cream of London's green-fingered and flower-mad gardeners.

June

👁 Royal Academy Summer Exhibition

From June through August, this exhibition (www.royalacademy.org.uk/exhibitions/summer) showcases works submitted by artists from all over Britain.

✪ Trooping the Colour

The Queen's official birthday is celebrated with much flag-waving, parades, pageantry and noisy flyover (www.trooping-the-colour.co.uk).

✪ Wimbledon Lawn Tennis Championships

For two weeks each year this quiet South London village falls under a sporting spotlight as the world's best tennis players gather to battle for the championships.

July

✪ Pride London

The gay and lesbian community paints the town pink in this annual extravaganza, featuring a morning parade and a huge afternoon event on Trafalgar Sq (check website as locations can change).

✪ BBC Promenade Concert (Proms)

Starting in mid-July and ending in early September, the Proms offer two months of outstanding classical concerts (www.bbc.co.uk/proms) at the Royal Albert Hall.

✪ Lovebox

This now huge three-day music extravaganza in Victoria Park is mainly about dance music, but there are plenty of other genres too.

August

✪ Notting Hill Carnival

Europe's biggest – and London's most vibrant – outdoor carnival (p162) is a two-day celebration of Caribbean London, with music, dancing and extravagant costumes.

September

✪ The Mayor's Thames Festival

Celebrating the River Thames, this cosmopolitan festival (www.thamesfestival.org) features fairs, street theatre, music, food stalls, fireworks and river races culminating in the superb Night Procession.

◉ London Open House

During the third weekend in September the public is invited in to see over 800 heritage buildings throughout the capital that are normally off-limits (www.londonopenhouse.org).

October

✪ London Film Festival

The city's premier film event (www.bfi.org.uk/lff) attracts big overseas names and you can catch over 100 British and international films before their cinema release. Masterclasses are given by world-famous directors.

November

✪ Guy Fawkes Night (Bonfire Night)

Bonfire Night recalls Guy Fawkes' foiled attempt to blow up Parliament in 1605, with bonfires and fireworks lighting up the night across London on 5 November.

✪ Lord Mayor's Show

The newly elected Lord Mayor of the City of London travels in a state coach from Mansion House to the Royal Courts of Justice to take an oath of allegiance to the Crown amidst colourful floats, bands and fireworks (www.lordmayorsshow.org).

December

◉ Lighting of the Christmas Lights & Tree

A celebrity is normally brought in to switch on all the festive lights that line Oxford, Regent and Bond streets, and a towering Norwegian spruce is set up in Trafalgar Sq.

What's New

For this new edition of Discover London, our authors hunted down the fresh, the transformed, the hot and the happening. Here are a few of our favourites. For up-to-the-minute recommendations, see lonelyplanet.com/London.

1 VIEW FROM THE SHARD
London's latest statement skyscraper, the spinter of glass that is the Shard, pierces the sky from the south bank of the river. Head up top for sweeping panoramas. (p133)

2 CUTTY SARK RELAUNCHED
It was six years in the remaking, but the refurbishment of this legendary clipper ship was worth it: the Cutty Sark is now one of Greenwich's top sights. (p226)

3 COCKTAIL CRAZE
Londoners have always loved their cocktails, but they keep upping the ante with ever-fancier bars and concoctions: it's all about rare spirits, flower infusions and exotic fruit syrups. (p177)

4 CHARLES DICKENS AT HOME
After a £3.5 million renovation, the only surviving London residence of the great 19th-century novelist is bigger and better than ever and now open to the public as the Charles Dickens Museum. (p63)

5 ALL CHANGE AT THE BBC
The BBC moved from its old home in Bush House in Aldwych to the equally historic but recently refurbished and extended Broadcasting House in 2012. (p63)

6 HIGH-FLYING CABLE CAR
Forget about bridges, boats or tunnels, the newest and coolest way to cross the Thames is by Emirates Air Line, a cable car between the O2 on the Greenwich Peninsula and the Excel Centre in East London's Docklands. (p226)

7 THEATRICAL TOURS OF BENJAMIN FRANKLIN HOUSE
The American statesman spent 17 years in London trying to broker peace with Britain in the late 18th century. Visit the modest Benjamin Franklin House where the 'First American' spent his London years. (p70)

Get Inspired

Books

Oliver Twist (Charles Dickens) Dickens' classic and melodramatic tale of grinding Victorian London poverty is filled with vivid social detail.

Sour Sweet (Timothy Mo) Vivid, moving and sometimes humorous portrayal of a Hong Kong Chinese family moving to London in the 1960s.

London Fields (Martin Amis) A dark and gripping tale of London lowlife in the 1980s; one of the first great postmodernist novels.

White Teeth (Zadie Smith) Poignant and big-hearted look at friendship and cultural differences through the eyes of three unassimilated North London families.

 Films

The King's Speech A verbally challenged Colin Firth playing George VI sets about conquering his demons (partly filmed in London).

Notting Hill Soppy rom-com with Hugh Grant and Julia Roberts in a not-so-typical Notting Hill but still much fun.

Bridget Jones's Diary Everyone's favourite chick flick, set in and around London's South Bank.

 Music

Abbey Road (The Beatles) The ultimate London album.

Animals (Pink Floyd) 1970s psychedelic group's concept album with iconic Battersea Power Station and a flying pig on the cover.

London Calling (The Clash) A 1979 call to arms by the legendary London band.

Alright, Still (Lily Allen) This upbeat debut album of London life became an instant classic.

Websites

Transport for London (www.tfl.gov.uk) Check the best routes and journey times and keep up to date with frequent engineering works at weekends.

Visit London (www. visitlondon.com) London's official tourism website is packed with useful information.

Time Out (www. timeout.com/london) What's on at everything from galleries to clubs from London's weekly online freebie.

Short on time?

This list will give you an instant insight into the city.

Read *London: The Biography* (Peter Ackroyd), a colourful, thematically arranged history of the city, is a modern classic.

Watch The offbeat classic comedy *Withnail and I* is set partly in Camden in the closing years of the 1960s.

Listen *Waterloo Sunset* (The Kinks) Unimpeachable classic from the 1960s.

Log On All the latest London news, gossip and listings can be found on the daily *Evening Standard* newspaper's website (www. thisislondon.co.uk).

Abbey Road road sign covered in graffiti by Beatles fans
PHOTOGRAPHER: DOUG ARMAND/GETTY IMAGES ©

Need to Know

●●●

Currency
Pound sterling (£)

Language
English

Visas
Not required for US, Canadian, Australian, New Zealand or South African visitors for stays of up to six months.

Money
ATMs widespread. Major credit cards accepted everywhere.

Mobile Phones
Buy local SIM cards for European and Australian phones or a pay-as-you-go phone. Set other phones to international roaming.

Time
London is on GMT.

Wi-Fi
In most hotels and cafes.

Tipping
In restaurants 12.5% is standard and often included in the bill.

For more information, see Survival Guide (p282).

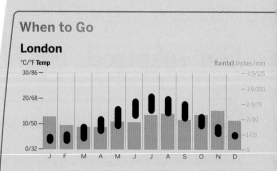

When to Go

London

Summer is peak season: days are long, festivals are afoot, but it's busy and crowded and the queues can be endless.

Spring and autumn are cooler and often wet, but delightful.

Winter is cold but quiet, with the possibility of snow.

Advance Planning

Three months Book weekend performance of top shows; dinner at renowned restaurants; tickets for must-see exhibitions; a room at a popular or boutique hotel.

One month Check listings on entertainment sites such as www.timeout.com for fringe theatre, live music, festivals and then book your tickets.

A few days Check the weather on www.tfl.gov.uk/weather.

Daily Costs

Budget under £80
- Dorm bed: £10–£30
- Market-stall lunch: £5, supermarket sandwich: £3–£4
- Many museums: free
- Standby theatre tickets: £5–£15
- Barclays bike daily charge: £2

Midrange £80–£180
- Double room: £100–£150
- Two-course dinner with glass of wine: £30
- Theatre ticket: £10–£50

Top End over £180
- Four-star/boutique hotel room: £200
- Three-course dinner in top restaurant with wine: £60–£90
- Black cab trip: £30
- Top theatre ticket: £65

Arriving in London

Heathrow Airport Trains, London Underground (tube) and buses to central London from 5.25am to midnight (night buses run later) £5–£20; taxi £45–£65.

Gatwick Airport Trains to central London from 4.30am to 1.35am £8–£20; hourly buses to central London from 6am to 9.45pm £7–£10; taxi £90.

Stansted Airport Trains to central London from 5.30am to around midnight £23.40; round-the-clock buses to central London £8–£10; taxi £90.

Luton Airport Trains to central London from 7am to 10pm £15; round-the-clock buses to central London £10–£15; taxi £75.

London City Airport Trains to central London from 5.30am to 12.30am Monday to Saturday, 7am to 11.30pm Sunday £2.10–£4.50; taxi £30.

St Pancras International Train Station In central London (for Eurostar train arrivals from Europe) and connected by many underground lines to other parts of the city.

Getting Around

Prepaid Oyster cards can be used across London's transport network, offering the cheapest fares. Buy one (and top up) at most tube stations, most train stations and many newsagents.

o **Underground (tube)** The quickest way to get around; trains run 5.30am to 12.30am (7am to 11.30pm Sunday).

o **Bus** Slow going but great views from double-deckers; large number of night and 24-hour buses.

o **Train** Mostly useful for outlying areas such as Hampton Court and day trips.

o **Bicycle** The Barclays Cycle Hire Scheme is excellent value, and free for short hops.

o **Taxi** Black cabs can be hailed on the street when the yellow light is lit.

o **Boat** A number of companies operate along the River Thames but only Thames Clippers really offers commuter services.

o **Walking** A lot of central sightseeing is best done on foot.

o **Car hire** It's generally better to use a combination of the walking, bike and public transport; if you drive, beware the congestion charge.

Sleeping

Hanging your hat in London can be expensive and as the city is busy at the best of times, you'll need to book your room well in advance to secure your top choice.

Decent, centrally located hostels are easy enough to find and offer reasonably priced double rooms. Bed and breakfasts are a dependable and inexpensive, if rather simple, option. Hotels range from cheap, no-frills chains to boutique choices to luxury five-star historic hotels.

Useful Websites

o **Lonely Planet** (www.lonelyplanet.com/london) Hundreds of properties from budget hostels to luxury apartments.

o **London Town** (www.londontown.com) Excellent last-minute offers on boutique hotels and B&Bs.

o **Alastair Sawdays** (www.sawdays.com) Hand-picked selection of abodes in the capital.

o **Visit London** (www.visitlondon.com) Huge range of listings from the city's official tourism portal.

What to Bring

o **Rain jacket** The rumours about the weather are mostly true.

o **Comfortable shoes** Cushion those endless strolls.

o **Small day-pack** For stowing that rain jacket when the sun does shine.

Be Forewarned

London is a safe city in general, but employ common sense.

o **Cabs** After a night's clubbing, ensure you go for a black cab or a licensed minicab.

o **Areas to avoid** Avoid wandering alone at night in certain areas of King's Cross, Dalston and Peckham, though sticking to the main roads offers a degree of safety.

o **Pickpocketing** Keep an eye on your handbag, especially in bars, nightclubs and outdoor cafes, and in crowded areas such as the Underground.

The West End

This exciting and chaotic place is undoubtedly where your London adventure will begin.

It's London's shopping, eating and entertainment heart and consists of Soho, Chinatown and Covent Garden, stretching out in a rough rectangle between Oxford Circus, Piccadilly Circus, Aldwych and Holborn. This is the best place for an introduction to fast-paced London life, and you will find glitz, glamour and crowds of shoppers any day of the year.

There is no better way to appreciate the energy of the West End than by walking around and taking it all in. Atmospheric places for a breather include Covent Garden, Trafalgar Sq and St James's Park.

World-famous West End theatres dominate the main avenues, while in the back streets cocktail bars, cutting-edge fashion stores and superb restaurants can be found almost anywhere you go, bar Westminster and Whitehall.

Carnaby Street
SYLVAIN SONNET/GETTY IMAGES ©

West End Highlights

Houses of Parliament (p60)

The Gothic splendour of the Houses of Parliament, overlooking the Thames with impressive Big Ben towering above, is one of London's most unforgettable sights. Not many visitors to London actually go inside, but few countries allow such unrestricted access to their parliament. It's a unique experience to be able to watch Members of Parliament debate the latest bills.

British Museum (p54)

The British Museum is one of London's great wonders and holds a most impressive collection spanning seven millennia. It's truly a museum of the world, and in the space of a day you can explore the history and culture of all the world's great civilisations. The museum is free, so you can line up a string of visits if you find yourself overwhelmed.

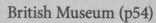

Covent Garden (p67)

Lovely but packed in fine weather, Covent Garden is great for fine architecture, street performers, shopping at Covent Garden Market, a glut of fine restaurants, pubs and bars, and a host of important sights and entertainment venues, including the London Transport Museum and the Royal Opera House.

3

4

5

Westminster Abbey (p52)

Majestic Westminster Abbey has witnessed more historical events than most major cities. Indeed, this was where William the Conqueror was crowned in 1066 after the Battle of Hastings, and it has been the place of coronation of every monarch but two since then. It is also the final resting place of 17 monarchs as well as that of such luminaries as Chaucer, Dickens and Laurence Olivier.

Trafalgar Square & the National Gallery (p67)

Once encircled with snarling traffic and swarming with flocks of feral pigeons, Trafalgar Sq today is quite a magnificent plaza, and is a great place to take in London and the views down Whitehall. Immediately north of the square is the standout National Gallery with its jaw-dropping collection of masterful art.

West End Walk

This walk starts from the tourist mecca of Covent Garden, snakes through colourful Chinatown and bohemian Soho and ends at glorious Trafalgar Sq. There are plenty of places to stop for a drink and soak up the heart of London.

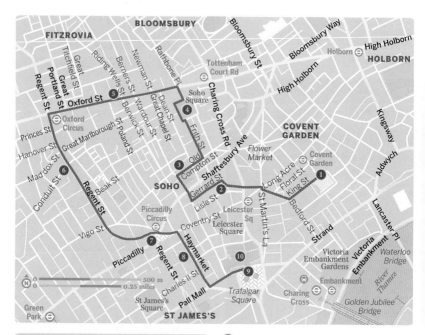

WALK FACTS

- **Start** Covent Garden Piazza
- **Finish** National Gallery
- **Distance** 2.5 miles
- **Duration** One hour and a half hours

1 Covent Garden Piazza

Touristy perhaps, but it's worth seeing this piazza (p69), designed by Inigo Jones, and the street performers doing their thing in front of St Paul's Church, the modern-day descendants of street performers who put on the first ever Punch and Judy show here in 1662.

2 Chinatown

Avoid Leicester Sq and pop down Gerrard St under the Chinese *paifang* (memorial gateway) of Chinatown (p67). Take in the exotic fruits and vegetables for sale, and stop for Chinese food at one of the many restaurants.

3 Soho

Wander across Shaftesbury Ave, the main street of London's 'theatreland' and home to some of the West End's most prestigious theatres. Continue up Wardour St, turning right onto Old Compton St, London's gayest thoroughfare and the main street of Soho (p66).

4 Soho Square

Take Frith St, past Mozart's erstwhile home at No 20, and emerge into the open space of Soho Sq (p67), the perfectly formed park at the heart of the West End.

5 Oxford Street

Head into **Oxford St**, past many of London's premier shops and department stores including **John Lewis** and Selfridges (p93).

6 Regent Street

At Oxford Circus, turn left into Regent St, the centrepiece of John Nash's design for Regency London. You'll pass world-famous toyshop Hamleys (p91) and one of London's smartest department stores, Liberty (p92), both on the left as you walk south.

7 Piccadilly Circus

Piccadilly Circus (p67) is like New York's Times Sq, full of flashing ads, shops and tourists. Don't miss the famous statue, incorrectly (but affectionately) known as Eros (p67).

8 Haymarket

Escape the chaos of Piccadilly Circus by plunging down grand Haymarket. On the way take note of terribly chic **Jermyn St**, noted for its gentlemen's clothing and accessories shops. From Haymarket turn left onto Pall Mall.

9 Trafalgar Square

Tourist magnet Trafalgar Sq (p67) is a beauty of a square. Check out the views of Big Ben from its southern side, and don't miss the so-called fourth plinth (p70).

10 National Gallery

Take a few hours to admire the artwork at the National Gallery (p71). Then sit down for a well-deserved lunch or dinner in the stylish National Dining Rooms, where you can enjoy British cuisine in its finest form.

✦ The Best...

PLACES TO EAT

Providores & Tapa Room Fusion food at its absolute best. (p85)

Yauatcha Top-drawer dim sum in a contemporary environment. (p83)

Green Man & French Horn First-rate French flavours in an intimate bistro. (p84)

Newman Street Tavern The ultimate London gastropub with excellent seafood. (p81)

PLACES TO DRINK

Opium Inventive cocktail creations in a Chinatown speakeasy. (p86)

Lamb & Flag Everyone's favourite historic pub in the heart of the West End. (p87)

Gordon's Wine Bar Superbly atmospheric wine bar with historic charms. (p87)

FREE SIGHTS

British Museum Supreme collection of international artefacts and an inspiring testament to human creativity. (p54)

National Gallery Tremendous gathering of largely pre-modern masters, with free entry for all. (p71)

Houses of Parliament When parliament is in session, it's free to watch UK democracy in action. (p60)

Piccadilly Circus (p67)
SYLVAIN SONNET/GETTY IMAGES ©

Don't Miss
Westminster Abbey

Westminster Abbey is such an important com-
memoration site for both the British royalty and
the nation's political and artistic idols that it's dif-
ficult to overstress its symbolic value or imagine
its equivalent anywhere else in the world. With
the exception of Edward V and Edward VIII, every
English sovereign has been crowned here since
William the Conqueror in 1066, and most of the
monarchs from Henry III (died 1272) to George II
(died 1760) are buried here too.

Map p68

☎ 020-7222 5152

www.westminster-
abbey.org

20 Dean's Yard,
SW1

adult/child £18/8,
verger tours £3

⏱ 9.30am-4.30pm
Mon, Tue, Thu &
Fri, to 7pm Wed, to
2.30pm Sat

Ⓔ Westminster

Sanctuary & Quire

The heart and soul of the Abbey, **sanctuary** is where coronations, royal weddings and funerals take place. The flooring is the celebrated 13th-century **Cosmati Pavement**. The **quire** (choir), a sublime structure of gold, blue and red Victorian Gothic, dates to the mid-19th century.

Shrines & Chapels

The sacred **Shrine of St Edward the Confessor** lies behind the high altar; access is generally restricted to one daily visit to protect the 13th-century floor. St Edward was the founder of the Abbey and the original building was consecrated a few weeks before his death.

Henry VII's Lady Chapel is the most spectacular with its circular vaulting on the ceiling, colourful banners and dramatic oak stalls. Behind the altar is the elaborate sarcophagus of Henry VII and his queen. Several monarchs, including Henry VIII's only son, Edward VI, are buried in the crypt below.

Coronation Chair & Tomb of the Unknown Warrior

Opposite the entrance to the Lady Chapel is the rather ordinary-looking **Coronation Chair**, upon which almost every monarch since the early 14th century is said to have been crowned. Nearby is the **Tomb of the Unknown Warrior** from WWI, the nation's most sacred war memorial.

Poet's Corner

The south transept contains **Poets' Corner**, where many of England's finest writers – from Chaucer to former poet laureate Ted Hughes – are buried or commemorated.

Chapter House

The oldest part of the cloister is the East Cloister (or East Walk), dating to the 13th century. The octagonal **Chapter House** has one of Europe's best-preserved medieval tile floors and retains traces of religious murals on the walls.

1 **LADY CHAPEL & ST EDWARD'S CHAPEL**
My favourite part of Westminster Abbey church has to be the Lady Chapel with its absolutely exquisite architecture. Next for me in importance, however, is the Shrine of St Edward the Confessor and the great kings and queens buried around it.

2 **OUR LADY OF PEW**
Our Lady of Pew is a quite unique shrine – fully restored with much of its 14th-century paintwork still in place. As I am Warden of the Society of Our Lady of Pew, the shrine is of particular importance to me.

3 **OTHER CHAPELS**
Of the other chapels, Islip Chapel is special to me for its sense of intimacy – a sensation rarely found in Westminster Abbey. St Faith's Chapel is the most prayerful and contemplative chapel in the abbey. Also of great significance is St Edmund's Chapel for its fine tombs and monuments, many of national importance.

4 **POET'S CORNER & ST BENEDICT'S CHAPEL**
Poet's Corner, with its great poets and writers, is naturally an important part of the Abbey but there is also the sometimes-forgotten chapel of St Benedict, where, if you know where to look, you can still see where St Benedict's head was enshrined before the Reformation.

5 **CHAPTER HOUSE & THE PYX CHAPEL**
In the cloister, the wonderful Chapter House – with its floor tiles and wall paintings – is one of my favourite parts of the Abbey. Finally, the Pyx Chapel, the oldest altar in the Abbey still in use, is a place where you can really connect with the earliest days of the Abbey's long history.

Don't Miss
British Museum

Still London's most visited attraction, the British Museum draws an average of 5.5 million visitors each year. It's an exhaustive and exhilarating stampede through world cultures, with galleries devoted to the ancient civilisations of Egypt, the Middle East, Rome, Greece, Britain and much more. It's huge, so make a few focused visits if you have time, and consider the choice of tours: there are 15 free 30- to 40-minute eyeOpener tours of individual galleries, multimedia iPad tours (adult/child £5/3.50), offering six themed one-hour tours and highlights tours.

Map p64

☎ 020-7323 8000

www.british museum.org

Great Russell St, WC1

🕙 10am-5.30pm Sat-Thu, to 8.30pm Fri

Russell Sq, Tottenham Court Rd

Great Court

With a spectacular glass-and-steel roof designed by Norman Foster in 2000, the Great Court is the largest covered public square in Europe. In its centre is the famous **Reading Room**, formerly containing the British Library, which has been frequented by all the big brains of history, from Mahatma Gandhi to Karl Marx.

Ancient Egypt

The star of the show at the British Museum is the Ancient Egypt collection. It comprises sculptures, fine jewellery, papyrus texts, coffins and mummies, including the beautiful and intriguing **Mummy of Katebet** (Room 63). Perhaps the most prized item in the collection is the **Rosetta Stone** (Room 4), the key to deciphering Egyptian hieroglyphics.

Ancient Greece

The **Parthenon Sculptures** (aka Parthenon Marbles; Room 18) are thought to show the great procession to the temple that took place during the Great Panathenaea, a blow-out version of an annual festival in honour of Athena.

Other Highlights

Kids will love the North American (Room 26) and Mexican (Room 27) galleries, with the 15th-century Aztec **Mosaic Mask of Tezcatlipoca** (or Skull of the Smoking Mirror), a human skull decorated with turquoise mosaic, and the **Lewis Chessmen** (Room 40), which appeared larger than life in the first Harry Potter film.

There are also superb collections on ancient Middle East civilisations, including rare artefacts from the **Royal Tombs of Ur** (Room 56) in modern-day Iraq and the exquisite gold figurines from the **Oxus Treasure** (Room 52), originating from the ancient Persian capital of Persepolis around 400 BC.

The stunning **Enlightenment Galleries** (Room 1) is a neoclassical space built between 1823 and 1827. It traces how such disciplines as biology, archaeology, linguistics and geography emerged during the 18th century.

1 **ENLIGHTENMENT GALLERY (ROOM 1)**
This magnificent room contains an informative display that shows how collectors, antiquaries and travellers viewed and classified objects at the time the museum was founded (1753). It's an excellent introduction to the British Museum.

2 **ASSYRIAN LION HUNT FROM NINEVEH (ROOM 10)**
These are some of the greatest carvings from the ancient world. They originate from the city of Nineveh, in what is now modern-day Iraq. They've become especially important given the events of recent years in Iraq.

3 **CLOCKS & WATCHES GALLERY (ROOMS 38–9)**
These rooms contain a collection of mechanical devices for telling the time. My favourite clock is driven by a ball that rolls back and forward along a grooved plate that releases the mechanism. It's quite a strange experience to be surrounded by the ticking, striking and chiming of hundreds of clocks!

4 **EAST STAIRS**
An impressive collection of casts of Persian, Mayan and Egyptian reliefs line the stairs. These were made in the 19th and early 20th centuries and are historically important as the original objects left at the sites have been damaged or have disappeared.

5 **JAPAN GALLERIES (ROOMS 92–4)**
Climb to the very top of the museum for a fascinating insight into the art, religion, and everyday life of the Japanese, ranging from Samurai warrior swords to Manga comic books.

The British Museum

A HALF-DAY TOUR

The British Museum, with almost eight million items in its permanent collection, is so vast and comprehensive that it can be daunting for the first-time visitor. To avoid a frustrating trip – and getting lost on the way to the Egyptian mummies – set out on this half-day exploration, which takes in some of the museum's most important sights. If you want to see and learn more, join a tour or hire a multimedia iPad.

A good starting point is the **Rosetta Stone ❶**, the key that cracked the code to ancient Egypt's writing system. Nearby treasures from Assyria – an ancient civilisation centred in Mesopotamia between the Tigris and Euphrates Rivers – including the colossal **Khorsabad Winged Bulls ❷**, give way to the **Parthenon Sculptures ❸**, highpoints of classical Greek art that continue to influence

Winged Bulls from Khorsabad
This awesome pair of alabaster winged bulls with human heads once guarded the entrance to the palace of Assyrian King Sargon II at Khorsabad in Mesopotamia, a cradle of civilisation in present-day Iraq.

Parthenon Sculptures
The Parthenon, a white marble temple dedicated to Athena, was part of a fortified citadel on the Acropolis in Athens. There are dozens of sculptures and friezes with models and interactive displays explaining how they all once fitted together.

Ancient Greece & Rome ❸

Lion Hunt Reliefs from Nineveh ❷

West Stairs

❶ ❹

South Stairs

Main Entrance

Great Court

Reading Room

Great Court Shop

China, India & Southeast Asia

North America

Paul Hamlyn Library

Ticket Desk (Temporary Exhibtions)

GROUND FLOOR

Rosetta Stone
Written in hieroglyphic, demotic (cursive ancient Egyptian script used for everyday use) and Greek, the 762kg stone contains a decree exempting priests from tax on the first anniversary of young Ptolemy V's coronation.

Bust of Ramesses the Great
The most impressive sculpture in the Egyptian galleries, this 7.5-tonne bust portrays Ramesses II, scourge of the Israelites in the Book of Exodus, as great benefactor.

us today. Be sure to see both the sculptures and the monumental frieze celebrating the birth of Athena. En route to the West Stairs is a huge bust of **Pharaoh Ramesses II** ④, just a hint of the large collection of **Egyptian mummies** ⑤ upstairs. (The earliest, affectionately called Ginger because of wispy reddish hair, was preserved simply by hot sand.) The Romans introduce visitors to the early Britain galleries via the rich **Mildenhall Treasure** ⑥. The Anglo-Saxon **Sutton Hoo Ship Burial** ⑦ and the medieval **Lewis Chessmen** ⑧ follow.

EATING OPTIONS

» **Court Cafes** At the northern end of the Great Court; takeaway counters with salads and sandwiches; communal tables

» **Gallery Cafe** Slightly out of the way near Room 12; quieter; offers hot dishes

» **Court Restaurant** Upstairs overlooking the former Reading Room; sit-down meals

Lewis Chessmen
The much-loved 78 chess pieces portray faceless pawns, worried-looking queens, bishops with their mitres turned sideways and rooks as 'warders', gnawing away at their shields.

FEARGUS COONEY / GETTY IMAGES ©

Egyptian Mummies
Among the rich collection of mummies and funerary objects is 'Ginger', who was buried at the site of Gebelein, in Upper Egypt, more than 5000 years ago, and Katebet, a one-time chantress (ritual performer) at the Amun temple in Karnak.

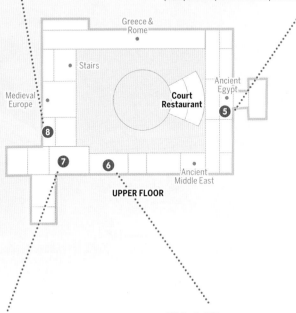

Greece & Rome

Stairs

Medieval Europe

Ancient Egypt

Court Restaurant

⑤

⑧

⑦ ⑥

Ancient Middle East

UPPER FLOOR

Sutton Hoo Ship Burial
This unique grave of an important (but unidentified) Anglo-Saxon royal has yielded drinking horns, gold buckles and a stunning helmet with face mask.

Mildenhall Treasure
Roman gods such as Neptune and Bacchus share space with early Christian symbols like the *chi-rho* (short for 'Christ') on the find's three dozen silver bowls, plates and spoons.

Don't Miss
Buckingham Palace

Built in 1705 as Buckingham House for the duke of the same name and purchased by George III, the palace has been the Royal Family's London lodgings only since 1837 when Queen Victoria moved in from her childhood home at Kensington Palace. St James's Palace was judged too old-fashioned and insufficiently impressive, although Buckingham had to undergo a number of modifications before it was deemed fit.

Map p68

☏ 020-7766 7300

www.royal collection.org.uk

Buckingham Palace Rd, SW1

adult/child £19/10.85

🕑 9.30am-7pm late Jul-Aug, to 6.30pm Sep

🚇 St James's Park, Victoria, Green Park

State Rooms

The tour of the 19 rooms (of 775) open to the public starts in the Grand Hall at the foot of the monumental Grand Staircase, commissioned by George IV in 1828. It takes in architect John Nash's Italianate Green Drawing Room, the State Dining Room (all red damask and Regency furnishings), the Blue Drawing Room (which has a gorgeous fluted ceiling) and the White Drawing Room, where foreign ambassadors are received.

The Ballroom, where official receptions and state banquets are held, was built between 1853 and 1855 and opened with a ball a year later to celebrate the end of the Crimean War. The Throne Room is rather anticlimactic, with his-and-hers pink chairs initialled 'ER' and 'P', sitting under a curtained theatre arch.

Picture Gallery & Gardens

The most interesting part of the tour is the 47m-long Picture Gallery, featuring splendid works by such artists as Van Dyck, Rembrandt, Canaletto, Poussin, Claude Lorrain, Rubens, Canova and Vermeer.

Wandering around the 18-hectare garden is another highlight – as well as admiring some of the 350 or so species of flowers and plants and listening to the many birds, you'll get beautiful views of the palace and a peek at its famous lake.

Queen's Gallery

Since the reign of Charles I, the Royal Family has amassed a priceless collection of paintings, sculpture, ceramics, furniture and jewellery. The splendid Queen's Gallery showcases some of the palace's treasures on a rotating basis.

The gallery was originally designed as a conservatory by Nash. It was converted into a chapel for Queen Victoria in 1843, destroyed in a 1940 air raid and reopened as a gallery in 1962. A £20-million renovation for Elizabeth II's Golden Jubilee in 2002 enlarged the entrance and added a Greek Doric portico, a multimedia centre and three times as much display space.

Royal Mews

Southwest of the palace, the Royal Mews started life as a falconry but is now a working stable looking after the royals' three dozen immaculately groomed horses, along with the opulent vehicles – motorised and horse-driven – the monarch uses for transport

Highlights for visitors include the enormous and opulent Gold State Coach of 1762, which has been used for every coronation since that of George III; the 1911 Glass Coach used for royal weddings and the Diamond Jubilee in 2012; Queen Alexandra's State Coach (1893), used to transport the Imperial State Crown to the official opening of Parliament in May, and a Rolls-Royce Phantom VI from the royal fleet.

Changing of the Guard

At 11.30am daily from April to July, and on alternate days, weather permitting, from August to March, the old guard (Foot Guards of the Household Regiment) comes off duty to be replaced by the new guard on the forecourt of Buckingham Palace. Crowds come to watch the carefully choreographed marching and shouting of the guards in their bright red uniforms and bearskin hats. It lasts about 40 minutes and is very popular so arrive early if you want to get a good spot.

Royal Christenings

At the centre of Royal Family life is the Music Room, where four royal babies have been christened: the Prince of Wales (Prince Charles), the Princess Royal (Princess Anne), the Duke of York (Prince Andrew), the Duke of Cambridge (Prince William).

⭐ Don't Miss
Houses of Parliament

Both the House of Commons and the House of Lords sit in the sumptuous Palace of Westminster, a neo-Gothic confection dating from the mid-19th century. The House of Commons is where Members of Parliament (MPs) meet to propose and discuss new legislation and to grill the prime minister and other ministers. The House of Lords contains Lords Spiritual, linked with the established church, and Lords Temporal, who are both appointed and hereditary.

Map p68

www.parliament.uk

Parliament Sq, SW1

⊖ Westminster

Towers

The most famous feature of the Houses of Parliament is the Clock Tower, officially named Elizabeth Tower to mark the Queen's Diamond Jubilee in 2012 but commonly known as **Big Ben**. Ben is actually the 13-tonne bell hanging inside and is named after Benjamin Hall, the rotund commissioner of works when the tower was completed in 1858. At the base of the taller **Victoria Tower** at the southern end is the Sovereign's Entrance, which is used by the Queen.

Westminster Hall

One of the most stunning features of the Palace of Westminster, seat of the English monarchy from the 11th to the early 16th centuries, is Westminster Hall. Originally built in 1099, it is the oldest surviving part of the complex; the awesome hammer-beam roof was added around 1400.

Westminster Hall was used for coronation banquets in medieval times. It also served as a courthouse until the 19th century; the trials of William Wallace (1305), Thomas More (1535), Guy Fawkes (1606) and Charles I (1649) all took place here. In the 20th century, monarchs and Winston Churchill lay in state here after their deaths.

House of Commons

The layout of the Commons Chamber is based on St Stephen's Chapel in the original Palace of Westminster. The chamber, designed by Giles Gilbert Scott, replaced the one destroyed by a 1941 bomb.

Although the Commons is a national assembly of 650 MPs, the chamber has seating for only 437. Government members sit to the right of the Speaker and Opposition members to the left.

House of Lords

The House of Lords is visited via the amusingly named Strangers' Gallery. The intricate 'Tudor Gothic' interior led its poor architect, Pugin (1812–52), to an early death from overwork and nervous strain.

Most of the 760-odd members of the House of Lords are life peers (appointed for their lifetime by the monarch); there is also a small number of hereditary peers and a group of 'crossbench' members (not affiliated to the main political parties).

Tours

On Saturdays year-round and daily when Parliament is in summer recess (mid-July to early September), visitors can join a 75-minute **guided tour** (☎ 0844 847 1672; www.parliament.uk/guided-tours; adult/child £16.50/7) of both chambers, Westminster Hall and other historic buildings conducted by qualified Blue Badge Tourist Guides in six languages. Tour schedules change with every recess, so check ahead. It's best to book.

Debates

When Parliament is in session, visitors may attend debates. The best time to watch a debate is during Prime Minister's Question Time at noon on Wednesday, but it's also the busiest. To find out what's being debated on a particular day, check the notice board beside the entrance, or check online at www. parliament.uk. The debating style in the Commons is quite combative but not all debates are flamboyant duelling matches. In fact, many are rather boring and long-winded, although they are an essential feature of British democracy.

Access & Security

Enter via St Stephen's Entrance. It's not unusual to have to wait up to two hours to access the chambers. Following a series of protest incidents in 2004, security was tightened, and a bulletproof screen now sits between members of the public and the debating chamber.

Discover the West End

Getting There & Away

○ **Underground** Every tube line goes through the West End so wherever you're staying in London, you'll have no difficulty getting here. The tube is also good for getting from one end of the West End to the other (Russell Sq to Green Park or Baker St to Embankment).

○ **Walking** The West End is relatively compact so it'll be cheaper and generally more enjoyable to walk from one place to another.

○ **Barclays Bikes** There are docking stations everywhere within the West End and cycling is your best bet for short journeys.

Leicester Square (p67)
MAREMAGNUM/GETTY IMAGES ©

⊙ Sights

Westminster

Westminster Abbey　　　Church
See p52.

Houses of Parliament　　Historic Building
See p60.

Supreme Court　　　Landmark
Map p68 (www.supremecourt.gov.uk; Parliament Sq, SW1; ⊗9.30am-4.30pm Mon-Thu ; ⊖Westminster) FREE The highest court in the UK, the Supreme Court was the Appellate Committee of the House of Lords until 2009. It is now housed in neo-Gothic Middlesex Guildhall (1913), and members of the public are welcome to observe cases when the court is sitting.

Bloomsbury & Fitzrovia

British Museum　　　Museum
See p54.

Squares of Bloomsbury　　Square
At the heart of Bloomsbury is **Russell Square** (Map p64) laid out in 1800 by Humphrey Repton. It was dark and bushy until a striking facelift a decade ago pruned the trees and gave it a 10m-high fountain.

The centre of literary Bloomsbury was **Gordon Square** (Map p64) where lived Bertrand Russell (No 57), Lytton Strachey (No 51) and Vanessa and Clive Bell, Maynard Keynes and the Woolf family (No 46).

Lovely oval-shaped **Bedford Square** (Map p64)is the only completely Georgian square still surviving in Bloomsbury.

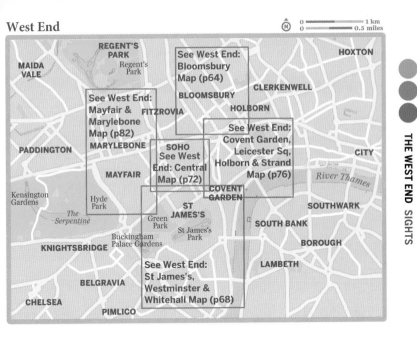

THE WEST END SIGHTS

New London Architecture
Exhibition

Map p64 (www.newlondonarchitecture.org; Building Centre, 26 Store St, WC1; ⊙9am-6pm Mon-Fri, 10am-5pm Sat; ⊖Goodge St) FREE
This is an excellent place to see which way London's architectural development is going, and the frequently changing exhibitions will capture the imagination of anyone who loves the city. A large, constantly updated model of the capital highlights the planned and new buildings.

Charles Dickens Museum
Museum

(www.dickensmuseum.com; 48 Doughty St, WC1; adult/child £8/4; ⊙10am-5pm; ⊖Chancery Lane, Russell Sq) After a £3.5 million renovation, this museum in a handsome four-storey house – the great Victorian novelist's sole surviving residence in London (1837-39) – is bigger and better than ever. A period kitchen in the basement and a nursery in the attic have been added, and newly acquired 49 Doughty St increases the exhibition space substantially.

Broadcasting House
TV Location

Map p82 (☎0370 901 1227; www.bbc.co.uk/showsandtours; Portland Pl, W1; ⊙tour days & times vary; ⊖Oxford Circus) This is the iconic building from which the BBC began radio broadcasting in 1932 and from where all TV and radio broadcasting in London has taken place since March 2013. You can visit radio and TV studios on a 1½-hour tour departing up to nine times a day (check the website for details).

St James's

Buckingham Palace
Palace

See p58.

St James's Park
Park

Map p68 (www.royalparks.gov.uk; The Mall, SW1; deckchairs per hr/day £1.50/7; ⊙5am-midnight, deckchairs Mar-Oct daylight hours; ⊖St James's Park, Green Park) At just 23 hectares, St James's is the smallest but most groomed of London's royal parks. It has brilliant views of the London Eye, Westminster, St James's Palace, Carlton Tce and Horse Guards Parade; the sight of Buckingham Palace from the footbridge spanning the central lake is photo-perfect. The lake is full of different types of waterfowl, and the rocks on its southern side serve as a rest stop for a half-dozen pelicans (fed at 2.30pm daily).

63

West End: Bloomsbury

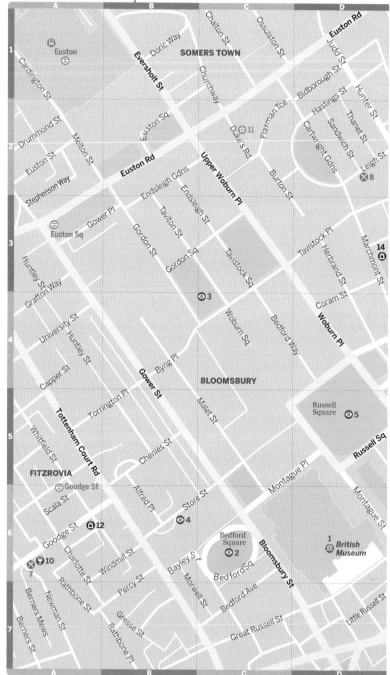

West End: Bloomsbury

Royal Academy of Arts   Gallery

Map p72 (www.royalacademy.org.uk; Burlington House, Piccadilly, W1; adult/child £10/6; ⊙10am-6pm Sat-Thu, to 10pm Fri; ⊖Green Park) Britain's oldest society devoted to fine arts was founded in 1768, but the organisation moved to Burlington House exactly a century later. The collection contains drawings, paintings, architectural designs, photographs and sculptures by past and present Academicians such as Joshua Reynolds, John Constable, Thomas Gainsborough, JMW Turner, David Hockney and Norman Foster.

Highlights are displayed in the **John Madejski Fine Rooms** on the 1st floor, which are accessible by free guided tours (1pm & 3pm Wednesday to Friday, 1pm Tuesday, 11.30am Saturday). The displays change regularly.

The **Summer Exhibition** (⊙Jun–mid-Aug), which has showcased contemporary art for sale by unknown as well as established artists for nearly 250 years, is the Academy's biggest annual event.

Burlington Arcade Shopping Arcade

Map p68 (www.burlington-arcade.co.uk; 51 Piccadilly, W1; ⊙10am-9pm Mon-Fri, 9am-6.30pm Sat, 11am-5pm Sun; ⊖Green Park) Beside the

Royal Academy, this delightful arcade was built in 1819. Today it is a shopping precinct for the wealthy, and is most famous for the Burlington Berties, uniformed guards who patrol the area keeping an eye out for such offences as running, chewing gum or whatever else might lower the tone.

St James's Piccadilly   Church
Map p72 (www.st-james-piccadilly.org; 197 Piccadilly, W1; ⏰8am-8pm; ⊖Piccadilly Circus) The only church (1684) Christopher Wren built from scratch and on a new site (most of the other London churches are replacements for ones razed in the Great Fire), this simple building is exceedingly easy on the eye and substitutes what some might call the pompous flourishes of Wren's most famous churches with a warm and elegant user-friendliness.

St James's Palace   Palace
Map p68 (www.royal.gov.uk/theroyalresidences/stjamesspalace/stjamesspalace.aspx; Cleveland Row, SW1; ⊖Green Park) The striking Tudor gatehouse of St James's Palace, the only surviving part of a building initiated by the palace-mad Henry VIII in 1530, is best approached from St James's St to the north of St James's Park. This was the official residence of kings and queens for more than three centuries.

Guards Museum   Museum
Map p68 (www.theguardsmuseum.com; Wellington Barracks, Birdcage Walk, SW1; adult/child £5/free; ⏰10am-4pm; ⊖St James's Park) Learn the the history of the five regiments of foot guards and their role in military campaigns from Waterloo onwards at this little museum in Wellington Barracks. There are uniforms, oil paintings, medals, curios and memorabilia that belonged to the soldiers. Perhaps the biggest draw is the huge collection of toy soldiers for sale in the shop.

Institute of Contemporary Arts   Arts Centre
Map p68 (ICA; ☎020-7930 9493; www.ica.org.uk; Nash House, The Mall, SW1; ⏰11am-11pm Tue-Sun, exhibition times vary; 🛜; ⊖Charing Cross) FREE Housed in a John Nash building along the Mall, the untraditional ICA is where Picasso and Henry Moore had their first UK shows. Since then the ICA has been at the cutting (and controversial) edge of the British arts world, with an excellent range of experimental and progressive films, music nights, photography, art, lectures, multimedia works and book readings.

Soho & Chinatown

Soho   Neighbourhood
Map p72 (⊖Tottenham Court Rd, Leicester Sq) Soho's reputation as the epicentre of nightlife and a proud gay neighbourhood is legendary and well deserved. It definitely comes into its own in the evenings, but during the day you'll be charmed by the area's bohemian side and the sheer energy of the place.

Chinatown
GARY YEOWELL/GETTY IMAGES ©

Getting High in London

Not so long ago, getting a good view of London was a near-impossible endeavour. There was the **London Eye** (p128), to be sure, but been-there-done-that, yeah? And **Vertigo 42** (p116) involved a lot of forward planning.

Now things are a lot more democratic and, well, the sky's the limit. The 72nd-floor open-air platform of the **Shard** (p133) is as high as you'll get in the EU. For nibbles and views head for the 40th-floor location of **Duck & Waffle** (p115) or to **Madison** (p117). For drinks we love **Galvin at Windows** (p88) and the expanded **Paramount** (p87) at Centre Point is fabulously placed. The **5th View** (p84) atop Waterstones bookshop in Piccadilly is admittedly low on the totem pole but, having taken afternoon tea there, you can legitimately use the ultimate intellectual's chat-up line: 'I get high on books'.

At Soho's northern end, leafy **Soho Square** (Map p72) is the area's back garden (1681). **Old Compton Street** is Soho's gay village. It's a street loved by all, gay or other, for its great bars, risqué shops and general good vibes.

Chinatown — Neighbourhood

Map p72 (www.chinatownlondon.org; ⊖Leicester Sq) Immediately north of Leicester Sq – but a world away in atmosphere – are Lisle and Gerrard Sts, the focal point for London's Chinese community. Although not as big as Chinatowns in many other cities – it's just two streets really – this is a lively quarter with oriental gates, Chinese street signs, red lanterns, many restaurants and great Asian supermarkets.

Piccadilly Circus — Square

Map p72 (⊖Piccadilly Circus) John Nash had originally designed Regent St and Piccadilly in the 1820s to be the two most elegant streets in town. He would certainly be disappointed with what Piccadilly Circus has become: swamped with visitors, flanked by flashing advertisement panels and surrounded by shops flogging tourist tat.

At the centre of the circus is the famous aluminium statue, Anteros, twin brother of Eros, dedicated to the philanthropist and child-labour abolitionist Lord Shaftesbury. The sculpture was at first cast in gold, but it was later replaced by newfangled aluminium, the first outdoor statue in that metal. Down the years the angel has been mistaken for Eros, the God of Love, and the misnomer has stuck (you'll even see signs for 'Eros' from the Underground).

Photographers' Gallery — Gallery

Map p72 (www.photonet.org.uk; 16-18 Ramillies St, W1; ⏱10am-6pm Mon-Wed, Fri & Sat, to 8pm Thu, 11.30am-6pm Sun; ⊖Oxford Circus) FREE With seven galleries over three floors, an excellent cafe and a shop brimming with prints and photography books, the Photographers' Gallery has risen phoenix-like from a massive refurbishment and looks positively stunning.

Covent Garden & Leicester Square

Trafalgar Square — Square

Map p76 (WC2; ⊖Charing Cross) This is the true centre of London, where rallies and marches take place, tens of thousands of revellers usher in the New Year and locals congregate for anything from communal open-air cinema to various political protests.

The square commemorates the victory of the British navy at the Battle of Trafalgar against the French and Spanish navies in 1805 during the Napoleonic Wars. Standing in the centre of the square since 1843, the 52m-high

West End: St James's, Westminster & Whitehall

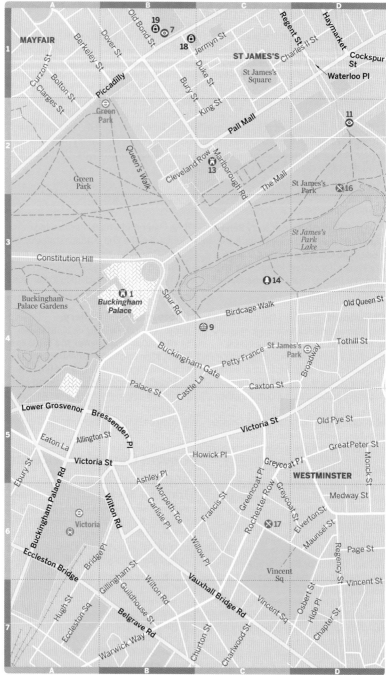

Nelson's Column Map p76 (upon which the admiral surveys his fleet of ships to the southwest) honours Admiral Lord Nelson, who led the fleet's victory over Napoleon. The column is flanked by four enormous bronze statues of lions, which were sculpted by Sir Edwin Landseer. If you look southwest down Whitehall, you'll also get a glimpse of **Big Ben** (Map p68) down at the Houses of Parliament.

Covent Garden Piazza   Square
Map p76 (www.coventgardenlondonuk.com/-/covent-garden-piazza; ⊖ Covent Garden) London's first planned square is now the exclusive preserve of tourists who flock here to shop in the quaint old arcades and watch street performers. On the square's west side is lovely **St Paul's Church** Map p76 (www.actorschurch.org; Bedford St, WC2; ⊙8.30am-5pm Mon-Fri, varies Sat, 9am-1pm Sun; ⊖ Covent Garden), built by Inigo Jones in 1633 and known as the 'Actors' Church'.

National Portrait Gallery   Gallery
Map p76 (www.npg.org.uk; St Martin's Pl, WC2; ⊙10am-6pm Sat-Wed, to 9pm Thu & Fri; ⊖ Charing Cross, Leicester Sq) **FREE** Visiting the

Fourth Plinth

Three of the four plinths at Trafalgar Sq's corners are occupied by notables: King George IV on horseback, and military men General Sir Charles Napier and Major General Sir Henry Havelock. One, originally intended for a statue of William IV, has largely remained vacant for the past 150 years. The Royal Society of Arts conceived the unimaginatively titled **Fourth Plinth Project** (Map p76; www.london.gov.uk/fourthplinth) in 1999, deciding to use the empty space for works by contemporary artists. It was replaced by Katharina Fritsch's *Hahn/Cock*, a huge, bright blue sculpture of a cockerel. Each artwork will be exhibited for 18 months.

fascinating National Portrait Gallery is like stepping into a picture book of English history. Founded in 1856, the permanent collection counts 10,000 works, which are rotated regularly.

The collection is organised chronologically (starting with the early Tudors on the 2nd floor), and then by theme. A highlight is the famous 'Chandos' portrait of William Shakespeare, the first artwork the gallery acquired (1856) and believed to be the only one to have been painted during the playwright's lifetime. Other highlights include the 'Ditchley' portrait of Queen Elizabeth I displaying her might by standing on a map of England, and a touching sketch of novelist Jane Austen by her sister.

The 1st-floor portraits illustrate the rise and fall of the British Empire through the Victorian era and the 20th century. The ground floor is dedicated to modern figures, using a variety of media (sculpture, photography, video etc).

The audio guide (£3) highlights 200 portraits and allows you to hear the voices of some of the subjects. The **Portrait** (p84) restaurant has views towards Westminster and does wonderful food.

London Transport Museum   Museum

Map p76 (www.ltmuseum.co.uk; Covent Garden Piazza, WC2; adult/child £15/free; ⊙10am-6pm Sat-Thu, 11am-6pm Fri; ⊖Covent Garden) One of our favourite 'other' museums, this one looks at how London developed as a result of better transport and contains everything from horse-drawn omnibuses, early taxis, underground trains you can drive yourself and everything in between. Check out the museum shop for original and interesting souvenirs, including a great selection of historical tube posters.

St Martin-in-the-Fields   Church

Map p76 (www.stmartin-in-the-fields.org; Trafalgar Sq, WC2; ⊙8.30am-6pm Mon, Tues, Thu & Fri, 8.30am-5pm Wed, 9.30am-6pm Sat, 3.30-5pm Sun, usually shuts 1hr at lunch; ⊖Charing Cross) The 'royal parish church' is a delightful fusion of classical and baroque styles that was completed by James Gibbs in 1726 and serves as a model for many churches in New England. The church is well known for its excellent classical music concerts, many by candlelight, and its links to the Chinese community (services in English, Mandarin and Cantonese).

Benjamin Franklin House   Museum

Map p76 (www.benjaminfranklinhouse.org; 36 Craven St, WC2; adult/concession £7/5; ⊙10.30am-5pm Wed-Mon; ⊖Charing Cross, Embankment) This modest house south-east of Trafalgar Sq is where American statesman Benjamin Franklin lived from 1757 to 1775 as he tried to broker peace with Britain and (unsuccessfully) avert war. Visits are by guided tour only, which depart at noon, 1pm, 2pm, 3.15pm and 4.15pm Wednesday to Sunday (architectural tours on Monday only).

PETER D NOYCE/ALAMY ©

⭐ Don't Miss
National Gallery

With some 2300 European paintings on display, this is one of the richest art galleries in the world. There are seminal paintings from every important epoch in the history of art from the mid-13th to the early 20th century, including works by Leonardo da Vinci, Michelangelo, Titian, Van Gogh and Renoir.

The modern Sainsbury Wing on the gallery's western side houses paintings from 1260 to 1510. Here you will find largely religious paintings commissioned for private devotion (eg the *Wilton Diptych*) as well more unusual masterpieces such as Boticelli's *Venus & Mars* and Van Eyck's *Arnolfini Portrait*.

The High Renaissance (1510–1600) is covered in the West Wing where Michelangelo, Titian, Raphael, Correggio, El Greco and Bronzino hold court; Rubens, Rembrandt and Caravaggio can be found in the North Wing (1600–1700). Notable are two self-portraits of Rembrandt (age 34 and 63) and the beautiful *Rockeby Venus* by Velázquez.

The most popular section is the East Wing (1700–1900), with works by 18th-century and 19th-century British artists such as Gainsborough, Constable and Turner, and highbrow Impressionist and post-Impressionist masterpieces by Van Gogh and Monet.

The comprehensive audioguide (£3.50) is highly recommended, as are the free one-hour introductory guided tours that leave from the information desk in the Sainsbury Wing daily at 11.30am and 2.30pm, and at 7pm Friday. There are also special trails and activity sheets for children.

The **National Dining Rooms** (p84) have high-quality British food and an all-day bakery.

NEED TO KNOW

Map p76 www.nationalgallery.org.uk; Trafalgar Sq, WC2; ⏰10am-6pm Sat-Thu, to 9pm Fri; ⊖Charing Cross

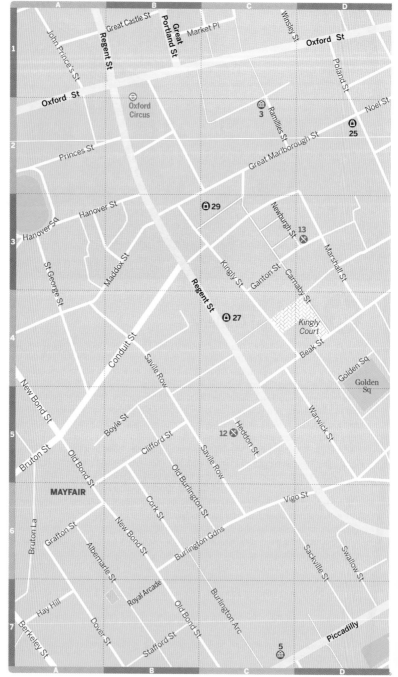

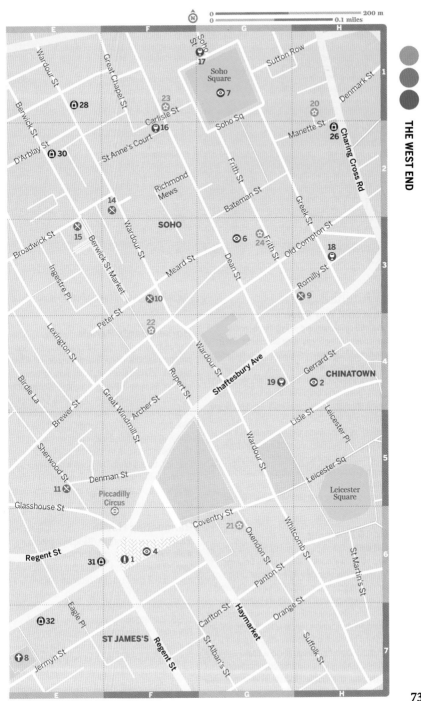

West End: Central

Whitehall

Churchill War Rooms   Museum

Map p68 (www.iwm.org.uk/visits/churchill-war-rooms; Clive Steps, King Charles St, SW1; adult/child £17/free; ⏰9.30am-6pm, last entry 5pm; ⊖Westminster) Winston Churchill coordinated the Allied resistance against Nazi Germany on a Bakelite telephone from this underground military HQ during WWII. The Cabinet War Rooms remain much as they were when the lights were flicked off in 1945, capturing the drama and dogged spirit of the time, while the multimedia Churchill Museum affords intriguing insights into the resolute, cigar-smoking wartime leader. Highly recommended.

No 10 Downing Street   Historic Building

Map p68 (www.number10.gov.uk; 10 Downing St, W1; ⊖Westminster) The official office of British leaders since 1732, when George II presented No 10 to Robert Walpole, this has also been the prime minister's London residence since refurbishment in 1902. For such a famous address, No 10 is a small-looking building on a plain-looking street, hardly warranting comparison with, say, the White House. The street was cordoned off with a rather large iron gate

during Margaret Thatcher's time so you won't see much.

Horse Guards Parade   Historic Site

Map p68 (www.changing-the-guard.com/london-programme.html; Horse Guards Parade, off Whitehall, W1; ⏰11am Mon-Sat, 10am Sun; ⊖Westminster, St James's Park) In a more accessible version of Buckingham Palace's Changing of the Guard, the mounted troops of the Household Cavalry change guard here daily, at the official vehicular entrance to the royal palaces. A slightly scaled down version takes place at 4pm when the dismounted guards are changed. On the Queen's official birthday in June, Trooping the Colour is staged here.

Banqueting House   Palace

Map p68 (www.hrp.org.uk/BanquetingHouse; Whitehall, SW1; adult/child £5/free; ⏰10am-5pm; ⊖Westminster) This is the only surviving part of the Tudor Whitehall Palace (1532), which once stretched most of the way down Whitehall and burned down in 1698. Designed by Inigo Jones in 1622, Banqueting House was England's first purely Renaissance building. In a huge, virtually unfurnished hall on the 1st floor there are nine ceiling panels painted by Peter Paul Rubens in 1635.

JOHNNIE PAKINGTON/GETTY IMAGES ©

⭐ Don't Miss
Tate Britain

The more elderly and venerable of the two Tate galleries, this riverside Portland stone edifice, which was built in 1897 by Henry Tate (the man who invented the sugar cube), celebrates British painting from 1500 to the present, exhibiting works from artists such as Blake, Hogarth, Gainsborough, Barbara Hepworth, Whistler, Constable and Turner – in particular. It doesn't stop there and vibrant modern and contemporary art finds expression in pieces from Lucian Freud, Francis Bacon and Tracey Emin.

The star of the show at the Tate Britain is JMW Turner. After he died in 1851, his estate was settled by a decree declaring that whatever had been found in his studio – 300 oil paintings and about 30,000 sketches and drawings – would be bequeathed to the nation. You will find such classics as *The Scarlet Sunset* and *Norham Castle, Sunrise*.

As well as Turner's art, there are seminal works by such artists as Constable, Gainsborough and Reynolds as well as pre-Raphaelites (Rossetti, Holman Hunt, Millais), but also more modern artists, such as Lucian Freud, Francis Bacon and Tracey Emin. Tate Britain also hosts the prestigious and often controversial Turner Prize for contemporary art, which is held from October to early December every year.

There are free 45-minute **thematic tours** (🕙11am, noon, 2pm & 3pm), along with free 15-minute **Art in Focus** (🕙1.15pm Tue, Thu & Sat) talks on specific works. Audioguides (£3.50) are also available.

NEED TO KNOW
Map p68 www.tate.org.uk; Millbank, SW1; 🕙10am-6pm, to 10pm some Fri; 🚇Pimlico

West End: Covent Garden, Leicester Sq, Holborn & Strand

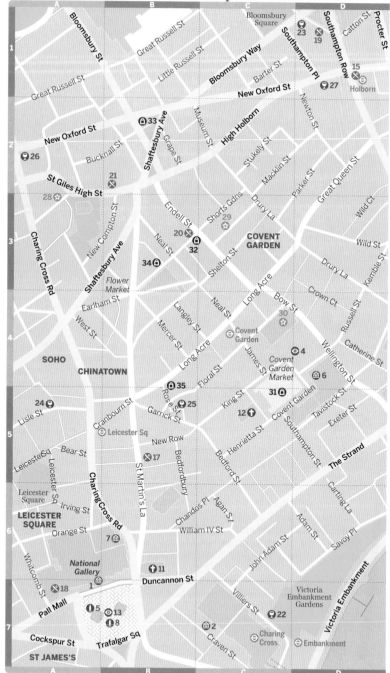

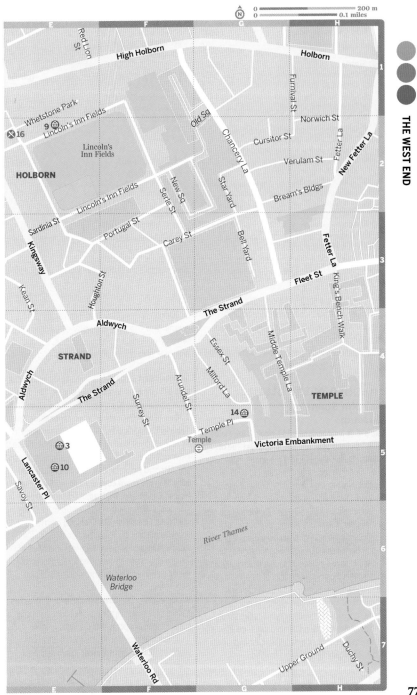

0 ———————— 200 m
0 ———————— 0.1 miles

High Holborn

Holborn

Red Lion St

Whetstone Park

Furnival St

Norwich St

Lincoln's Inn Fields

Old Sq

Cursitor St

Fetter La

New Fetter La

16

9

Chancery La

Verulam St

Lincoln's
Inn Fields

HOLBORN

Bream's Bldgs

Lincoln's Inn Fields

New Sq

Serle St

Star Yard

Sardinia St

Portugal St

Bell Yard

Fetter La

Kingsway

Carey St

Houghton St

Fleet St

King's Bench Walk

Kean St

The Strand

Aldwych

STRAND

Essex St

The Strand

Milford La

Middle Temple La

TEMPLE

Aldwych

Arundel St

Surrey St

14

Temple Pl

Lancaster Pl

3

Temple

Victoria Embankment

10

Savoy St

River Thames

Waterloo
Bridge

Waterloo Rd

Upper Ground

Duchy St

A bust outside commemorates 30 January 1649, when Charles I, accused of treason by Oliver Cromwell after the Civil War, was executed on a scaffold built against a 1st-floor window here.

Holborn & the Strand

Sir John Soane's Museum
Museum

Map p76 (www.soane.org; 13 Lincoln's Inn Fields, WC2; ⏰10am-5pm Tue-Sat, 6-9pm 1st Tue of month; ⊖Holborn) FREE This little museum is one of the most atmospheric and fascinating in London. The building is the beautiful, bewitching home of architect Sir John Soane (1753–1837), which he left brimming with surprising personal effects and curiosities, and the museum represents his exquisite and eccentric taste.

The heritage-listed house is largely as it was when Soane died and is itself a main part of the attraction. It has a canopy dome that brings light right down to the crypt, a colonnade filled with statuary, rooms within rooms, and a picture gallery where paintings are stowed behind each other on folding wooden panes.

Audioguides are free. Tours (£10) depart at 11.30am Tuesday and Friday and at 3.30pm Wednesday and Thursday. The evening of the first Tuesday of each month, when the house is lit by candles, is very popular and there are always long queues.

Somerset House
Historic Building

Map p76 (www.somersethouse.org.uk; The Strand, WC2; ⏰galleries 10am-6pm, Safra Courtyard 7.30am-11pm; ⊖Charing Cross, Embankment, Temple) Designed by William Chambers in 1775 for royal societies, Somerset House now contains two fabulous galleries. Near the Strand entrance, the **Courtauld Gallery** Map p76 (www.courtauld.ac.uk; Somerset House, The Strand, WC2; adult/child £6/free Tue-Sun, £3/free Mon; ⏰10am-6pm; ⊖Charing Cross, Embankment or Temple) contains masterpieces by Rubens, Botticelli, Cézanne, Degas, Renoir, Manet and Monet. There are free, 15-minute lunchtime talks on specific works or themes at 1.15pm every Monday and Friday and sometimes Wednesday. The **Embankment Galleries** focus on contemporary fashion, architecture, photography and design.

The courtyard is transformed into a popular **ice-skating rink** in winter and used for concerts and events in summer. Particularly popular is the outdoor cinema in the Great Court in early August, **Film4 Summer Screen**.

Two Temple Place   Gallery

Map p76 (www.twotempleplace.org; 2 Temple Pl, WC2; ⏰10am-4.30pm Mon & Thu-Sat, to 9pm Wed, 11am-4.30pm Sun; ⊖Temple) FREE This neo-Gothic house built in the late 1890s for William Waldorf Astor, of hotel fame and once the richest man in America, is now the only gallery in London showcasing art from outside the capital. Visit here as much to see the opulent house as the collections on display.

Marylebone

Wallace Collection   Museum

Map p82 (www.wallacecollection.org; Hertford House, Manchester Sq , W1; ⏰10am-5pm; ⊖Bond St) FREE Arguably London's finest smaller gallery, the Wallace Collection is an enthralling glimpse into 18th-century aristocratic life. The sumptuously restored Italianate mansion houses a treasure-trove of 17th- and 18th-century paintings, porcelain, artefacts and furniture collected by generations of the same family and bequeathed to the nation by the widow of Sir Richard Wallace (1818–90) on condition it remain displayed in the same fashion.

Among the highlights are paintings by Rembrandt, Delacroix, Titian, Rubens, Poussin, Velázquez and Gainsborough in the **Great Gallery**. Particularly rich is its collection of Rococo paintings and furniture and porcelain that belonged to Queen Marie-Antoinette of France. There's also an array of medieval and Renaissance armour and a sweeping staircase – deemed one of the best examples of French interior architecture anywhere. The excellent audio guide costs £3.

The fabulous glass-roofed courtyard restaurant **Wallace** (p84) is in the heart of the museum

Madame Tussauds   Museum

Map p82 (📞0870 400 3000; www.madametussauds.com/london; Marylebone Rd, NW1; adult/child £30/26; ⏰9/10am-5/7pm (seasonal); ⊖Baker St) It may be kitschy and terribly overpriced (a family ticket will set you back £108), but Madame Tussauds still makes for a fun-filled day. It offers photo ops for days with your dream celebrity at the A-List Party (Daniel Craig, Lady Gaga, George Clooney, David and Victoria

Trooping the Colour (p41)

Below: Wax figure display of Queen Elizabeth II at Madame Tussauds (p79);
Right: Somerset House (p78)

Beckham) and the Royal Appointment (the Queen, Harry, William and Kate). If you're into politics, get up close and personal with London Mayor Boris Johnson or even Barack Obama.

The Spirit of London taxi ride through the history of the city is a bit hokey but good educational fun, the Chamber of Horrors is as scary as ever and the excellent 3-D Super Heroes extravaganza is very high-tech.

Sherlock Holmes Museum
Museum

Map p82 (www.sherlock-holmes.co.uk; 221b Baker St, NW1; adult/child £8/5; ⊙9.30am-6pm; ⊖Baker St) Fans of Arthur Conan Doyle's classic detective novels will enjoy examining the three floors of reconstructed Victoriana, complete with deerstalkers, burning candles and flickering grates, but may baulk at the dodgy waxworks of Professor Moriarty and 'the Man with the Twisted Lip' at the top. It's a pity too that there is so little information on the author himself.

Eating

Many of the city's most eclectic, fashionable and, quite simply, best restaurants are dotted around the West End. As with most things in London, it pays to be in the know: while there's a huge concentration of mediocre places to eat along the main tourist drags, the best eating experiences are frequently tucked away on backstreets and not at all obvious.

Westminster

Vincent Rooms   Modern European £
Map p68 (☎020-7802 8391; www.thevincentrooms.com; Westminster Kingsway College, Vincent Sq, SW1; mains £8-12; ⊙noon-2pm Mon-Fri, 6-8pm Wed & Thu; ⊖Victoria) Care to be a guinea pig for student chefs at Westminster Kingsway College, where celebrity

THE WEST END EATING

chef Jamie Oliver was trained? Service is eager to please, the atmosphere in both the **Brasserie** and the **Escoffier Room** smarter than expected, and the food (including veggie options) ranges from wonderful to exquisite.

Bloomsbury & Fitzrovia

Newman Street
Tavern   Brasserie ££

Map p64 (📞020-3667 1445; www.newmanstreet-tavern.co.uk; 48 Newman St, W1; mains £12-20; 🕙noon-11pm Mon-Sat, 10.30am-5pm Sun; ⊖Goodge St) As you'll gather from the tray of large crabs and other briny things on display in the front window, the emphasis here is on seafood, with Colchester oysters, Devon crab and local cod in profusion. But fish-fearing carnivores need not worry; they're accommodated with the likes of venison and mushroom stew and the signature hay-baked black-faced-lamb breast.

Abeno   Japanese ££

Map p64 (www.abeno.co.uk; 47 Museum St, WC1; mains £9.50-21; 🕙noon-10pm Mon-Sat; ⊖Tottenham Court Rd) This Japanese restaurant specialises in *okonomiyaki,* a savoury pancake from Osaka. The pancakes consist of cabbage, egg and flour combined with the ingredients of your choice (there are more than two dozen varieties, including anything from sliced meats and vegetables to egg, noodles and cheese) and they're cooked on the hotplate at your table.

North Sea Fish
Restaurant   Fish & Chips ££

Map p64 (www.northseafishrestaurant.co.uk; 7-8 Leigh St, WC1; mains £10-20; 🕙noon-2.30pm & 5.30-11pm Mon-Sat; ⊖Russell Sq) The North Sea sets out to cook fresh fish and potatoes – a simple ambition in which it succeeds admirably. Look forward to jumbo-sized plaice or halibut fillets, deep-fried or grilled, and a huge serving of chips. There's takeaway next door.

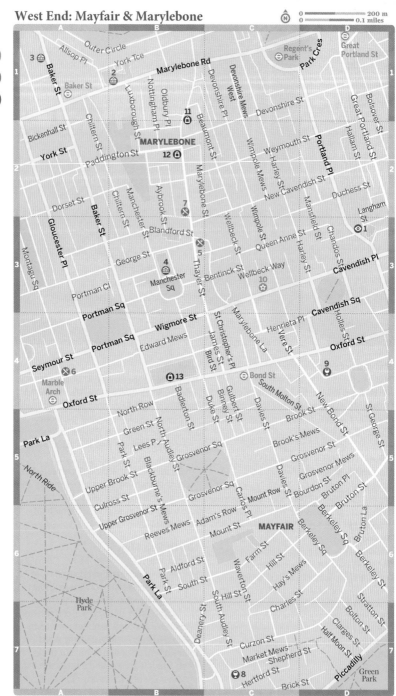

West End: Mayfair & Marylebone

THE WEST END EATING

0 — 200 m
0 — 0.1 miles

Great Portland St

Regent's Park

Park Cres

Outer Circle

Allsop Pl

3

Baker St

Baker St

York Tce

York Tce

Marylebone Rd

2

Luxborough St

Nottingham Pl

Oldbury Pl

Beaumont St

11

Devonshire Mews West

Devonshire Pl

Devonshire St

Great Portland St

Bolsover St

Bickenhall St

Chiltern St

York St

Paddington St

MARYLEBONE

12

Wimpole Mews

Weymouth St

Harley St

New Cavendish St

Portland Pl

Hallam St

Duchess St

Dorset St

Baker St

Chiltern St

Manchester St

Aybrook St

Marylebone St

7

Blandford St

5

Wellbeck St

Wimpole St

Queen Anne St

Harley St

Mansfield St

Chandos St

Langham St

1

George St

4

Manchester Sq

Thayer St

Bentinck St

Wellbeck Way

10

Cavendish Pl

Montagu Sq

Portman Cl

Portman Sq

Portman Sq

Portman Sq

Wigmore St

Edward Mews

St Christopher's Pl

James St

Bird St

Marylebone La

Wellbeck Way

Henrieta Pl

Vere St

Cavendish Sq

Holles St

Oxford St

Seymour St

6

Marble Arch

Oxford St

13

Duke St

Gilbert St

Binney St

Bond St

South Molton St

9

New Bond St

St George St

Gloucester Pl

North Row

Green St

Lees Pl

North Audley St

Badderton St

Davies St

Brook St

Brook's Mews

Grosvenor St

Grosvenor Mews

Park La

Upper Brook St

Blackburne's Mews

Grosvenor Sq

Grosvenor Sq

Carlos Pl

Mount Row

Davies St

Bourdon St

Bruton Pl

Bruton St

North Ride

Culross St

Upper Grosvenor St

Reeves Mews

Adam's Row

Mount St

MAYFAIR

Berkeley Sq

Bruton La

Berkeley St

Hyde Park

Park St

Park La

Aldford St

South St

Hill St

Waverton St

Farm St

Hill St

Hay's Mews

Charles St

Stratton St

Bolton St

Deanery St

South Audley St

South Hill St

Curzon St

Market Mews

Shepherd St

8

Hertford St

Brick St

Half Moon St

Clarges St

Piccadilly

Green Park

82

West End: Mayfair & Marylebone

St James's

Inn the Park   British ££
Map p68 (☏020-7451 9999; www.innthepark.
com; St James's Park, SW1; mains £14.50-22.50;
⊙8am-6pm Oct-Mar, 8am-11pm Apr-Sep;
⊖Charing Cross, St James's Park) This stunning wooden cafe and restaurant in St
James's Park is run by Irish chef Oliver
Peyton and offers cakes and tea as well
as excellent British food, with the menu
changing monthly. The terrace, which
overlooks one of the park's fountains with
views of Whitehall's grand buildings, is
wonderful in warm weather.

Soho & Chinatown

Princi   Italian £
Map p72 (www.princi.co.uk; 135 Wardour St, W1;
mains £7.50-12.50; ⊙8am-11.30pm Mon-Sat,
8.30am-10pm Sun; 🛜; ⊖Tottenham Court
Rd, Piccadilly Circus) Most people come to
Princi by accident rather than design;
they were just walking by and suddenly
noticed a mouth-watering array of breads
and Italian pastries through the restaurant's huge bay windows. Before they
know it, they're tucking into focaccia,
authentic pizzas or a hearty salad with a
slice of tiramisu.

Bone Daddies Ramen Bar   Noodles £
Map p72 (www.bonedaddiesramen.com; 21 Peter
St, W1; dishes £8-11; ⊙noon-3pm Mon-Fri & 5.30-
10pm Mon, to 11pm Tue & Wed, to midnight Thu &
Fri, noon-midnight Sat, noon-9pm Sun; ⊖Totten-
ham Court Rd) For a bowl of sustaining ra-
men noodles you couldn't do better than
Bone Daddies (and we'll come back just
for the name). Choose your 'foundation'
– be it noodles in broth or a salad – and
then add a topping or two (chashu pork,
pulled chicken, bean sprouts etc).

Yauatcha   Chinese ££
Map p72 (☏020-7494 8888; www.yauatcha.com;
15 Broadwick St, W1; dishes £4-17; ⊙noon-
11.30pm Mon-Sat, to 10.30pm Sun; ⊖Piccadilly
Circus, Oxford Circus) This most glamorous
of dim sum restaurants is divided into two
parts: the upstairs dining room offers a
delightful blue-bathed oasis of calm from
the chaos of Berwick St Market, while
downstairs has a smarter, more atmospheric feel with constellations of 'star'
lights. Both serve exquisite dim sum and
have a fabulous range of teas.

Bar Shu   Chinese ££
Map p72 (☏020-7287 8858; www.bar-shu.co.uk;
28 Frith St, W1; mains £10-31; ⊖Piccadilly Circus,
Leicester Sq) This is the restaurant that
introduced London to the joys of fiery
Szechuan cuisine and it remains more
authentic than much of the competition.
Dishes are redolent of smoked chillies
and the all-important (and ubiquitous)
peppercorn. Service can be a little
brusque, but the food is delicious and the
portions huge.

Brasserie Zédel   French ££
Map p72 (☏020-7734 4888; www.brasseriezedel.
com; 20 Sherwood St, W1; mains £8-20; ⊙8am-
11pm Mon-Fri, noon-11pm Sat, noon-8pm Sun;
⊖Piccadilly Circus) This brasserie in the
renovated art deco ballroom of a former
Piccadilly hotel is the French-est eatery
west of Calais. Choose from among the
usual favourites, including choucroute
alsacienne (sauerkraut with sausages and
charcuterie, £14) and duck leg confit with
Puy lentils. The set menus (£8.25/11.75

Museum Restaurants

National Dining Rooms (Map p76; ☎020-7747 2525; www.peytonandbyrne.co.uk; 1st fl, Sainsbury Wing, National Gallery, Trafalgar Sq, WC2 ; mains £15.50-20.50; ☺10am-5.30pm Sat-Thu, till 8.30pm Fri; ⊖Charing Cross) The menu at chef Oliver Peyton's restaurant at the National Gallery features an extensive and wonderful selection of British cheeses for a light lunch. For something more filling, go for the monthly changing County Menu, honouring regional specialities from across the British Isles. Set lunch is £19.50/23.50 for two/three courses.

Portrait (Map p76; ☎020-7312 2490; www.npg.org.uk/visit/shop-eat-drink.php; 3rd fl, National Portrait Gallery, St Martin's Pl, WC2; mains £18.50; ☺11.45am-2.45pm daily, 5.30-8.15pm Thu-Sat; ⊖Charing Cross) This stunningly located restaurant above the excellent National Portrait Gallery – with views over Trafalgar Sq and Westminster – is a great place to relax after a morning or afternoon at the gallery. The brunch (10am to 11.30am) and afternoon tea (3.30pm to 4.45pm) come highly recommended; set meals are £25/30 for two/three courses.

Wallace (Map p82; ☎020-7563 9505; www.wallacecollection.org/visiting/thewallacerestaurant; Hertford House, Manchester Sq, W1; mains £15.50-22.50; ☺10am-5pm Sun-Thu, to 11pm Fri & Sat; ⊖Bond St) There are few more idyllically placed restaurants than this brasserie in the enclosed courtyard of the Wallace Collection. The emphasis is on seasonal French-inspired dishes, with the daily menu offering two- or three-course meals for £22/26. Afternoon tea is £17.

for two/three courses) and *plats du jour* (£12.95) offer excellent value.

5th View
International ££

Map p72 (☎020-7851 2433; www.5thview.co.uk; 5th fl, Waterstone's Piccadilly, 203-205 Piccadilly, W1; mains £9-15; ☺9am-10pm Mon-Sat, noon-5pm Sun; ⊖Piccadilly Circus) The views of Westminster from the top floor of Waterstone's on Piccadilly are just the start. Add a relaxed, sophisticated dining room and some lovely food, and you have a gem of a place. We love the Greek meze and antipasti platters (small/large £9/15) to share, and the large breakfast selection.

Pitt Cue
Barbecue ££

Map p72 (www.pittcue.co.uk; 1 Newburgh St, W1; mains £11.50-16.50; ☺noon-3pm & 5.30-10.30pm Mon-Sat, noon-5pm Sun; ⊖Oxford Circus) This one-time food truck selling American-style barbecue and other meaty dishes has parked permanently and moved into funny little digs with seating up and downstairs just around

the corner from Carnaby St. Choose from pulled pork, beef ribs or smoked chipotle wings, add pickles and coleslaw then wash it all down with a Sam Adams or (for the abstemious) A&W root beer.

Covent Garden & Leicester Square

Rock & Sole Plaice
Fish & Chips £

Map p76 (47 Endell St, WC2; mains £10-11.50; ☺11.30am-10.30pm Mon-Sat, noon-9.30pm Sun; ⊖Covent Garden) The approach at this no-nonsense fish-and-chip shop dating back to Victorian times is simplicity itself: basic wooden tables under the trees in summer (downstairs in the cooler months), simple decor inside and delicious cod, haddock or skate in batter served with a generous portion of chips.

Green Man & French Horn
Modern European ££

Map p76 (☎020-7836 2645; www.green-manfrenchhorn.co; 54 St Martin's Lane, WC2; £11.50-25; ☺noon-3pm & 5.30-11pm Mon-Sat;

Leicester Sq, Charing Cross) Set in a long narrow space that was once a Victorian pub but has now been given a post-modern patina, this new eatery does some wonderful new things with class-A British produce (eg squid and black pudding). More bistro than restaurant, it's very relaxed and service is seamless.

Union Jacks   British ££
Map p76 (www.unionjacksrestaurants.com; 4 Central St Giles Piazza, WC2; mains £8-14.50; ⊙noon-11pm Mon-Sat, to 10.30pm Sun; ⊖Tottenham Court Rd) Celebrity chef Jamie Oliver's latest venture is a salute to all things British. Order a bunch of sharing plates (fish fingers, black pudding, beans on toast) and then launch into the main act – from empire chicken and cauliflower cheese to pizza. Graffiti pop art and genuinely welcoming service makes this a fun night out.

Holborn

Orchard   Vegetarian £
Map p76 (www.orchard-kitchen.co.uk; 11 Sicilian Ave, WC1; mains £6.50-7; ⊙8am-8pm Mon-Sat, 10am-7pm Sat; 🖋; ⊖Holborn) A boon for vegetarians in central London is this delightful retro-style cafe on a quiet pedestrian street. Mains include specialities like broccoli and Yorkshire blue cheese pie, a sarnie (that's a sandwich to Londoners) and mug of soup is just £4.95 and desserts are unusual – try the toasted oat and currant cake with Horlicks icing.

Fleet River Bakery   Cafe £
Map p76 (www.fleetriverbakery.com; 71 Lincoln's Inn Fields, WC2; dishes £6-10; ⊙7am-7pm Mon-Wed, to 9pm Thu & Fri, 9am-6pm Sat; ⊖Holborn) Our favourite new cafe in London has gained even a few more points now it has extended its hours on Thursday and Friday. Good for lunch (quiche, soup, sandwiches), great for coffee, wi-fi that always works and some supper club events. But Saturday brunch is our favourite: heavenly eggs Benedict.

Asadal   Korean ££
Map p76 (www.asadal.co.uk; 227 High Holborn, WC1; mains £8-20; ⊙noon-2.30pm & 6-10.30pm

Mon-Sat, 6-10pm Sun ; ⊖Holborn) If you fancy Korean but want a bit more style thrown into the act, head for this spacious basement restaurant next to the Holborn tube station. The *kimchi* (pickled Chinese cabbage with chillies) is searing and the barbecues (£8 to £14) are done on your table.

Marylebone

Golden Hind   Fish & Chips £
Map p82 (73 Marylebone Lane, W1; mains £5-11; ⊙noon-3pm & 6-10pm Mon-Fri; ⊖Bond St) This 90-year-old chippie has a classic interior, chunky wooden tables and builders sitting alongside folks in suits. And from the vintage fryer come ace fish and chips.

Providores & Tapa Room   Fusion £££
Map p82 (📞020-7935 6175; www.theprovidores.co.uk; 109 Marylebone High St, W1; 2/3/4/5 courses £33/47/57/63; ⊙9am-10.30pm Mon-Fri, 10am-10pm Sat & Sun; ⊖Baker St) This place is split over two levels: tempting tapas (£2.50 to £17) on the ground floor (no bookings); and outstanding fusion cuisine in the elegant and understated dining room above. The food at Providores is truly original and tastes divine: the Sri Lankan spiced short ribs, Cajun pork belly with Puy lentils and beef fillet with Szechuan-pickled shiitake mushrooms.

Mayfair

La Porte des Indes   Indian ££
Map p82 (📞020-7224 0055; www.laportedesindes.com; 32 Bryanston St, W1; mains £15-25; ⊖Marble Arch) 'Indian cuisine with a difference' might sound like hyberbole but it's a fact: 'Gateway to the Indies' serves the food of Pondicherry (now Puducherry), a French colony on the southeast coast until 1962. Gallic-inspired dishes include *kari de mouton* (actually a goat curry) and *magret de canard pulivaar* (Barbary duck breast fillets with tamarind).

Momo   Moroccan £££
Map p72 (📞020-7434 4040; www.momoresto.com; 25 Heddon St, W1; mains £18-28; ⊙noon-2.15pm Mon-Sat, 6.30-11.30 daily; ⊖Piccadilly Circus) This atmospheric Moroccan

restaurant is stuffed with cushions and lamps, and staffed by tambourine-playing waiters. Service is very friendly and the dishes are as exciting as you dare to be, so after the meze eschew the traditional and ordinary *tajine* (stew cooked in a traditional clay pot) and couscous, and tuck into the splendid Moroccan specialty *pastilla* (pigeon pie).

🍷 Drinking & Nightlife

The West End is a wonderful place for a night out – Friday and Saturday nights are buzzing with excitement and decadence, particularly the areas around Soho, Leicester Sq and Covent Garden where you'll find people, booze and rickshaws in the streets till the early hours, and bars and clubs that range from the swanky to the skanky.

Bloomsbury & Fitzrovia

Lamb   Pub
Map p64 (www.thelamblondon.com; 94 Lamb's Conduit St, WC1; ⏱noon-11pm Mon-Wed, to midnight Thu-Sat, to 10.30pm Sun; ⊖Russell Sq) The Lamb's central mahogany bar with beautiful Victorian dividers (also called 'snob screens' as they allowed the well-to-do to drink in private) has been a favourite with locals since 1729. Nearly three centuries later, its popularity hasn't waned, so come early to bag a booth.

London Cocktail Club   Cocktail Bar
Map p64 (www.londoncocktailclub.co.uk; 61 Goodge St, W1; ⏱4.30pm-midnight Mon-Fri, from 5pm Sat; ⊖Goodge St) There are cocktails and then there are cocktails. The guys in this slightly tatty subterranean bar will shake, stir, blend and smoke (yes, smoke) you some of the most inventive, colourful and punchy concoctions in creation. Try the smoked apple martini or the squid ink sour.

Soho & Chinatown

Opium   Cocktail Bar
Map p72 (📞020-7734 7276; www.opiumchinatown.com; 15-16 Gerrard St, W1; ⏱5pm-midnight Mon-Wed, to 2am Thu-Sat, noon-midnight Sun) Towering above Chinatown's main drag, what touts itself as a 'cocktail and dim sum parlour' could easily pass as an opium den-cum-brothel with Suzie Wong as host. Everything is in various shades of scarlet, there's a bartender's table with unmarked bottles (surprise, surprise) and the dim sum (£7 to £11) is made with ingredients available at the moment.

Edge   Gay
Map p72 (www.edgesoho.co.uk; 11 Soho Sq, W1; ⏱3pm-1am Mon-Thu, to 3am Fri & Sat, to 11.30pm Sun; ⊖Tottenham Court Rd) Over-

Drinking in Soho
MAREMAGNUM/GETTY IMAGES ©

looking Soho Sq in all its four-storey glory, the Edge is London's largest gay bar and heaves every night of the week: there are dancers, waiters in skimpy outfits, good music and a generally super friendly vibe. There's a heavy straight presence, as it's so close to Oxford St.

Candy Bar   Lesbian
Map p72 (www.ku-bar.co.uk; 4 Carlisle St, W1; ⊙3pm-3am Mon & Wed-Fri, from 1pm Sat, 1-9.30pm Sun; ⊖Tottenham Court Rd) Also called Ku Bar Girls and busy most nights of the week, this is very much a girls' space (though one male guest per two women are allowed) and this should definitely be your first port of call on the London lesbian scene.

Norman's Coach & Horses   Pub
Map p72 (www.coachandhorsessoho.co.uk; 29 Greek St, W1; ⊙11am-11.30pm Mon-Thu, to midnight Fri & Sat, noon-10.30pm Sun; ⊖Leicester Sq) Oh, the times they are a-changing. Once famous as the unreconstructed boozer where *Spectator* columnist Jeffrey Bernard drank himself to death amidst a regular clientele of soaks, writers, hacks, tourists and those too drunk to lift their heads off the counter, this is now London's first vegetarian pub (mains £7.50 to £9). We wish them all the luck in the world.

Loop Bar   Bar
Map p82 (www.theloopbar.co.uk; 19 Dering St, W1; admission £10 after 10pm Fri & Sat; ⊙noon-11pm Mon, to midnight Tue, to 1am Wed, to 3am Thu & Fri, 5pm-3am Sat; ⊖Oxford Circus) Just off Oxford Circus, Loop has three floors of fun: a street-level bar, a sleek basement bar with leather booths and chandeliers and, on the level below that, Groovy Wonderland, a disco-style club with flashing dance floors, platform shoes on the walls and mirror balls everywhere. Fun, fun, fun.

Covent Garden & Leicester Square

Lamb & Flag   Pub
Map p76 (www.lambandflagcoventgarden.co.uk; 33 Rose St, WC2; ⊙11am-11pm Mon-Sat, noon-10.30pm Sun ; ⊖Covent Garden) Pocket-sized but packed with charm and history, the Lamb & Flag is still going strong after three and a half centuries (indeed, the poet John Dryden was mugged outside in 1679). Rain or shine, you'll have to elbow your way to the bar through the merry crowd drinking outside. Inside, it's all brass fittings and creaky wooden floors.

Ku Bar Lisle St   Gay
Map p76 (www.ku-bar.co.uk; 30 Lisle St, WC2; ⊙noon-3am Mon-Sat, to midnight Sun; ⊖Leicester Sq) With its smart interior, geometric black-and-white patterns on the walls and busy events schedule (disco, cabaret, DJ sets etc) in the basement, the Lisle St branch of this gay mini-chain attracts a young, fun-loving crowd. It's student night on Mondays. And all the noodles of Chinatown are close to hand.

Paramount   Bar
Map p76 (☏020-7420 2900; www.paramount. uk.net; 33rd fl, Centre Point, 101-103 New Oxford St, WC1; ⊙8am-1.30am Mon-Wed, to 2.30am Thu-Sat, noon-4pm Sun ; ⊖Tottenham Court Rd) The second best thing about sipping a cocktail from the top of Centre Point, taking in the 360-degree view, is not having to look at the godawful 1960s listed monstrosity you're sitting in. This is probably the best view you'll get in central London. Booking is essential.

Holborn & the Strand

Gordon's Wine Bar   Bar
Map p76 (www.gordonswinebar.com; 47 Villiers St, WC2; ⊙11am-11pm Mon-Sat, noon-10pm Sun; ⊖Embankment) Gordon's is a victim of its own success; it is relentlessly busy and unless you arrive before the office crowd does (generally around 6pm), you can forget about getting a table. It's cavernous and dark, and the French and New World wines are heady and reasonably priced. You can nibble on bread, cheese and olives. Outside garden seating in summer.

Holborn Whippet   Pub
Map p76 (www.holbornwhippet.com; Sicilian Ave, WC1; ⊙11am-1am; ⊖Holborn) This new breed of pub – tiny, all wood, at the end of a pedestrian-only street – stocks a

commendable range of ales (we counted two dozen) from small craft breweries. Staff are more than keen to offer a taste from the spouts on the 'brick wall' to help you decide.

Princess Louise — Pub
Map p76 (208 High Holborn, WC1; ⏰11.30am-11pm Mon-Fri, noon-11pm Sat, to 10.30pm Sun; ⊖Holborn) This late-19th-century Victorian pub is spectacularly decorated with a riot of fine tiles, etched mirrors, plasterwork and a stunning central horseshoe bar. The old Victorian wood partitions give punters plenty of nooks and alcoves to hide in. Beers are from the Sam Smith brewery only but cost just under £3 a pint, so it's no wonder many elect to spend the whole evening here.

Mayfair
Galvin at Windows — Bar
Map p82 (www.galvinatwindows.com; London Hilton on Park Lane, 28th fl, 22 Park Lane, W1; ⏰11am-1am Mon-Wed, to 3am Thu-Sat, to 11pm Sun; ⊖Hyde Park Corner) This swish bar on the edge of Hyde Park opens onto stunning views, especially at dusk. Cocktail prices reach similar heights (£11.50 to £15.25) but the leather seats are comfortable and the marble bar is gorgeous. The restaurant (same views, one Michelin star) offers a two- and three-course lunch menu for £25 and £29.

☆ Entertainment

Madame Jo Jo's — Club
Map p72 (www.madamejojos.com; 8 Brewer St, W1; ⏰8pm-3am Tue, from 10pm Wed-Sat, from 9.30pm Sun; ⊖Leicester Sq, Piccadilly Circus) The renowned subterranean crimson cabaret bar and all its sleazy fun comes into its own with Kitsch Cabaret on Saturday and Burlesque Idol on the last Friday of the month. Andy Smith's Lost & Found club night on Saturdays is legendary, attracting a cool crew of breakdancers, jazz dancers and party people. It's Tranny Shack (drag queen night) on Wednesdays.

12 Bar Club — Live Music
Map p76 (www.12barclub.com; Denmark St, WC2; admission £6-10; ⏰7pm-3am Mon-Sat, to 12.30am Sun; ⊖Tottenham Court Rd) Small, intimate, with a rough-and-ready feel, the 12 Bar is a favourite live-music venue, with anything from solo acts to bands performing nightly. The emphasis is on songwriting and the music is very much indie rock, with anything from folk and jazzy influences to full-on punk and metal sounds.

Royal Opera House — Opera
Map p76 (☎020-7304 4000; www.roh.org.uk; Bow St, WC2; tickets £7-175; ⊖Covent Garden) The £210 million redevelopment for the millennium gave classic opera a fantastic setting in London, and coming here for a night is a sumptuous – if pricey – affair. Although the program has been fluffed up by modern influences, the main attractions are still the opera and classical ballet – all are wonderful productions and feature world-class performers.

Comedy Store — Comedy
Map p72 (☎0844 871 7699; www.thecomedystore.co.uk; 1a Oxendon St, SW1; admission £15-22.50; ⊖Piccadilly Circus) This was one of the first (and is still one of the best) comedy clubs in London. Wednesday and Sunday night's Comedy Store Players is the most famous improvisation outfit in town, with the wonderful Josie Lawrence; on Thursdays, Fridays and Saturdays Best in Stand Up features the best on London's comedy circuit.

Pizza Express Jazz Club — Jazz
Map p72 (☎0845 602 7017; www.pizzaexpresslive.com; 10 Dean St, W1; admission £15-20; ⊖Tottenham Court Rd) Believe it or not, Pizza Express is one of the best jazz venues in London. It's a bit of a strange arrangement, in a basement beneath the main chain restaurant, but it seems to work. Lots of big names perform here and such promising artists as Norah Jones, Jamie Cullum and the late Amy Winehouse played here in their early days.

ADINA TOVY/GETTY IMAGES ©

Ronnie Scott's — Jazz

Map p72 (📞020-7439 0747; www.ronniescotts. co.uk; 47 Frith St, W1; 🕙6.30pm-3am Mon-Sat, to midnight Sun; 🚇Leicester Sq, Tottenham Court Rd) Ronnie Scott originally opened his jazz club on Gerrard St in 1959 under a Chinese gambling den. The club moved to its current location six years later and became widely known as Britain's best jazz club. Gigs are at 8.30pm (8pm Sunday) with a second one at 11.15pm Friday and Saturday, and are followed by a late show until 2am. Expect to pay between £20 and £50.

Borderline — Concert Venue

Map p72 (www.mamacolive.com/theborderline; Orange Yard, off Manette St, W1; 🚇Tottenham Court Rd) Through the Tex-Mex entrance off Orange Yard and down into the basement you'll find a packed, 275-capacity venue that really punches above its weight. Read the gig list: Crowded House, REM, Blur, Counting Crows, PJ Harvey, Lenny Kravitz, Debbie Harry, plus many anonymous indie outfits, have all played here. The crowd is equally diverse but full of music journos and record-company talent spotters.

Place — Dance

Map p64 (www.theplace.org.uk; 17 Duke's Rd, WC1; 🚇Euston Sq) One of London's most exciting cultural venues, this was the birthplace of modern British dance; it still concentrates on challenging and experimental choreography. Behind the late-Victorian facade you'll find a 300-seat theatre, an arty, creative cafe atmosphere and a dozen training studios. The Place sponsors an annual Place Prize, which awards new and outstanding dance talent. Tickets cost £12 to £25.

Wigmore Hall — Classical Music

Map p82 (www.wigmore-hall.org.uk; 36 Wigmore St, W1; 🚇Bond St) This is one of the best and most active (400 events a year) classical-music venues in town, not only because of its fantastic acoustics, beautiful art nouveau hall and great variety of concerts and recitals, but also because of the sheer standard of the performances. Built in 1901, it has remained one of the world's top places for chamber music.

🔒 Shopping

The West End's shopping scene hardly needs a formal introduction. Oxford St is heaven or hell, depending on what you're after; it's all about chains, from Marks & Spencer to H&M, Top Shop to Gap. Covent Garden is also beset with run-of-the-mill outlets, but they tend to be smaller and counterbalanced by independent boutiques, vintage ones in particular. As well as fashion, the West End is big on music. There are some great independent record shops, especially in Soho.

Westminster & St James's

Penhaligon's   Accessories

Map p68 (www.penhaligons.com; 16-17 Burlington Arcade, W1; ⊙10am-6pm Mon-Fri, to 6.30pm Sat, 11am-5pm Sun; ⊖Piccadilly Circus, Green Park) Penhaligon's is the antidote to buying your favourite scent at airport duty-free. Here attendants ask about your favourite smells, take you on an exploratory tour of the shop's signature range and help you discover new scents. There is a range of products, from traditional perfumes to home fragrances and bath and body products. Everything is made in Cornwall.

Fortnum & Mason   Department Store

Map p68 (www.fortnumandmason.com; 181 Piccadilly, W1; ⊙10am-8pm Mon-Sat, 11.30am-6pm Sun; ⊖Piccadilly Circus) London's oldest grocery store, now into its fourth century, refuses to yield to modern times. Its staff are still dressed in old-fashioned tailcoats and it keeps its glamorous food hall supplied with hampers, cut marmalade, speciality teas and so on. Downstairs is an elegant wine bar as well as elegant kitchenware, luxury gifts and perfumes.

Bloomsbury & Fitzrovia

Bang Bang Clothing
Exchange   Vintage

Map p64 (www.bangbangclothingexchange.co.uk;
21 Goodge St, W1; 🕐10am-6.30pm Mon-Fri, 11am-
6pm Sat; 🚇Goodge St) Got some designer or
high-street or vintage pieces you're tired
of? Bang Bang exchanges, buys and sells.
As they say, 'think of Alexander McQueen
cocktail dresses rubbing shoulders with
Topshop shoes and 1950s jewellery'.

James Smith & Sons   Accessories

Map p76 (www.james-smith.co.uk; 53 New Oxford
St, WC1; 🕐10am-6pm Mon-Fri, to 5.30pm Sat;
🚇Tottenham Court Rd) 'Outside every silver
lining is a big black cloud', claim the
cheerful owners of this quintessential
English shop. Nobody makes and stocks
such elegant umbrellas, walking sticks
and canes as this traditional place does.
They've been here since 1857 and, thanks
to London's notoriously bad weather,
they'll hopefully do great business for
years to come.

Soho & Chinatown

Joy   Fashion

Map p72 (www.joythestore.com; 162-170 Wardour
St, W1; 🕐10am-7pm Mon-Fri, to 8pm Sat, noon-
7pm Sun; 🚇Tottenham Court Rd, Oxford Circus)
Joy is an artistic blend of mainstream and
vintage: there are excellent clothes, from
silk dresses for women, fabulous shirts
for men and timeless T-shirts for both, as
well as funky gadgets such as moustache
clocks and lip-shaped ice cube trays.
Conventional shoppers abstain!

Hamleys   Toys

Map p72 (www.hamleys.com; 188-196 Regent
St, W1; 🕐10am-8pm Mon-Fri, 9.30am-8pm Sat,
noon-6pm Sun; 🚇Oxford Circus) Said to be
the largest toy store in the world, Hamleys
is a layer cake of playthings. Spread over
five floors are computer games next to
preschool toys, girls' playthings opposite
model cars and science kids next to the
latest playground trends. The confection
is topped off with Lego world and a cafe
on the 5th floor.

Liberty — Department Store

Map p72 (www.liberty.co.uk; Great Marlborough St, W1; ⏱10am-8pm Mon-Sat, noon-6pm Sun; ⊖Oxford Circus) An irresistible blend of contemporary styles in an old-fashioned mock-Tudor atmosphere, Liberty has a huge cosmetics department and an accessories floor, along with a breathtaking lingerie section, all at very inflated prices. A classic London souvenir is a Liberty fabric print, especially in the form of a scarf.

Beyond Retro — Vintage

Map p72 (www.beyondretro.com; 58-59 Great Marlborough St, W1; ⏱10.30am-7.30pm Mon-Wed & Sat, to 8.30pm Fri & Sat, 11am-6pm Sun; ⊖Oxford Circus) A more central basement outlet of an enormous warehouse off Brick Lane in East London, Beyond Retro sells vintage and some vintage repro clothes for men and women, with the requisite stilettos, bowler and top hats and satin wedding dresses.

Sister Ray — Music

Map p72 (www.sisterray.co.uk; 34-35 Berwick St, W1; ⏱10am-8pm Mon-Sat, noon-6pm Sun; ⊖Oxford Circus, Tottenham Court Rd) If you were a fan of the late, great John Peel on the BBC/BBC World Service, this specialist in innovative, experimental and indie music is just right for you.

Covent Garden & Leicester Square

Neal's Yard Dairy — Food

Map p76 (www.nealsyarddairy.co.uk; 17 Shorts Gardens, WC2; ⏱10am-7pm Mon-Sat; ⊖Covent Garden) A fabulous, fragrant cheese house that would fit in rural England, this place is proof that the British can do just as well as the French when it comes to big rolls of ripe cheese. There are more than 70 varieties that the shopkeepers will let you taste, including independent farmhouse brands. Condiments, pickles, jams and chutneys are also on sale.

Benjamin Pollock's Toy Shop — Toys

Map p76 (www.pollocks-coventgarden.co.uk; 1st fl, 44 Market bldg, Covent Garden, WC2; ⏱10.30am-6pm Mon-Sat, 11am-4pm Sun; ⊖Covent Garden) Here's a traditional toyshop stuffed with the things that kids of all ages love. There are Victorian paper theatres, wooden marionettes and finger puppets, and antique teddy bears that might be too fragile to play with.

Do Shop — Homewares

Map p76 (www.do-shop.com; 34 Shorts Gardens, WC2; ⏱10am-6.30pm Mon-Wed, Fri & Sat, to 8pm Thu, noon-6pm Sun; ⊖Covent Garden) A great collection of always functional furniture, kitchenware and home accessories from independent designers, including students at the Royal College of Art. Check out the versatile tables that double as bookshelves, the neon bento boxes or scrunched-up paper cups that are made of porcelain. Perfect for presents.

Liberty
LONELY PLANET/GETTY IMAGES ©

Bookworm Paradise: The West End's Best Bookshops

Daunt Books (Map p82; www.dauntbooks.co.uk; 83 Marylebone High St, W1; ⊙9am-7.30pm Mon-Sat, 11am-6pm Sun; ⊖Baker St) An original Edwardian bookshop, with oak panels and gorgeous skylights, Daunt is one of London's loveliest travel bookshops. It has two floors and stocks general fiction and nonfiction titles as well.

London Review Bookshop (Map p64; www.lrb.co.uk; 14 Bury Pl, WC1; ⊙10am-6.30pm Mon-Sat, noon-6pm Sun; ⊖Holborn) The flagship bookshop of the *London Review of Books* magazine doesn't believe in piles of books, taking the clever approach of stocking wide-ranging titles in one or two copies only. It hosts high-profile author talks (tickets £7), and there is a **cafe** where you can peruse your new purchases.

Foyle's (Map p72; www.foyles.co.uk; 113-119 Charing Cross Rd, WC2; ⊙9.30am-9pm Mon-Sat, 11.30am-6pm Sun; ⊖Tottenham Court Rd) This is London's most legendary bookshop, where you can bet on finding even the most obscure of titles. The lovely **cafe** is on the 1st floor where you'll also find **Grant & Cutler** (Map p72; www.grantandcutler.com; 113-119 Charing Cross Rd, WC2; ⊖Oxford Circus), the UK's largest foreign-language bookseller. **Ray's Jazz** (Map p72; www.foyles.co.uk; 113-119 Charing Cross Rd, WC2; ⊙9.30am-9pm Mon-Sat, 11.30am-6pm Sun; ⊖Tottenham Court Rd) is on the 3rd floor.

Stanford's (Map p76; www.stanfords.co.uk; 12-14 Long Acre, WC2; ⊙9am-8pm Mon-Fri, from 10am Sat, noon-6pm Sun; ⊖Leicester Sq, Covent Garden) As a 150-year-old seller of maps, guides and literature, the grand-daddy of travel bookshops is a destination in its own right. Ernest Shackleton and David Livingstone and, more recently, Michael Palin and Brad Pitt have all popped in here.

Skoob Books (Map p64; www.skoob.com; 66 The Brunswick, off Marchmont St, WC1; ⊙10.30am-8pm Mon-Sat, to 6pm Sun; ⊖Russell Sq) Skoob (you work out the name) has got to be London's largest secondhand bookshop, with some 60,000 titles spread over 2500 sq ft of floor space. If you can't find it here, it probably doesn't exist.

Marylebone

Cath Kidston Homewares, Clothing
Map p82 (www.cathkidston.co.uk; 51 Marylebone High St, W1; ⊙10am-7pm Mon-Wed, Fri & Sat, to 8pm Thu, 11am-6pm Sun; ⊖Baker St) If you favour the colourful preppy look, you'll love Cath Kidston with her signature floral prints and 1950s fashion (dresses cinched at the waist, shawls and old-fashioned pyjamas). There's also a range of homewares.

Mayfair

Sting Fashion
Map p72 (www.thesting.nl; 55 Regent St, W1; ⊙10am-10pm Mon-Sat, noon-6pm Sun; ⊖Piccadilly Circus) This Dutch chain is a 'network of brands': most of the clothes it stocks are European labels that are little known in the UK. Spread over three floors are anything from casual sweatpants and fluorescent T-shirts to elegant dresses, frilly tops and handsome shirts.

Selfridges Department Store
Map p82 (www.selfridges.com; 400 Oxford St, W1; ⊙9.30am-8pm Mon-Wed, to 9pm Thu-Sat, 11.30am-6.15pm Sun; ⊖Bond St) Selfridges loves innovation – it's famed for its inventive window displays by international artists, gala shows and its amazing range of products. It's the trendiest of London's one-stop shops, with labels such as Boudicca, Luella Bartley, Emma Cook, Chloé and Missoni; an unparalleled food hall; and Europe's largest cosmetics department.

The City

The City's ancient, hallowed streets are among London's most fascinating. The Square Mile occupies pretty much exactly the same patch of land around which the Romans first flung up a defensive wall almost 2000 years ago, and probably contains more history within it than the rest of London combined.

The tiny backstreets and ancient churches are today juxtaposed with skyscrapers, office blocks and major financial institutions. Very few people – about 8000 – live here and so, while Monday to Friday the City is very animated, the frantic industry and hum stops at the weekend. Although you'll find most places shut tight until Monday, the City is trying to reverse this by opening such places as One New Change (p113).

Don't miss the standout sights, including St Paul's Cathedral, the Gherkin, the Monument and London's ultimate sight – the Tower of London. All of the big-hitting sights are open at least one weekend day.

Tower Bridge (p106)
JANE SWEENEY/GETTY IMAGES ©

City Highlights

Tower of London (p100)

Of cardinal importance to London as a historic town and a magnificent counterpoint to the modern architecture rising above the City, the Tower of London is crucial to an understanding of this ancient metropolis. The tower's most famous residents are the marvellously attired Yeoman Warders (nicknamed 'Beefeaters') and the ravens who must never leave the tower lest the kingdom fall.

30 St Mary Axe (p109)

London has never strived for absolute altitude in its towers, instead aiming for modest height achieved with innovation and imagination. As much an icon of London as St Paul's Cathedral or Big Ben, the Norman Foster–designed 'Gherkin' sums up the city's fusion of style and originality. It's inaccessible to visitors but makes for some excellent photos.

Tower Bridge (p106)

This London icon is a masterpiece of Victorian engineering and a sight you're unlikely to miss if you spend any time around the City. Some of the best views of Tower Bridge can be had from the embankment in front of the Tower of London. You might get lucky and be in the vicinity when this drawbridge opens dramatically to allow large boats to pass through.

JOHN HAY/GETTY IMAGES ©

NEIL SETCHFIELD/GETTY IMAGES ©

Historic City Pubs (p116)

Whetting your whistle in a London pub is essential to catch Londoners in their element, and where better than a pub with lashings of history? Some of London's most venerable pubs are found in the City, including the hoary Ye Olde Cheshire Cheese (p117) – where a pub has stood since the 16th century, although this one was rebuilt soon after the Great Fire – and the museum-quality Black Friar (p116).

St Paul's Cathedral (p104)

This astonishing church is known to all, but a visit to its hallowed ground must be made to fully appreciate its sublime architecture. The key experience is the climb up into the dome, rewarded with some truly majestic all-around views of London, but the rest of the cathedral is equally rewarding, on all levels.

City Walk

Beginning at Chancery Lane tube station, this saunter through the ancient heart of the City can take under two hours or fill an entire day, depending on how long you spend at each sight. You'll finish at landmark Tower Bridge.

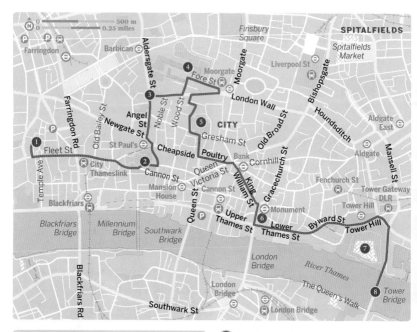

WALK FACTS

- **Start** Dr Johnson's House
- **Finish** Tower Bridge
- **Distance** 3 miles
- **Duration** Two hours

① Dr Johnson's House

Find your way to this miraculously well-preserved early 18th-century mansion (p114) in the heart of the City and explore the story of Dr Johnson's amazing life. Perhaps even drop by his nearby local, Ye Olde Cheshire Cheese (p117), which is just a few steps away to the southeast closer to Fleet St.

② St Paul's Cathedral

Wren's beautiful domed masterpiece, St Paul's Cathedral (p104) somehow eluded Luftwaffe bombs during the Blitz and is one of the London skyline's best-loved features. View the dazzling interior, intriguing crypt, overhead whispering gallery and breathtaking views from the cupola.

③ Museum of London

Head north to this wonderful museum (p107). It may not look like much from the outside, but it's one of the city's best, totally devoted to documenting the multifaceted history of the capital through its many stages of development – from Saxon village to three-time Olympic host.

4 Barbican

Built on the site of an old Roman watch-tower (hence its name), the modern Barbican (p112) is the City's fabulous arts centre and Brutalist masterpiece – check out the public areas with lakes and ponds and John Milton's parish church, St Giles' Cripplegate.

5 Guildhall

Once the very heart of the City, the seat of power and influence, the Guildhall (p111) is today home to the Corporation of London. See the excellent Guildhall Art Gallery (p112) and go back in time two millennia to see the remains of London's Roman Amphitheatre (p112).

6 Monument

This historic column (p107) commemorates the Great Fire of London and, while not for those suffering vertigo, is a superb way to see the City from on high. Despite the number of high-rises all around, the Monument still feels high altitude, giving you an idea of how massive it would have looked in the late 17th century.

7 Tower of London

The sheer amount of history within the enormous stone walls of the Tower of London (p100) is hard to fathom. The **White Tower**, the **Crown Jewels**, the **Yeoman Warders** and **Traitor's Gate** are all equally fascinating. Spend as much time as you can here.

8 Tower Bridge

A symbol of London since the day it opened, Tower Bridge (p106) is a must-see. A walk across it (and a visit to the interesting exhibition, from which the views are spectacular) is crucial to appreciate old Father Thames at its widest and most spectacular.

⭐ The Best...

PLACES TO EAT

Sweeting's The place for seafood in the City, with real pedigree. (p116)

Duck & Waffle Brasserie fare from on high in the heart of the City. (p115)

Bread Street Kitchen The latest from Gordon Ramsay in the City's favourite new mall. (p116)

Restaurant at St Paul's Fine Modern British fare in a classic setting. (p116)

PLACES TO DRINK

Vertigo 42 Plump for a day with clear skies and settle down for the bravura performance of sunset. (p116)

Blackfriar Fine pub with distinctive, much-loved interior and bags of character. (p116)

Folly Leafy bar-cum-cafe around the corner from the Monument. (p116)

CHURCHES

St Bartholomew-the-Great Authentic Norman remains and an age-old sense of tranquility. (p113)

St Stephen Walbrook Seventeenth-century Wren masterpiece in the City. (p111)

Temple Church Ancient church with a lineage back to the Crusades. (p114)

Beefeater and raven, Tower of London (p100)
MAX ALEXANDER/GETTY IMAGES ©

Don't Miss
Tower of London

The absolute heart of London, with a history as bleak and bloody as it is fascinating, the Tower of London should be very near the top of anyone's list of London's sights. Begun during the reign of William the Conqueror (1066–87), the Tower is in fact a castle, and has served over the years as a palace, an observatory, a storehouse and a mint. But it is, of course, most famous for its grizzly past as a prison and place of execution.

Map p108

☎ 0844 482 7777

www.hrp.org.uk/
toweroflondon

Tower Hill, EC3

adult/child
£21.45/10.75,
audioguide £4/3

🕑 9am-5.30pm Tue-
Sat, from 10am Sun
& Mon, to 4.30pm
Nov-Feb

⊖ Tower Hill

White Tower

Begun in 1078, this was the original 'Tower' of London, built as a palace and fortress; its name arose after Henry III whitewashed it in the 13th century. Standing just 30m, it's not exactly tall by modern standards. But in the Middle Ages it would have dwarfed the wooden huts surrounding the castle walls and intimidated the peasantry.

Apart from Norman **St John's Chapel**, most of its interior is given over to a Royal Armouries collection of cannons, guns and suits of mail and armour for men and horses. Among the most remarkable exhibits are Henry VIII's two suits of armour, one made for him when he was a dashing 24-year-old and the other when he was a bloated 50-year-old with a waist measuring 51 inches (129cm).

Tower Green Scaffold Site

Those 'lucky' enough to meet their fate here (rather than suffering the embarrassment of execution on Tower Hill observed by tens of thousands of jeering and cheering onlookers) numbered but a handful and included two of Henry VIII's wives (and alleged adulterers) Anne Boleyn and Catherine Howard; 16-year-old Lady Jane Grey, who fell foul of Henry's daughter Mary I for attempting to have herself crowned queen; and Robert Devereux, Earl of Essex, once a favourite of Elizabeth I.

Crown Jewels

To the east of the chapel and north of the White Tower is the building that visitors most want to see: **Waterloo Barracks**, the home of the Crown Jewels. Inside are dozens of orbs, sceptres and crowns that are the centrepiece, including the Imperial State Crown, set with diamonds (2868 of them, to be exact), sapphires, emeralds, rubies and pearls, and the platinum crown of the late Queen Mother, Elizabeth, which is famously set with the 106-carat Koh-i-Noor (Mountain of Light) diamond from India.

Don't Miss List

BY ALAN KINGSHOTT, CHIEF YEOMAN WARDER AT THE TOWER OF LONDON

1 **TOWER TOUR**
To understand the Tower's history, I suggest visitors take a guided tour by a Yeoman Warder. Few people appreciate that the Tower is actually our home as well as our place of work; all the Warders live inside the outer walls. With such a vast amount of history within the walls, you should allow at least three hours to fully enjoy your experience.

2 **CROWN JEWELS**
The new presentation of the Crown Jewels is a must-see with a new layout, which will help visitors easily explore our sometimes complex history and ceremonies. Just ask a member of the Jewel House staff about any item: you will be amazed at their wealth of knowledge and it will enhance your visit.

3 **RAVENS**
We must have six ravens at the Tower at any one time by a Royal Decree put in place by Charles II. According to an old legend, should the birds leave, the monarchy and the White Tower will crumble and fall. We tend not to provoke legends so generally we have eight birds.

4 **CEREMONY OF THE KEYS**
There are many ceremonies at the Tower of London, most of which can be viewed by visitors. However, many happen around royal events such as the Queen's Birthday and the State Opening of Parliament. Alternatively there is the Ceremony of the Keys (the locking up of the Tower of London), which takes place, as it has done for 700 years, at 9.53pm every night. (Note: attendance is free but requires that you apply by post at least two months in advance and supply a return-address envelope.)

Tower of London

TACKLING THE TOWER

Although it's usually less busy in the late afternoon, don't leave your assault on the Tower until too late in the day. You could easily spend hours here and not see it all. Start by getting your bearings on one of the Yeoman Warder (Beefeater) tours; they are included in the cost of admission, entertaining and the easiest way to access the **Chapel Royal of St Peter ad Vincula** ❶, which is where they finish up.

When you leave the chapel, the **Tower Green Scaffold Site** ❷ is directly in front. The building immediately to your left is Waterloo Barracks, where the **Crown Jewels** ❸ are housed. These are the absolute highlight of a Tower visit, so keep an eye on the entrance and pick a time to visit when it looks relatively quiet. Once inside, take things at your own pace. Slow-moving travelators shunt you past the dozen or so crowns that are the treasury's centrepiece, but feel free to double-back for a second or even third pass – particularly if you ended up on the rear travelator the first time around. Allow plenty of time for the **White Tower** ❹, the core of the whole complex, starting with the exhibition of royal armour. As you continue onto the 1st floor, keep an eye out for **St John's Chapel** ❺. The famous **ravens** ❻ can be seen in the courtyard south of the White Tower. Head next through the towers that formed the **Medieval Palace** ❼, then take the **East Wall Walk** ❽ to get a feel for the castle's mighty battlements. Spend the rest of your time poking around the many other fascinating nooks and crannies of the Tower complex.

Chapel Royal of St Peter ad Vincula

This chapel serves as the resting place for the royals and other members of the aristocracy who were executed on the small green out front. Several other historical figures are buried here too, including Thomas More.

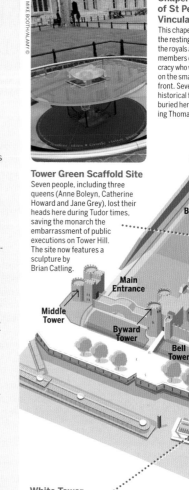

Dry Moat

Tower Green Scaffold Site

Seven people, including three queens (Anne Boleyn, Catherine Howard and Jane Grey), lost their heads here during Tudor times, saving the monarch the embarrassment of public executions on Tower Hill. The site now features a sculpture by Brian Catling.

Beauchamp Tower

Main Entrance

Middle Tower

Byward Tower

Bell Tower

White Tower

Much of the White Tower is taken up with an exhibition on 500 years of royal armour. Look for the virtually cuboid suit made to match Henry VIII's bloated body, complete with an oversized armoured pouch to protect, ahem, the crown jewels.

BEAT THE QUEUES

» **Buy** your fast-track ticket in advance online or at the City of London Information Centre in St Paul's Churchyard.

» **Become a member** An annual Historic Royal Palaces membership allows you to jump the queues and visit the Tower (and four other London palaces) as often as you like.

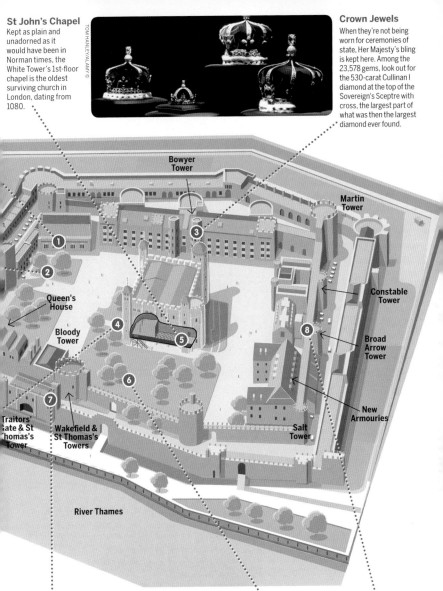

St John's Chapel
Kept as plain and unadorned as it would have been in Norman times, the White Tower's 1st-floor chapel is the oldest surviving church in London, dating from 1080.

Crown Jewels
When they're not being worn for ceremonies of state, Her Majesty's bling is kept here. Among the 23,578 gems, look out for the 530-carat Cullinan I diamond at the top of the Sovereign's Sceptre with cross, the largest part of what was then the largest diamond ever found.

Bowyer Tower

Martin Tower

Constable Tower

Broad Arrow Tower

Queen's House

Bloody Tower

New Armouries

Traitors' Gate & St Thomas's Tower

Wakefield & St Thomas's Towers

Salt Tower

River Thames

Medieval Palace
This part of the Tower complex was begun around 1220 and was home to England's medieval monarchs. Look for the recreations of the bedchamber of Edward I (1272–1307) in St Thomas's Tower and the throne room of his father, Henry III (1216–72) in the Wakefield Tower.

Ravens
This stretch of green is where the Tower's half-dozen ravens are kept, fed on raw meat and blood-soaked bird biscuits. According to legend, if the birds were to leave the Tower, the kingdom would fall.

East Wall Walk
Follow the inner ramparts, starting from the 13th-century Salt Tower, passing through the Broad Arrow and Constable Towers, and ending at the Martin Tower, where the Crown Jewels were stored till the mid-19th century.

⊛ Don't Miss
St Paul's Cathedral

Towering over Ludgate Hill, in a superb position that has been a place of worship for more than 1400 years, St Paul's Cathedral is one of London's most majestic and iconic buildings. For Londoners, the vast dome, which still manages to dominate the skyline despite the far higher skyscrapers of the Square Mile, is a symbol of resilience and pride, standing tall for over 300 years.

Map p108

www.stpauls.co.uk

St Paul's Churchyard, EC4

adult/child £16/7

🕑8.30am-4.30pm Mon-Sat, last entry 4pm

⊖St Paul's

Architecture

St Paul's was designed by Sir Christopher Wren and is one of the first examples of the English Baroque style of architecture. It is crowned with a magnificent dome, the second largest in Europe. The exterior and interior are ornately carved with the most wonderful swags of fruit and flowers and cherubs and everything is sparkling after a decade-long £40 million cleaning that included an outside 'face peel' and filled 2000 vacuum-cleaner bags.

Dome & Upper Galleries

Wren's tour de force, the dome consists of three parts: a brick inner dome, a lead outer dome and a brick cone in between supporting the latter. Appropriately enough, it's a three-stage journey to the top: through a door on the western side of the southern transept and some 30m (257 steps) above, you reach the interior walkway around the dome's base. This is the **Whispering Gallery**, where if you talk into the wall it can be heard on the other side. It also has a view down to the cathedral floor. Climbing another 119 steps brings you to the **Stone Gallery**, an exterior viewing platform rather obscured by pillars. The 152 iron steps to the **Golden Gallery** are steeper and narrower than below but are really worth the effort. From here, 85m above London, you can enjoy superb 360-degree views.

Interior

The magnificent interior is flooded with light and is decorated with statues commemorating celebrated Britons. In the northern aisle you'll find the grandiose **Duke of Wellington Memorial**, completed in 1912. In the north transept chapel is William Holman Hunt's painting, *The Light of the World*, which depicts Christ knocking at an overgrown door that can only be opened from the inside. Beyond, in the cathedral's heart, are the particularly spectacular **quire** (or chancel) – its ceilings and arches dazzling with green, blue, red and gold mosaics – and **high altar**. The **dome** is painted with scenes from the life of St Paul. On the floor just beneath the dome is a compass and epitaph written for Wren by his son: *Lector, si monumentum requiris, circumspice* (Reader, if you seek his monument, look around you).

American Memorial Chapel

Located behind the high altar, this chapel commemorates the 28,000 Americans who were killed on their way to, or stationed in, the UK during WWII. Their names are recorded in a 500-page illuminated **Roll of Honour** and a page of it has been turned by a gloved hand every day since the chapel was dedicated in 1958. American visitors will enjoy spotting the depictions of the flora and fauna of North America and references to historical events that adorn the chapel's carved wood panelling and metalwork.

Crypt

On the eastern side of both the north and south transepts are stairs leading down to the crypt and **OBE Chapel**, where services are held for members of the Order of the British Empire. The crypt has memorials to some 300 military demigods, including Florence Nightingale and Lord Kitchener.

Wren's tomb is also in the crypt, and near it is a kind of **'Painters' Corner'** to match Poets' Corner in Westminster Abbey, with the tombs of Sir Joshua Reynolds, Sir John Everett Millais, Frederic, Lord Leighton; JMW Turner; and William Holman Hunt.

Discover the City

Getting There & Away

o **Underground** The handiest tube lines are Bank (Central, Northern, DLR and Waterloo & City) and St Paul's (Central Line), but Blackfriars (Circle and District), Barbican (Circle, Metropolitan and Hammersmith & City) and Tower Hill (Circle & District) are useful for sights further afield.

o **Bus** For a west-to-east sweep from Oxford Circus through St Paul's, Bank and Liverpool St, hop on the 8; and from Piccadilly Circus via Fleet St and the Tower, the 15. The 11 sets off from Liverpool St and passes Bank and Mansion House on its way to Chelsea. The 26 follows the same route through the City but branches off for Waterloo.

Sights

St Paul's Cathedral   Church
See p104.

Tower of London   Castle
See p100.

Tower Bridge   Bridge
Map p108 (Θ Tower Hill) One of London's most recognisable sights, Tower Bridge doesn't disappoint up close. Built in 1894 as a much-needed crossing point in the east, it was equipped with a then revolutionary bascule (see-saw) mechanism that could clear the way for oncoming ships in three minutes. Although London's days as a thriving port are long over, the bridge still does its stuff, lifting around 1000 times a year and as often as 10 times a day in summer.

Housed within is the **Tower Bridge Exhibition** Map p108 (www.towerbridge.org.uk; adult/child £8/3.40; ⊙10am-6pm Apr-Sep, 9.30am-5.30pm Oct-Mar; Θ Tower Hill), which explains the nuts and bolts of it all. If you're not technically minded, it's still fascinating to get inside the bridge and look along the Thames from its two walkways. A lift takes you to the top of the structure, 42m above the river, from where you can walk along the east- and west-facing walkways, lined with information boards. There are a couple of stops on the way down before you exit and continue on to the Engine Rooms, which provide the real mechanical detail, and also house a few interactive exhibits and a couple of short films.

Leadenhall Market (p110)
DAVID BANK/GETTY IMAGES ©

Museum of London · Museum

Map p108 (www.museumoflondon.org.uk; 150 London Wall, EC2; ⏰10am-6pm; ⊖Barbican) **FREE** One of the capital's best museums, this is a fascinating walk through the various incarnations of the city from Anglo-Saxon village to 21st-century metropolis contained in two-dozen galleries.

The first gallery, London Before London, brings to life the ancient settlements that predated the capital and is followed by the Roman era, full of excellent displays, models and archaeological finds. The rest of the floor takes you through the Saxon, medieval (don't miss the 1348 Black Death video), Tudor and Stuart periods, culminating in the Great Fire of London in 1666. After a glimpse of the real Roman wall from the window, head down to the modern galleries where, in Expanding City, you'll find exquisite fashion and jewellery, the graffited walls of a prison cell (1750) and the Rhinebeck Panorama, an incredibly detailed watercolour of London in 1806-7.

After a quick spin through the recreated Pleasure Gardens, you emerge onto a glorious re-creation of a Victorian street. Highlights of the galleries leading up to the present day include a 1908 taxi cab, an art deco 1928 lift from Selfridges, an interactive water pump that makes clear the perils of the once insanitary water system and costumes worn by East End Pearly Kings and Queens. The testimonies of ordinary people from WWII are particularly moving, and in the last gallery you'll find the rather impressive Lord Mayor's Coach dating from 1757.

There's also a great shop and two cafes. Free highlights tours lasting a half-hour depart daily at 11am (not Saturday), noon, 3pm and 4pm.

Monument · Tower

Map p108 (www.themonument.info; Fish Street Hill, EC3; adult/child £3/1; ⏰9.30am-5.30pm; ⊖Monument) Sir Christopher Wren's 1677 column, known simply as the Monument, is a memorial to the Great Fire of London of 1666, whose impact on London's history cannot be overstated. An immense Doric column made of Portland stone, it is 4.5m wide, and 60.6m tall – the exact distance it stands from the bakery in Pudding Lane where the fire reputedly started – and is topped with a gilded bronze urn of flames that some think looks like a big gold pincushion. Although Lilliputian by today's standards, the Monument would have been gigantic when built, and towered over London.

Climbing up the column's 311 spiral steps rewards you with some of the best 360-degree views over London (due to its central location as much as its height). And after your descent, you'll also be the proud owner of a certificate that commemorates your achievement.

All Hallows by the Tower · Church

Map p108 (www.ahbtt.org.uk; Byward St, EC3; ⏰8am-6pm Mon-Fri, 10am-5pm Sat, 10am-1pm Sun; ⊖Tower Hill) **FREE** A church by this name (meaning 'all saints') has stood here since AD 675. Despite its proximity to the spot where the Great Fire started (Samuel Pepys watched the blaze from the brick tower), All Hallows survived virtually unscathed, only to be hit by German bombs in 1940.

In the atmospheric Saxon undercroft (crypt) you'll find a pavement of 2nd-century Roman tiles and walls of the 7th-century Saxon church. In the nave, note the pulpit taken from a Wren church on Cannon St destroyed in WWII and the beautiful 17th-century font cover decorated by the master woodcarver Grinling Gibbons. The church has a strong American connection: William Penn, founder of Pennsylvania, was baptised here in 1644, and John Quincy Adams, sixth president of the USA, was married here in 1797.

Trinity Square Gardens · Gardens

Map p108 (⊖Tower Hill) Just west of Tower Hill tube station, this was once the site of the Tower Hill scaffold where many met their fate, the last in 1747. Now it's a much more peaceful place, ringed with important buildings and bits of the Roman wall.

To the north is **Trinity House** (1795), topped with a ship weather vane and housing the General Lighthouse Authority

The City

THE CITY SIGHTS

The City

for England and Wales. To the west is the massive former **Port of London Authority building** (1922) lorded over by Father Thames; it's now being converted into a residential block and hotel. To the south is Edwin Lutyens' **Tower Hill Memorial** (1928), dedicated to the 24,000 merchant sailors who died in both world wars and have no known grave except the sea. On a grassy area next to the tube's main exit there's a stretch of the **medieval wall** built on Roman foundations, with a modern **statue of Emperor Trajan** (r AD 98–117) standing in front of it.

St Olave's   Church
Map p108 (www.sanctuaryinthecity.net; 8 Hart St, EC3; ⏰9am-5pm Mon-Fri Sep-Jul; ⊖Tower Hill) FREE Tucked at the end of quiet Seething Lane, St Olave's was built in the mid-15th century and survived the Great Fire. It was bombed in 1941 and restored in the 1950s. The diarist Samuel Pepys worshipped and is buried here; see the

tablet on the south wall. Dickens called the place 'St Ghastly Grim' because of the skulls above its main entrance.

30 St Mary Axe   Notable Building
Map p108 (Gherkin; www.30stmaryaxe.co.uk; 30 St Mary Axe, EC3; ⊖Aldgate) Nicknamed 'the Gherkin' for its pickle-like shape, 30 St Mary Axe remains the City's most distinctive skyscraper, dominating the skyline though actually being slightly smaller than the neighbouring NatWest Tower. Built in 2003 by award-winning Norman Foster, the Gherkin's futuristic exterior has become an emblem of modern London.

Lloyd's of London   Notable Building
Map p108 (www.lloyds.com/lloyds/about-us/the-lloyds-building; 1 Lime St, EC3; ⊖Aldgate, Monument) While the world's leading insurance brokers are inside underwriting everything from cosmonauts' lives to film stars' legs, people outside still stop to gawp at the stainless-steel external ducting and

Below: Mosaic of St Stephen at St Stephen Walbrook; **Right:** Guildhall
(BELOW) NEIL HOLMES/GETTY IMAGES ©; (RIGHT) LONELY PLANET/GETTY IMAGES ©

staircases of this 1986 building. Designed by Richard Rogers, one of the architects responsible for the Pompidou Centre in Paris, its brave-new-world postmodernism strikes a particular contrast with the olde-worlde Leadenhall Market situated next door.

Leadenhall Market   Market
Map p108 (www.leadenhallmarket.co.uk; Whittington Ave, EC3; ☉public areas 24hr, shop times vary; ⊖Bank) Like stepping into a small slice of Victorian London, a visit to this covered mall off Gracechurch St is a step back in time. There's been a market on this site since the Roman era, but the architecture that survives is all cobblestones and late–19th-century ironwork; even modern restaurants and chain stores decorate their facades in period style here.

The market appears as Diagon Alley in *Harry Potter and the Philosopher's Stone* and an optician's shop was used for the entrance to the Leaky Cauldron wizarding pub in *Harry Potter and the Goblet of Fire.*

Bank of England Museum   Museum
Map p108 (www.bankofengland.co.uk/museum; Bartholomew Lane, EC2; ☉10am-5pm Mon-Fri; ⊖Bank) FREE The centrepiece of this museum, which explores the evolution of money and the history of the venerable Bank of England founded in 1694, is a reconstruction of architect John Soane's original Bank Stock Office, complete with original mahogany counters. A series of rooms leading off the office are packed with exhibits ranging from silverware and coins to a 13kg gold bar you can lift up.

Royal Exchange   Historic Building
Map p108 (www.theroyalexchange.co.uk; Royal Exchange, EC3; ☉shops 10am-6pm, restaurants 8am-11pm; ⊖Bank) Founded by Thomas Gresham in 1564, this imposing, colonnaded building at the juncture of Thread-

needle St and Cornhill is the third building on the site; the first was officially opened by Elizabeth I in 1571. It has not had a role as a financial institution since the 1980s and now houses a posh shopping centre and food outlets including the **Royal Exchange Grand Café & Bar** (p116).

Mansion House   Historic Building

Map p108 (📞020-7626 2500; www.cityoflondon. gov.uk; btwn King William St & Walbrook; tour adult/concession £7/5; ⏱2pm Tue; 🚇Bank) Opposite the Bank of England stands porticoed Mansion House, the official residence of the Lord Mayor of the City of London. Built in 1752 by George Dance the Elder, its magnificent interiors, including an impressive art collection and stunning banqueting hall, can be visited on a weekly tour, which leaves from the porch entrance on Walbrook. The 40 tickets are sold on a first-come-first-served basis.

St Stephen Walbrook   Church

Map p108 (www.ststephenwalbrook.net; 39 Walbrook, EC4; ⏱10am-4pm Mon-Fri; 🚇Bank)

FREE Just south of Mansion House, St Stephen Walbrook (1672) is considered to be the finest of Wren's City churches and, as it was his first experiment with a dome, a forerunner to St Paul's Cathedral. Some 16 pillars with Corinthian capitals rise up to support the dome; the modern travertine marble altar nicknamed 'the Camembert' is by sculptor Henry More.

St Mary-le-Bow   Church

Map p108 (📞020-7248 5139; www.stmarylebow. co.uk; Cheapside, EC2; ⏱7.30am-6pm Mon-Wed, to 6.30pm Thu, to 4pm Fri; 🚇St Paul's, Bank) FREE Another of Wren's great churches, St Mary-le-Bow (1673) is famous as the church with the medieval curfew bells that still dictate who is – and who is not – a true cockney; it's said that a true cockney has to have been born within earshot of Bow Bells. The church's delicate steeple is one of Wren's finest works.

Guildhall   Historic Building

Map p108 (📞020-7606 3030; www.guildhall. cityoflondon.gov.uk; Gresham St, EC2; 🚇Bank)

Bang in the centre of the Square Mile, the Guildhall has been the City's seat of government for more than 800 years. The present building dates from the early 15th century, making it the only secular stone structure to have survived the Great Fire of 1666, although it was severely damaged both then and during the Blitz of 1940.

Check in at reception to visit the impressive **Great Hall** (Gresham St, EC2; 9am-5pm, closed Sun Oct-Apr) where you can see the banners and shields of London's 12 principal livery companies, or guilds, which used to wield absolute power throughout the city. Among the monuments to look out for are statues of Winston Churchill, Admiral Nelson, the Duke of Wellington, and the two prime ministers Pitt the Elder and Younger. In the modern buildings to the west is the **Clockmakers' Museum** Map p108 (www.clockmakers.org; 9.30am-4.45pm Mon-Sat) FREE, which has a collection of more than 700 clocks and watches dating back 500 years.

Guildhall Art Gallery & Roman Amphitheatre   Gallery
Map p108 (www.guildhallartgallery.cityoflondon. gov.uk; Guildhall Yard, EC2; special exhibits £5; 10am-5pm Mon-Sat, noon-4pm Sun;

Barbican

Bank) FREE The gallery of the City of London provides a fascinating look at the politics of the Square Mile over the past few centuries, with a great collection of paintings of London in the 18th and 19th centuries. Below the gallery is a Roman amphitheatre dating back to the early 2nd century AD.

The archaeological site was only discovered in 1988 when work finally began on a new gallery after the original's destruction in the Blitz. While only a few remnants of the stone walls lining the eastern entrance still stand, they're imaginatively fleshed out with a black-and-fluorescent-green *trompe l'oeil* of the missing seating, and computer-meshed outlines of spectators and gladiators. Markings on the square outside the Guildhall indicate the original extent and scale of the amphitheatre, which could seat up to 6000 spectators.

Barbican   Historic Building
Map p108 (0845 1216823; www.barbican.org. uk; Silk St, EC2; architectural tours £8; arts centre 9am-11pm Mon-Sat, noon-1pm Sun, architectural tours 4pm Wed, 7pm Thu, 11am & 2pm Sat & 2pm Sun; Barbican or Moorgate) Londoners remain fairly divided about the

architectural legacy of this vast complex built on a huge bomb site abandoned since WWII and opened progressively between 1969 and 1982. The fact remains, however, that it is the City's pre-eminent cultural centre, boasting the main Barbican Hall, two theatres, a new cinema complex and two art galleries, the **Barbican Gallery** (⊙11am-8pm Fri-Tue, to 6pm Wed, to 10pm Thu), and the **Curve** (⊙11am-8pm Fri-Wed, to 10pm Thu).

Getting around the Barbican can be frustrating. There are stairs from the Barbican tube station that take you up onto the highwalks, from where a yellow line on the floor guides you to the arts complex. More straightforward is to walk through the Beech St road tunnel to the Silk St entrance. Guided architectural tours are the best way to make sense of the purpose and beauty of the estate.

St Bartholomew-the-Great
Church

Map p108 (www.greatstbarts.com; West Smithfield, EC1; adult/concession £4/3.50; ⊙8.30am-5pm Mon-Fri, 10.30am-4pm Sat, 8.30am-8pm Sun; ⊖Farringdon or Barbican) Dating to 1123 and adjoining one of London's oldest hospitals, this church was originally part of the monastery of Augustinian Canons, but became the parish church of Smithfield in 1539 when King Henry VIII dissolved the monasteries. William Hogarth was baptised here and the American statesman Benjamin Franklin worked on-site in his youth as an apprentice printer. The church has been used as the setting for many films and TV productions, including *Four Weddings and a Funeral*, *Shakespeare in Love* and *Sherlock Holmes*.

Smithfield Market
Market

Map p108 (www.smithfieldmarket.com; West Smithfield, EC1; ⊙3am-noon Mon-Fri; ⊖Farringdon) Smithfield is central London's last surviving meat market. Its name derives from 'smooth field' where animals could graze, although its history is far from pastoral.

Built on the site of the notorious St Bartholomew's Fair, where witches were traditionally burned at the stake, this

is where Scottish independence leader William Wallace was executed in 1305 (there's a plaque on the wall of St Bart's Hospital south of the market ending with the Gaelic words 'Bas agus Buaidh' or 'Death and Victory'), as well as the place where one of the leaders of the Peasants' Revolt, Wat Tyler, met his end in 1381. Described in terms of pure horror by Dickens in Oliver Twist, this was once the armpit of London, where animal excrement and entrails created a sea of filth. Today the surrounding area is a very smart annexe of Clerkenwell and full of bars and restaurants, while the market itself is a wonderful building. Visit the market before 7am to see it in full swing.

Postman's Park
Park

Map p108 (btwn King Edward & St Martin's-le-Grand Sts, EC1; ⊖St Paul's) FREE This peaceful patch of greenery just north of what was once London's General Post Office on St Martin's-le-Grand St would not rate special mention if it were not for the **Memorial to Heroic Self-Sacrifice**, a loggia with 54 ceramic plaques describing deeds of bravery by ordinary people who died saving the lives of others and who might otherwise have been forgotten.

Temple of Mithras

A site not visible at the time of writing is the City's 3rd-century **Temple of Mithras** (Map p108; ⊖ Bank). It was first uncovered in the 1950s during the construction of Bucklersbury House, an office block on Walbrook St, and then moved to Queen St where it remained until 2010. The peripatetic house of worship is now under wraps while construction of Walbrook Square, future headquarters of the financial media giant Bloomberg, continues and will be relocated to its original site when complete. In the meantime, if you're interested in this Persian god, artefacts found in the temple are on display at the **Museum of London** (p107).

Central Criminal Court (Old Bailey)   Historic Building

Map p108 (www.cityoflondon.gov.uk; cnr Newgate & Old Bailey Sts; ⏲ approx 10am-1pm & 2-4pm Mon-Fri; ⊖ St Paul's) FREE Just as fact is often better than fiction, taking in a trial in what's nicknamed the Old Bailey leaves watching a TV courtroom drama for dust. The Central Criminal Court gets its nickname from the street on which it stands: baillie was Norman French for 'enclosed courtyard'.

The entrance is on Old Bailey St opposite Limeburner Lane and the daily register of cases is outside to the right of the doorway. Choose from 18 courts, of which the oldest – courts one to four – usually have the most interesting cases. As cameras, video equipment, mobile phones, large bags and food and drink are all forbidden inside, and there are no cloakrooms or lockers, it's important not to take these with you. If you're interested in a high-profile trial, get there early.

Temple Church   Church

Map p108 (☎ 020-7353 8559; www.temple-church.com; Temple, EC4; adult/concession £4/2; ⏲ 11am-1pm & 2-4pm Mon-Fri, hrs vary) This magnificent church was built by the secretive Knights Templar, an order of crusading monks founded in the 12th century to protect pilgrims travelling to and from Jerusalem. Today the sprawling oasis of fine buildings and pleasant, traffic-free green space is home to two Inns of Court, which house the chambers of lawyers practising in the City: Inner Temple and Middle Temple.

The Temple Church has a distinctive design and is in two parts: the Round (consecrated in 1185 and modelled after the Church of the Holy Sepulchre in Jerusalem) adjoins the Chancel (built in 1240), which is the heart of the modern church. Both parts were severely damaged by a bomb in 1941 and have been completely reconstructed. Its most obvious points of interest are the life-size stone effigies of nine 13th-century knights lying on the floor of the Round. Some of them are cross-legged but contrary to popular belief this doesn't necessarily mean they were crusaders. In recent years the church has become a must-see for readers of *The Da Vinci Code* because a key scene was set here.

Check opening times in advance as they change frequently. During the week the easiest access to the church is via Inner Temple Lane, off Fleet St. At weekends you'll need to enter from Victoria Embankment.

Dr Johnson's House   Museum

Map p108 (www.drjohnsonshouse.org; 17 Gough Sq, EC4; adult/child £4.50/1.50, audioguide £2; ⏲ 11am-5.30pm Mon-Sat May-Sep, to 5pm Mon-Sat Oct-Apr; ⊖ Chancery Lane) This wonderful house, built in 1700, is a rare surviving example of a Georgian city mansion. It has been preserved, as it was the home of the great Georgian wit Samuel Johnson, the author of the first serious dictionary of the English language and the man who proclaimed 'When a man is tired of London, he is tired of life'.

Filled with antique furniture and artefacts from Johnson's life, the house is an atmospheric and worthy place to visit. The numerous paintings of Dr Johnson and his associates, including his black manservant Francis Barber and his clerk and biographer James Boswell, are, sadly, not particularly revealing of the great minds who would have considered the building a home away from home. A more revealing object in the parlour is a chair from Johnson's local pub, the Old Cock Tavern on Fleet St. On display in the 2nd-floor library is a copy of the first edition of the dictionary dating from 1755.

St Bride's, Fleet Street   Church

Map p108 (☏020-7427 0133; www.stbrides.com; Bride Lane, EC4; donation requested £2; ⊙8am-6pm Mon-Fri, hrs vary Sat, 10am-6.30pm Sun; ⊖St Paul's, Blackfriars) **FREE** Printing presses fell silent on Fleet St in the 1980s, but St Bride's, designed by Christopher Wren in 1671 and his tallest (and most expensive) church after St Paul's, is still referred to as 'the journalists' church'. There's quite a moving chapel in the north aisle honouring journalists who have died or been injured in the course of their work.

The add-on spire (1703) is said to have inspired the design of the tiered wedding cake. The church was hit by bombs in December 1940, and the interior layout is wood-panelled, modern and not particularly attractive. In the 11th-century crypt, however, there's a well-presented history of the church, its surrounding areas and the printing industry; don't miss the Roman pavement from the 2nd century AD.

⊗ Eating

The financial heart of London unsurprisingly caters to a well-heeled crowd and it can be a tough place to find a meal at the weekend, if not on a weekday evening. You'll find plenty of places to choose from in **One New Change** (p113), however. During the week, **Leadenhall Market** (p110) stalls offer a delicious array of food, from steaming noodles to mountains of sweets (11am to 4pm).

Café Below   Cafe £

Map p108 (www.cafebelow.co.uk; St Mary-le-Bow Church, Cheapside, EC2; mains £6.50-10; ⊙7.30am-2.30pm Mon-Fri; 🥄; ⊖Mansion House) This atmospheric cafe-restaurant, in the crypt of one of London's most famous churches, is breakfast and lunch only these days but offers excellent value and such tasty dishes as fish pie and Moroccan slow roast lamb in focaccia. There's always as many vegetarian choices as meat and fish ones.

St Bartholomew-the-Great (p113)

Duck & Waffle
Brasserie ££

Map p108 (☏020-3640 7310; www.duckandwaf-fle.com; 40th fl, Heron Tower, 110 Bishopsgate, EC2; mains £7-32; ⏱24hr; ⊖Liverpool St) If you like your views with sustenance round the clock, this is the place for you. Perched atop Heron Tower just down from Liverpool St Station, its hearty British dishes (lots of offal, some unusual seafood concoctions like pollack meatballs and chip-shop cod tongues) in small and large sizes by day, waffles by night and drinks any time.

Bread Street Kitchen
Brasserie ££

Map p108 (☏020-3030 4050; www.breadstreet-kitchen.com; 10 Bread St, EC4; mains £12-19; ⏱7am-midnight Mon-Fri, from noon Sat & Sun; ⊖St Paul's) Gordon Ramsay's latest foray into the City makes us wonder whether he thinks he's in East London. It's a huge warehouse-like space in One New Change with a raw bar, wine balcony and open kitchen that produces mostly Modern British favourites like mutton and potato pie and roasted cod. 'Lazy Loaf' brunch just might lure the crowds to the City on a Sunday.

Restaurant at St Paul's
Modern British ££

Map p108 (☏020-7248 2469; www.restauran-tatstpauls.co.uk; Crypt, St Paul's Cathedral, EC4; 2-/3-course lunch £21.50/25.95; ⏱noon-5pm; 📶; ⊖St Paul's) The quality of the dishes at this restaurant in the crypt of St Paul's lives up to the grandeur above. The menu offers two- or three-course lunches, including dishes like duck confit and venison burger with red onion relish. It also does a daily express lunch (£15, including a glass of wine) and afternoon tea (£15.95, with wine £21.95) served Monday to Saturday.

Royal Exchange Grand Café & Bar
Modern European ££

Map p108 (☏020-7618 2480; www.royalex-change-grandcafe.co.uk; Royal Exchange, Bank, EC3; mains £13.50-22; ⏱8am-11pm Mon-Fri; ⊖Bank) This lovely cafe-restaurant sits in the middle of the covered courtyard of the beautiful Royal Exchange building and is a good place to people-watch. The food runs the gamut from breakfast, salads and sandwiches to oysters (from £11 a half-dozen) and rabbit *cassoulet* (£13.50).

Sweeting's
Seafood £££

Map p108 (☏020-7248 3062; www.sweetingsres-taurant.com; 39 Queen Victoria St, EC4; mains £13.50-35; ⏱11.30am-3pm Mon-Fri; ⊖Mansion House) Sweeting's is a City institution, having been around since 1889. It hasn't changed much, with its small sit-down dining area, mosaic floor and narrow counters, behind which stand waiters in white aprons. Dishes include sustainably sourced fish of all kinds (grilled, fried or poached), potted shrimps, eels and Sweeting's famous fish pie (£13.50).

🍷 Drinking & Nightlife

Folly
Bar

Map p108 (www.thefollybar.com; 41 Gracechurch St, EC3; ⏱7.30am-late Fri, from 10am Sat & Sun; ⊖Monument) We love this 'secret garden' bar-cum-cafe on two levels filled with greenery (both real and faux) and picnic-table seating. The aptly named Folly has a full menu on offer, with a strong emphasis on burgers and steaks, but we come for the excellent wine and champagne selection.

Vertigo 42
Bar

Map p108 (☏020-7877 7842; www.vertigo42.co.uk; Tower 42, 25 Old Broad St, EC2; ⏱noon-3.45pm Mon-Fri, 5-11pm Mon-Sat; ⊖Liverpool St) On the 42nd floor of a 183m-high tower, this circular bar has expansive views over the city that stretch for miles on a clear day. The classic drinks list is, as you might expect, pricier than average – wine by the glass starts from £9.50 and champagne and cocktails from £14, and there's also a limited food menu. Reservations essential; minimum spend £10.

Blackfriar
Pub

Map p108 (174 Queen Victoria St, EC4; ⊙10am-11.30 Mon-Thu, to midnight Fri & Sat, to 11pm Sun; ⊖Blackfriars) It may look like the corpulent friar just stepped out of this 'olde pub' just north of Blackfriars station, but the interior is actually an Arts and Crafts makeover dating back to 1905. Built on the site of a monastery of Dominicans (who wore black), the theme is appealingly celebrated throughout the pub. There's a good selection of ales.

Madison
Cocktail Bar

Map p108 (www.madisonlondon.net; Roof Terrace, One New Change, EC4; ⊙10am-midnight Mon-Sat, to 8pm Sun; ⊖St Paul's) Perched atop One New Change with a full-frontal view of St Paul's and beyond, Madison offers one of the largest public open-air roof terraces you'll ever encounter. There's a full restaurant on one side and a cocktail bar with outdoor seating on the other; we come for the latter and for inventive tapas (£4 to £14) like popcorn squid.

Ye Olde Cheshire Cheese
Pub

Map p8 (Wine Office Court, 145 Fleet St, EC4; ⊙11am-11pm Mon-Fri, from noon Sat; ⊖Chancery Lane) The entrance to this historic pub is via a narrow alley off Fleet St. Over its long history locals have included Dr Johnson, Thackeray and Dickens. Despite (or possibly because of) this, the Cheshire feels today like a bit of a museum. Nevertheless it's one of London's most famous pubs and it's well worth popping in for a pint.

⊛ Entertainment

Barbican
Performing Arts

Map p108 (☎0845 121 6823; www.barbican.org.uk; Silk St, EC2; ⊖Barbican) Home to the wonderful London Symphony Orchestra and the lesser-known BBC Symphony Orchestra, the arts centre hosts scores of other leading musicians each year as well, focusing in particular on jazz, folk, world and soul artists. Dance is another strong point here.

The centre's multidisciplinary **Barbican International Theatre Events**, which takes place year-round, showcases some great performances, as well as the work of exciting overseas drama companies alongside local fringe-theatre troupes.

Volupté
Cabaret

Map p108 (☎020-7831 1622; www.volupte-lounge.com; 9 Norwich St, EC4; ⊙4.30pm-1am Tue & Wed, to 3am Thu & Fri, noon-3am Sat; ⊖Chancery Lane) A gorgeous little cabaret venue north of Fleet St, Volupté offers a real variety of burlesque, vaudeville, comedy and live music. During the week, Baby Grand Burlesque offers cabaret stars complete with live music; there's often comedy or a gay club night on Thursday. At the weekend sit down to Afternoon Tease, with live music, cabaret or burlesque performances.

🔒 Shopping

London Silver Vaults
Silver

Map p108 (www.thesilvervaults.com; 53-63 Chancery Lane, WC2; ⊙9am-5.30pm Mon-Fri, to 1pm Sat; ⊖Chancery Lane) The 30 shops that work out of these incredibly secure subterranean vaults make up the largest collection of silver under one roof in the world. Everything from cutlery sets and picture frames to jewellery and tableware is on offer.

Hatton Garden
Jewellery

Map p172 (www.hatton-garden.net; Hatton Garden, EC1; ⊖Chancery Lane) If you're in the market for classic settings and unmounted stones, stroll along Hatton Garden – it's chock-a-block with gold, diamond and jewellery shops, especially at the southern end.

The South Bank

The South Bank has become one of London's must-see neighbourhoods in recent years. A roll call of riverside sights lines this section of the Thames, commencing with the London Eye, running past the cultural enclave of the Southbank Centre and on to the Tate Modern, the Millennium Bridge and Shakespeare's Globe. It continues: waterside pubs, busy boutique shopping quarters, a cathedral, one of London's most visited food markets, a handful of fun diversions for kids and the lofty Shard, the EU's tallest building. Indeed, a stunning panorama unfolds on the far side of the Thames, as head-swivelling architecture rises up on either bank.

The drawcard sights stretch out in a manageable riverside mix, so doing it on foot is the way to go. If you follow the Silver Jubilee Walkway and the South Bank section of the Thames Path along the southern riverbank – one of the most pleasant strolls in town – you can catch it all.

The Shard (p133)

South Bank Highlights

Tate Modern (p124)

London's world-class modern and contemporary art museum remains a firm favourite with visitors as much for its superb Pritzker Prize–winning conversion of the former Bankside Power Station as for its contents. Inside, count on encountering works by Georges Braque, Henri Matisse, Piet Mondrian, Andy Warhol, Mark Rothko and Jackson Pollock.

Eating & Drinking by the River (p134)

For some of London's tastiest and most photogenic views, you can't go wrong booking a table at one of the South Bank's swish riverside restaurants. Both Skylon (p135) and the Oxo Tower Restaurant & Brasserie (p135) pair excellent food with superb vistas, but if it's just a beer on your list, raise a glass to the views of St Paul's from the Anchor Bankside (p137). Oxo Tower Restaurant & Brasserie (p135)

GAIL MOONEY-KELLY/ALAMY ©

London Eye (p128)

③

WALTER ZERLA/GETTY IMAGES ©

Originally erected as a temporary structure to last just five years, the London Eye is now an integral part of the city's skyline and London would be unimaginable without it. Don't miss having a whirl – the views are spectacular and the entire experience is a highlight of many people's visit. Book online to avoid the lines or fast-track your way on.

LONELY PLANET/GETTY IMAGES ©

④

Shakespeare's Globe (p136)

Shakespeare's Globe, a meticulous reproduction of the theatre where the Bard worked and put on many of his plays for the first time, allows you to experience Elizabethan drama exactly as people four centuries ago would have done, including having to stand under roofless skies if you buy the cheapest tickets.

⑤

Borough Market (p132)

If you hear the way that some Londoners talk about Borough Market, you'd imagine it was a holy shrine or a sacred place of pilgrimage. And for foodies and incorrigible gastronomes, it's just that. Come and peruse the freshest produce in the city from Thursday to Saturday and keep an eye out for free samples.

South Bank Walk

This relaxed walk takes you past some of London's best views, standout cultural establishments and architectural highlights. It can be done in under an hour, though it's much better not to rush it. It follows the Thames, a tidal river and the powerhouse that helped put London on the map.

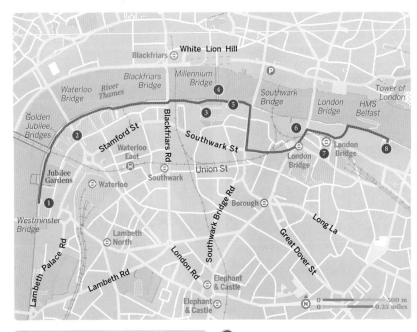

1 County Hall

Across Westminster Bridge from the splendid Houses of Parliament, the grand County Hall (p128) was once the seat of London's local government and affords glorious views of the river. It now houses the London Dungeon (p129), a film museum, the London Sea Life Aquarium (p128), as well as hotels and restaurants.

2 BFI Southbank

The headquarters of the BFI Southbank (p139) is a mecca for celluloid buffs and film historians alike. It screens thousands of films in four theatres each year, with archived films available for viewing in the mediatheque.

3 Tate Modern

London's second-most popular attraction after the august British Museum, the cutting-edge upstart Tate Modern (p124) is housed in the inventively converted Bankside Power Station overlooking Millennium Bridge and the river, and looking forward to its new extension in 2016. Don't miss the excellent installations in the main Turbine Hall.

4 Millennium Bridge

Crossed by up to 10,000 people each day, this pedestrian bridge (p129) links the north and south banks of the Thames. A slender 'blade of light' designed by Sir Norman Foster, it's everything contemporary architecture should be: modern, beautiful and useful.

5 Shakespeare's Globe

Firmly entrenched as a London must-see, the Globe (p136) is a superb recreation of the theatre where Shakespeare worked and saw many of his plays first performed. It is definitely worth visiting and, even if you don't see a play, you can join a tour.

6 Southwark Cathedral

This fantastic cathedral (p133) is well worth a visit, especially for its historical associations and medieval remnants. A monument to Shakespeare, whose great works were originally written for the Southwark playhouses nearby, takes pride of place. Borough Market (p132) is just around the corner.

7 The Shard

Rising up above you at London Bridge is the splinter-like Shard (p133), designed by Italian architect Renzo Piano. Now the tallest building in the EU and a stunning addition to London's architectural landscape, it houses a five-star hotel, restaurants and London's highest public viewing gallery.

8 City Hall

Nicknamed 'the egg' (or, more cheekily, 'the glass testicle'), this bulbous building has also been likened to Darth Vader's helmet. An interior spiral ramp ascends above the assembly chamber to the building's roof, fitted with energy-saving solar panels. Beyond is the gorgeous form of Tower Bridge (p106).

 The Best...

PLACES TO EAT

Anchor & Hope Gastropub famed for its flavourful British dishes. (p135)

Applebee's Fish Cafe Italian-inspired creations from the briny deep. (p137)

Skylon Thames vistas, '50s styling, modern international menu. (p135)

Magdalen Stylish restaurant with excellent cuisine and attentive staff. (p137)

PLACES TO DRINK

George Inn Historic coaching inn, bursting at the seams with age-old charm. (p138)

Baltic East European cocktail bar with enough vodka to float a ship. (p137)

Rake Just bigger than a pigeon hole, with an exemplary range of ales. (p138)

ATTRACTIONS

Tate Modern A feast of wonderfully housed modern and contemporary art. (p124)

London Eye The perfect perspective on town if the sun's out. (p128)

Borough Market A bustling cornucopia of gastronomic delights. (p132)

Shakespeare's Globe Theatre as it was when the Bard was alive and writing. (p139)

City Hall and Tower Bridge (p106) along South Bank
JANE SWEENEY/GETTY IMAGES ©

Don't Miss
Tate Modern

The public's love affair with this phenomenally successful modern art gallery shows no sign of cooling a decade after it opened. In fact, so enraptured are art goers with the Tate Modern that some 5.3 million visitors flock to the former power station every year. To accommodate this exceptional popularity, the world's most popular art gallery is converting the power station's three huge subterranean oil tanks and building a daring 11-storey geometric extension at the back. Grand opening planned for 2016.

Map p130

www.tate.org.uk

Queen's Walk, SE1

⊙10am-6pm Sun-Thu, to 10pm Fri & Sat

⊖Southwark, St Paul's

Architecture

The 200m-long Tate Modern is an imposing sight. The conversion of the empty Bankside Power Station – all 4.2 million bricks of it – to an art gallery in 2000 was a design triumph. Leaving the building's single central 99m-high chimney, adding a two-storey glass box onto the roof and employing the cavernous Turbine Hall as a dramatic entrance space were three strokes of genius. The new extension will similarly be constructed of brick, but artistically devised as a lattice through which interior lights will be visible.

Turbine Hall

Originally housing the power station's humungous turbines, the 3300-sq-m Turbine Hall is the commanding venue for large-scale, temporary exhibitions.

Permanent Collection

Tate Modern's permanent collection is displayed on levels 2, 3 and 4. More than 60,000 works are on constant rotation, which can be frustrating if you'd like to see one particular piece, but it's thrilling for repeat visitors.

The curators have at their disposal paintings by Georges Braque, Henri Matisse, Piet Mondrian, Andy Warhol, Mark Rothko and Jackson Pollock, as well as pieces by Joseph Beuys, Damien Hirst, Rebecca Horn, Claes Oldenburg, Auguste Rodin, Henry Moore and Barbara Helpworth.

Special Exhibitions

Special exhibitions (levels 2 and 3, subject to admission charge) have included retrospectives on Edward Hopper, Frida Kahlo, Roy Lichtenstein, August Strindberg and Joan Miró.

Tours

Audioguides (in five languages) are available for £4 – they contain explanations of about 50 artworks across the galleries and offer suggested tours for adults or children. Free guided highlights tours depart at 11am, noon, 2pm and 3pm daily.

Local Knowledge

Don't Miss

BY SARAH CIACCI, ART HISTORIAN, UNIVERSITY LECTURER AND BLUE BADGE TOURIST GUIDE.

1 THE HANG

The collection is not hung chronologically. Instead, it is arranged in four wings, with each one focusing on a key moment in 20th century art (eg Surrealism or Abstract art). Artists of the 20th century were inspired by the past, the present and the future. Thus modern art doesn't really have a beginning or an end; chronology wouldn't really work here. Instead, you are invited to make your own connections and to use your imagination!

2 SURREALISM

Tate has one of the world's greatest collections of art by the Surrealists, who believed that when you dream your unconscious mind bubbles to the surface. Find a work by Miro, Dali or Magritte, and have a look. So what do you dream about at night?

3 NON-WESTERN ART

One big change in the art world today is interest in art coming from outside Europe and the USA. Look out for works by artists from South America, Asia, Africa and the Middle East and try to see whether their themes and concerns are similar or different from those of Western artists.

4 THE TANKS

The Tanks are massive industrial chambers 30m high and 7m across that once held the oil to fuel the power station. Architecturally they are spectacular and will be used for new forms of art that need space – installations, performance, sound, moving images and works we can participate in.

5 THE VIEWS

Have a cocktail or a meal in the restaurant on level 6, with superb views of the Thames and St Paul's Cathedral. If the weather is fine, grab a coffee from the espresso bar on level 3 and drink it on one of the two riverside balconies.

The River Thames

A FLOATING TOUR

London's history has always been determined by the Thames. The city was founded as a Roman port nearly 2000 years ago and over the centuries since then many of the capital's landmarks have lined the river's banks. A boat trip is a great way to experience the attractions.

There are piers dotted along both banks at regular intervals where you can hop on and hop off

the regular services to visit places of interest. The best place to board is Westminster Pier, from where boats head downstream, taking you from the City of Westminster, the seat of government, to the original City of London, now the financial district and dominated by a growing band of skyscrapers. Across the river, the once shabby and neglected South Bank now bristles with as many top attractions as its northern counterpart, including the slender Shard.

In our illustration we've concentrated on the top highlights you'll enjoy from a waterborne vessel.

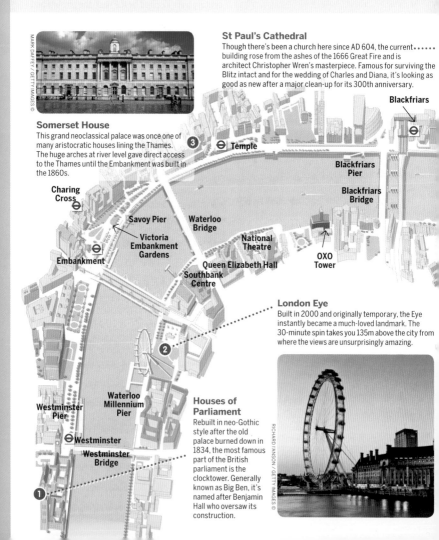

MARK DAFFEY / GETTY IMAGES ©

St Paul's Cathedral
Though there's been a church here since AD 604, the current building rose from the ashes of the 1666 Great Fire and is architect Christopher Wren's masterpiece. Famous for surviving the Blitz intact and for the wedding of Charles and Diana, it's looking as good as new after a major clean-up for its 300th anniversary.

Blackfriars

Somerset House
This grand neoclassical palace was once one of many aristocratic houses lining the Thames. The huge arches at river level gave direct access to the Thames until the Embankment was built in the 1860s.

❸ Temple

Blackfriars Pier

Blackfriars Bridge

Charing Cross

Savoy Pier

Waterloo Bridge

Victoria Embankment Gardens

National Theatre

OXO Tower

Embankment

Queen Elizabeth Hall

Southbank Centre

London Eye
Built in 2000 and originally temporary, the Eye instantly became a much-loved landmark. The 30-minute spin takes you 135m above the city from where the views are unsurprisingly amazing.

❷

Westminster Pier

Waterloo Millennium Pier

Houses of Parliament
Rebuilt in neo-Gothic style after the old palace burned down in 1834, the most famous part of the British parliament is the clocktower. Generally known as Big Ben, it's named after Benjamin Hall who oversaw its construction.

❸ Westminster

Westminster Bridge

❶

RICHARD l'ANSON / GETTY IMAGES ©

These are, from west to east, the **Houses of Parliament ❶**, the **London Eye ❷**, **Somerset House ❸**, **St Paul's Cathedral ❹**, **Tate Modern ❺**, **Shakespeare's Globe ❻**, the **Tower of London ❼** and **Tower Bridge ❽**.

Apart from covering this central section of the river, boats can also be taken upstream as far as Kew Gardens and Hampton Court Palace, and downstream to Greenwich and the Thames Barrier.

BOAT HOPPING

Thames Clippers hop-on/hop-off services are aimed at commuters but are equally useful for visitors, operating every 15 minutes on a loop from piers at Embankment, Waterloo, Blackfriars, Bankside, London Bridge and the Tower. Other services also go from Westminster. Oyster cardholders get a discount off the boat ticket price.

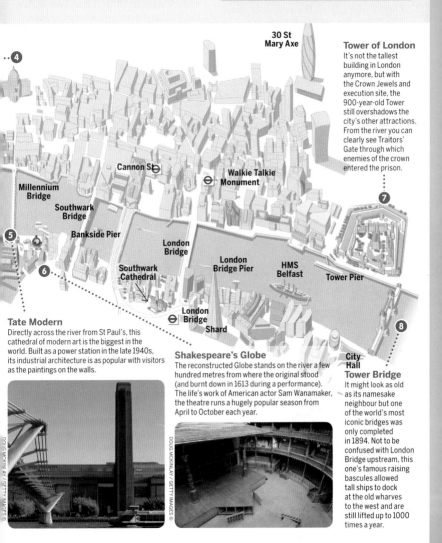

30 St Mary Axe

Tower of London
It's not the tallest building in London anymore, but with the Crown Jewels and execution site, the 900-year-old Tower still overshadows the city's other attractions. From the river you can clearly see Traitors' Gate through which enemies of the crown entered the prison.

❹

Cannon St

Walkie Talkie Monument

Millennium Bridge

Southwark Bridge

Bankside Pier

❺

❻

London Bridge

London Bridge Pier

HMS Belfast

Tower Pier

Southwark Cathedral

London Bridge

Shard

❼

❽

City Hall

Tate Modern
Directly across the river from St Paul's, this cathedral of modern art is the biggest in the world. Built as a power station in the late 1940s, its industrial architecture is as popular with visitors as the paintings on the walls.

Shakespeare's Globe
The reconstructed Globe stands on the river a few hundred metres from where the original stood (and burnt down in 1613 during a performance). The life's work of American actor Sam Wanamaker, the theatre runs a hugely popular season from April to October each year.

Tower Bridge
It might look as old as its namesake neighbour but one of the world's most iconic bridges was only completed in 1894. Not to be confused with London Bridge upstream, this one's famous raising bascules allowed tall ships to dock at the old wharves to the west and are still lifted up to 1000 times a year.

Discover the South Bank

Getting There & Away

Underground The South Bank is lashed into the tube system by stations at Waterloo, Southwark, London Bridge and Bermondsey, all on the Jubilee Line; the Northern Line runs through London Bridge and Waterloo (the Bakerloo line runs through the latter as well).

On Foot Cross to South Bank from the City over Tower Bridge or the Millennium Bridge, or from the West End across Waterloo Bridge or Golden Jubilee Bridge.

Bicycle Jump on a Barclays bike (p285).

Bus The RV1 runs around the South Bank and Bankside, linking all the main sights and runs between Covent Garden and Tower Gateway.

Summer crowds near the Southbank Centre
ADINA TOVY/GETTY IMAGES ©

Sights

Waterloo

London Eye   Viewpoint
Map p130 (☎ 0871 781 3000; www.londoneye.com; adult/child £19.20/12.30; ⊙10am-8pm; ⊖Waterloo) It's hard to remember what London looked like before the landmark 135m-tall London Eye began twirling at the south-western end of Jubilee Gardens in 2000. A ride in one of the wheel's 32 glass-enclosed pods holding up to 28 people draws 3.5 million visitors annually. At peak times (July, August and school holidays) it may seem like they are all in the queue with you; save money and shorten queues by buying tickets online, or cough up an extra £10 to jump the queue. Alternatively, try to visit before 11am or after 3pm to avoid peak density. It takes a gracefully slow 30 minutes and, weather permitting, you can see 25 miles in every direction from the top of the western hemisphere's tallest Ferris wheel. For factarians only: Together with its 23m-tall spindle, the hub of the London Eye weighs 330 tonnes – more than 20 times the weight of Big Ben.

County Hall   Historic Building
Map p130 (Riverside Bldg, Westminster Bridge Rd, SE1; ⊖Westminster or Waterloo) Begun in 1909 but not completed until 1922, this grand building with its curved, colonnaded facade contains a vast aquarium, a museum devoted to the local film industry and, since March 2013, the London Dungeon.

The excellent **London Sea Life Aquarium** Map p130 (www.visitsealife.com; Westminster Bridge Rd, SE1; adult/child £20.70/15; ⊙10am-6pm Mon-Fri, to 7pm Sat & Sun; ⊖Westminster or

Waterloo) is one of the largest in Europe. Fish and other creatures from the briny deep are grouped in 14 zones according to their geographic origin, from the Pacific to the Atlantic Ocean and from temperate waters to tropical seas. There are over 40 sharks, a colony of Gentoo penguins and other Antarctic creatures, ever-popular clownfish and a rewarding rainforests section. There are talks and feeding sessions throughout the day.

The **London Film Museum** Map p130 (✆020-7202 7040; www.londonfilmmuseum.com; County Hall, Westminster Bridge Rd; adult/student/child £13.50/11.50/9.50; ⏱10am-5pm Mon-Wed & Fri, from 11am Thu & Sun; ⏵) is a British film industry retrospective; it looks at the history of the main studios (Pinewod, Elstree etc) and iconic films shot there such as *Star Wars* and the Indiana Jones films. There are plenty of costumes, props, set drawings and scripts to look at. The only downside is the noise, with half a dozen videos constantly playing, which makes it hard to focus on what you want to hear.

Older kids tend to love the **London Dungeon** Map p130 (www.thedungeons.com/london; County Hall, Westminster Bridge Rd, SE1; adult/child £24.60/19.20; ⏱10am-5pm, extended hrs holidays; ⏵; ⊖Westminster, Waterloo), as the terrifying queues during school holidays and weekends testify. It's all spooky music, ghostly boat rides, macabre hangman's drop-rides, fake blood and actors dressed up as torturers and gory criminals (including Jack the Ripper and Sweeney Todd). Beware the interactive bits.

Southbank Centre   Concert Hall
Map p130 (✆020-7960 4200; www.southbank-centre.co.uk; Belvedere Rd, SE1; ⊖Waterloo) The flagship venue of the Southbank Centre, Europe's largest centre for performing and visual arts, is the **Royal Festival Hall**. Its gently curved facade of glass and Portland stone is more humane than its 1970s brutalist neighbours. It is one of London's leading music venues and the epicentre of life on this part of the South Bank, hosting cafes, restaurants, shops and bars.

Just north, the austere **Queen Elizabeth Hall** is a brutalist icon, the second-largest concert venue in the centre, hosting chamber orchestras, quartets, choirs, dance performances and sometimes opera. It also contains the smaller **Purcell Room**, while underneath its elevated floor is a long-term, graffiti-decorated skateboarders' hang-out.

The opinion-dividing 1968 **Hayward Gallery** Map p130 (www.southbankcentre.co.uk; Belvedere Rd, SE1; ⏱10am-6pm Sat-Wed, to 8pm Thu & Fri; ⊖Waterloo), another brutalist beauty, is a leading contemporary-art exhibition space.

The QEH and Hayward Gallery are about to receive a major overhaul. Works are due to start in 2014 and will temporarily dampen the buzz of the area. The finished result, however, with a floating glass box on top of the brutalist buildings and brand new art space, will be worth the wait.

Imperial War Museum   Museum
Map p130 (www.iwm.org.uk; Lambeth Rd, SE1; ⏱10am-6pm; ⊖Lambeth North) FREE Fronted by a pair of intimidating 15-inch naval guns, this riveting and recently renovated museum is housed in what was once Bethlehem Royal Hospital, also known as Bedlam. Although the museum's focus is on military action involving British or Commonwealth troops during the 20th century, it rolls out the carpet to war in the wider sense.

Stunning new **First World War Galleries** mark the centenary of the outbreak of WWI in 2014. **A Family in Wartime** tells the story of how ordinary people braved the challenges of life at home during WWII. The **Holocaust Exhibition** is especially harrowing and not recommended for children under 14 years of age.

Bankside & Southwark
Tate Modern   Museum
See p124.

Millennium Bridge   Bridge
Map p130 The elegant Millennium Bridge staples the south bank of the Thames, in

The South Bank

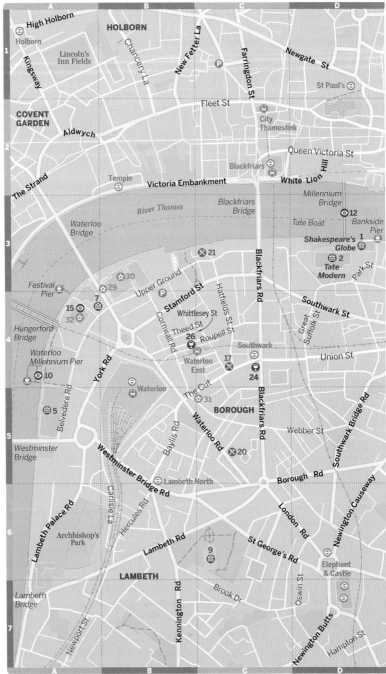

HOLBORN

High Holborn

Holborn

Kingsway

Lincoln's Inn Fields

Chancery La

New Fetter La

Farringdon St

Newgate St

St Paul's

Fleet St

COVENT GARDEN

Aldwych

City Thameslink

The Strand

Temple

Queen Victoria St

Blackfriars

White Lion

Hill

Victoria Embankment

River Thames

Blackfriars Bridge

Millennium Bridge

Tate Boat

Bankside Pier

12

Waterloo Bridge

Shakespeare's Globe 1

Tate Modern 2

21

Upper Ground

30

Festival Pier

29

7

Stamford St

Whittlesey St

Hatfields St

Park St

Southwark St

Great Suffolk St

15

32

Cornwall Rd

Theed St

Roupell St

26

Southwark

Blackfriars Rd

Hungerford Bridge

Waterloo Millennium Pier

10

York Rd

17

Waterloo East

24

Union St

5

Waterloo

31

The Cut

Waterloo Rd

BOROUGH

Belvedere Rd

Webber St

Southwark Bridge Rd

Westminster Bridge

Baylis Rd

20

Westminster Bridge Rd

Borough Rd

Lambeth North

Carlisle La

Hercules Rd

London Rd

Newington Causeway

Lambeth Palace Rd

Archbishop's Park

Lambeth Rd

9

St George's Rd

Elephant & Castle

Oswin St

LAMBETH

Lambeth Bridge

Newport St

Kennington Rd

Brook Dr

Newington Butts

Hampton St

THE SOUTH BANK

130

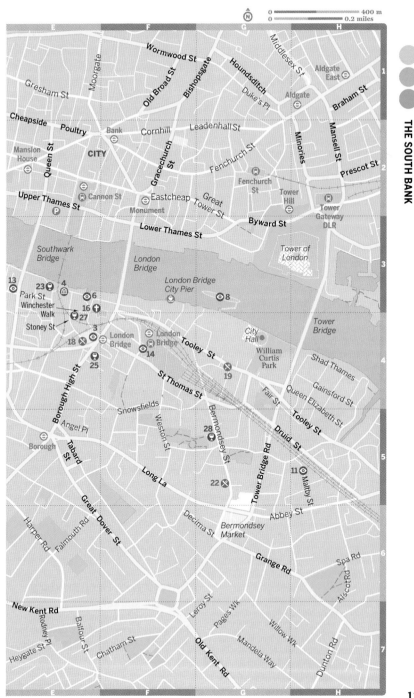

0 — 400 m
0 — 0.2 miles

Wormwood St
Houndsditch
Middlesex St
Aldgate East
Gresham St
Moorgate
Old Broad St
Bishopsgate
Duke's Pl
Aldgate
Braham St
Cheapside
Poultry
Bank
Cornhill
Leadenhall St
Minories
Mansell St
Prescot St
Mansion House
Queen St
CITY
Gracechurch St
Fenchurch St
Fenchurch St
Upper Thames St
Cannon St
Eastcheap
Monument
Great Tower St
Tower Hill
Tower Gateway DLR
Lower Thames St
Byward St
Southwark Bridge
London Bridge
Tower of London
13
23
4
6
Park St
Winchester Walk
16
27
Stoney St
3
18
London Bridge
London Bridge
14
25
Tooley St
City Hall
William Curtis Park
Tower Bridge
Shad Thames
St Thomas St
19
Fair St
Queen Elizabeth St
Gainsford St
Tooley St
Borough High St
Snowsfields
Weston St
Bermondsey St
Druid St
Angel Pl
28
Borough
Tabard St
Long La
22
Tower Bridge Rd
11
Maltby St
Great Dover St
Decima St
Abbey St
Bermondsey Market
Harper Rd
Falmouth Rd
Grange Rd
Spa Rd
Ascot Rd
New Kent Rd
Rodney Rd
Balfour St
Chatham St
Heygate St
Leroy St
Pages Wk
Old Kent Rd
Willow Wk
Mandela Way
Dunton Rd

The South Bank

front of Tate Modern, with the north bank, at the steps of Peter's Hill below St Paul's Cathedral. The low-slung frame designed by Sir Norman Foster and Antony Caro looks spectacular, particularly lit up at night with fibre optics.

Rose Theatre   Theatre
Map p130 (☑020-7261 9565; www.rosetheatre. org.uk; 56 Park St, SE1; ⊙10am-5pm Sat; 🛜; 🚇London Bridge) FREE The Rose (1587), for which Christopher Marlowe and Ben Jonson wrote their greatest plays and in which Shakespeare learned his craft, is unique: its original 16th-century foundations were discovered in 1989 beneath an office building and given a protective concrete cover. Plays are staged in the tiny theatre from February to November, often with a Sunday matinee. See the website for details.

Clink Prison Museum   Museum
Map p130 (☑020-7403 0900; www.clink.co.uk; 1 Clink St, SE1; adult/child £7.50/5.50; ⊙10am-6pm Mon-Fri, to 7.30pm Sat & Sun; 🚇London Bridge) This one-time private jail in the park of Winchester Palace, a 32-hectare area known as the Liberty of the Clink and under the jurisdiction of the bishops

of Winchester and not the City, was used to detain debtors, prostitutes, thieves and numerous Protestants and Catholics during the Reformation. The museum is a titch hokey but fun.

Golden Hinde   Ship
Map p130 (☑020-7403 0123; www.golden-hinde.com; St Mary Overie Dock, Cathedral St, SE1; adult/child £7/5; ⊙10am-5.30pm; 👪; 🚇London Bridge) Okay, it looks like a dinky theme-park ride and kids love it, but stepping aboard this replica of Sir Francis Drake's famous Tudor ship will inspire genuine admiration for the admiral and his rather short (average height: 1.6m) crew, which counted between 40 and 60 men. It was in a tiny five-deck galleon just like this that Drake and his crew circumnavigated the globe from 1577 to 1580.

Borough & Bermondsey
Borough Market   Market
Map p130 (www.boroughmarket.org.uk; cnr Southwark & Stoney Sts, SE1; ⊙11am-5pm Thu, noon-6pm Fri, 8am-5pm Sat; 🚇London Bridge) Located here in some form or another since the 13th century, 'London's Larder' has enjoyed an astonishing renaissance

in the past decade and a half. Now overflowing with food lovers, inveterate gastronomes, wide-eyed newcomers, guidebook-toting visitors and all types in between, this fantastic market has become firmly established as a sight in its own right.

Along with a section devoted to quality fresh fruit, exotic vegetables and organic meat, there's a fine-foods retail market, with the likes of home-grown honey and homemade bread plus loads of free samples. Throughout, takeaway stalls supply sizzling gourmet sausages, chorizo sandwiches and quality burgers in spades, filling the air with meaty aromas.

The market simply heaves on Saturdays so get here early for the best pickings or enjoy the craze at lunch time: if you'd like some elbow space to enjoy your takeaway, head to Southwark Cathedral gardens or walk five minutes in either direction along the Thames for river views.

If the crowds prove too much, head southeast past London Bridge station to **Maltby Street Market** Map p130 (www. maltby.st; Maltby St, SE1; ⏱10am-4pm Sat; ⊖London Bridge) 🍃, a rollicking little gem nicknamed the Ropewalk. It started a few years ago as an alternative to the juggernaut that is Borough Market and is now a bunting-lined gathering of small producers and boutique food stalls.

Shard Notable Building
Map p130 (www.the-shard. com; 32 London Bridge St, SE1; adult/child £29.95/23.95; ⏱9am-10pm; ⊖London Bridge) Puncturing the skies above South London, the dramatic splinter-like form of the Shard has rapidly become an icon of the town. The viewing platforms on floors 68, 69 and 72 are

open to the public, and the views are, as you'd expect from a 244m vantage point, sweeping. But they come at a price – book online to save £5. As well as the viewing platform, the Shard is to be home to apartments, hotels, and restaurants.

Southwark Cathedral Church
Map p130 (🖉020-7367 6700; cathedral. southwark.anglican.org; Montague Close, SE1; donations welcome; ⏱8am-6pm Mon-Fri, from 9am Sat & Sun; ⊖London Bridge) FREE The earliest surviving parts of this relatively small cathedral are the retrochoir at the eastern end, which contains four chapels and was part of the 13th-century Priory of St Mary Overie; some ancient arcading by the southwest door; 12th-century wall cores in the north transept; and an arch that dates to the original Norman church. But most of the cathedral is Victorian.

Enter via the southwest door and immediately to the left is a length of arcading dating to the 13th century; nearby is a selection of intriguing medieval roof bosses from the 15th

Southwark Cathedral
ROB MACDOUGALL/GETTY IMAGES ©

century. Walk up the north aisle of the nave and on the left you'll see the tomb of John Gower, the 14th-century poet who was the first to write in English. Cross into the choir to admire the 16th-century Great Screen separating the choir from the retrochoir.

In the south aisle of the nave have a look at the green alabaster monument to William Shakespeare. Beside the monument is a plaque to Sam Wanamaker (1919–93). Hunt down the exceedingly fine Elizabethan sideboard in the north transept.

HMS Belfast   Ship
Map p130 (hmsbelfast.iwm.org.uk; Queen's Walk, SE1; adult/child £14.50/free; ⏱10am-5pm; ⊕; ⊖London Bridge) White ensign flapping on the Thames breeze, HMS *Belfast* is a magnet for naval-gazing kids of all ages. This large, light cruiser – launched in 1938 – served in both WWII and the Korean War. The 6-inch guns could bombard a target 14 land miles distant.

Ranging over five decks and four platforms, HMS *Belfast* is surprisingly interesting – even for landlubbers – as an insight into the way of life on board a cruiser, from boiler room to living quarters. The operations room has been reconstructed to show its role in the 1943 Battle of North Cape off Norway, which ended in the sinking of the *Scharnhorst*. On the bridge you can visit the admiral's cabin and sit in his chair or peer through the sights of the 4-inch HA/LA guns on the open deck.

🍴 Eating

Waterloo
Masters Super Fish   Fish & Chips £
Map p130 (191 Waterloo Rd, SE1; mains £8-12; ⏱noon-3pm & 4.30-10.30pm Mon-Sat; ⊖Waterloo) This popular place serves excellent fish (brought in fresh daily from Billingsgate Market and grilled rather than fried if

desired); low on charm but full marks for flavour.

Anchor & Hope   Pub ££
Map p130 (36 The Cut, SE1; mains £12-20; ☺noon-2.30pm Tue-Sat, 6-10.30pm Mon-Sat, from 2pm Sun; ⊖Southwark) The hope is that you'll get a table without waiting hours because you can't book at this quintessential gastropub. Critics love this place inside out and despite the menu's heavy hitters (pork shoulder, salt marsh lamb shoulder cooked for seven hours and soy-braised shin of beef), vegetarians aren't completely left out.

Skylon   Modern European ££
Map p130 (☎020-7654 7800; www.skylon-restaurant.co.uk; 3rd fl, Royal Festival Hall, Southbank Centre, Belvedere Rd, SE1; grill mains £13-25, restaurant 2-/3-course menu £42/47.50; ☺grill noon-11pm; restaurant noon-2.30pm & 5.30-10.30pm Mon-Sat, noon-4pm Sun; ⊖Waterloo) Named after a defunct 1950s tower, this restaurant on top of the refurbished Royal Festival Hall is divided into grill and fine-dining sections by a large bar (open until 1am). The decor is cutting-edge 1950s: muted colours and period chairs while floor-to-ceiling windows bathe you in views of the Thames and the City.

Oxo Tower Restaurant & Brasserie   Fusion £££
Map p130 (☎020-7803 3888; www.harveyni-chols.com/restaurants/oxo-tower-london; Barge House St, SE1; mains £21.50-35; ☺restaurant noon-2.30pm & 6-11pm, brasserie noon-11pm; ✈; ⊖Waterloo) The iconic Oxo Tower's conversion, with this restaurant situated high up on the 8th floor, helped spur much of the local dining renaissance. In the stunning glassed-in terrace you have a front-row seat for the best view in London, and you pay for this handsomely in the brasserie and restaurant.

PETER PHIPP/GETTY IMAGES ©

⭐ Don't Miss
Shakespeare's Globe

The new Globe was designed to resemble the original as closely as possible, painstakingly constructed with 600 oak pegs (not a nail or a screw in the house), specially fired Tudor bricks and thatching reeds from Norfolk that pigeons supposedly don't like. Even the plaster contains goat hair, lime and sand, as it did in Shakespeare's time. It even means having the arena open to the fickle London skies and roar of passing aircraft, leaving the 700 'groundlings' to stand in London's notorious downpours.

Despite the worldwide popularity of Shakespeare over the centuries, the Globe was almost a distant memory when American actor (and, later, film director) Sam Wanamaker came searching for it in 1949. Undeterred by the fact that the theatre's foundations had vanished beneath a row of heritage-listed Georgian houses, Wanamaker set up the Globe Playhouse Trust in 1970 and began fundraising for a memorial theatre. Work started only 200m from the original Globe site in 1987, but Wanamaker died four years before it opened in 1997.

The Globe is also now applying the finishing touches to the new Sam Wanamaker Playhouse, an indoor Jacobean theatre (the first plays were due to be staged in early 2014). Shakespeare wrote for both outdoor and indoor theatre and the playhouse had always been part of the Globe's ambitions.

Visits include tours of the Globe and the playhouse (which depart half-hourly, generally in the morning so as not to clash with performances) as well as access to the exhibition space beneath the theatre, which has fascinating exhibits about Shakespeare and theatre in the 17th century (including costumes and props) and fun live talks and demonstrations. Or you can of course take in a play.

NEED TO KNOW
Map p130 www.shakespearesglobe.com; 21 New Globe Walk, SE1; adult/child £13.50/8; ⊙ 9am-5.30pm; ⊖ London Bridge

Borough & Bermondsey

Applebee's Fish Cafe
Seafood ££

Map p130 (☎020-7407 5777; www.applebees-fish.com; 5 Stoney St, SE1; mains £15.50-25.50; ⏰noon-3.30pm & 6-11pm Tue-Sat; ⊖London Bridge) Tempted by the seafood bounty of Borough Market? Then head for this excellent fishmonger with a cafe-restaurant attached: all manner of fresher-than-fresh fish and shellfish dishes – some with an Italian slant – are on the chalkboard.

Zucca
Italian ££

Map p130 (☎020-7873 6809; www.zuccalondon.com; 184 Bermondsey St; mains £15-18; ⏰noon-3pm Tue-Sun, 6-10pm Tue-Sat; ⊖London Bridge) In a crisp, minimalist dining room with wrap-around bay windows and an open kitchen, an (almost) all-Italian staff serves contemporary Italian fare. The pasta is made daily on the premises, and the menu is kept short to guarantee freshness.

Magdalen
Modern British ££

Map p130 (☎020-7403 1342; www.magdalenres-taurant.co.uk; 152 Tooley St, SE1; mains £17-18, lunch 2-/3-course £15.50/18.50; ⏰noon-2.30pm Mon-Fri, 6.30-10pm Mon-Sat; ⊖London Bridge) You can't go wrong with this formal dining room. The Modern British fare adds its own spin to familiar dishes (grilled calves' kidneys, creamed onion and sage, smoked haddock choucroute); the desserts and English cheese selection are delightful.

🍷 Drinking & Nightlife

The South Bank is a strange combination of good, down-to-earth boozers, which just happen to have been here for hundreds of years, and modern bars – all neon and alcopops – patronised by a younger crowd.

Waterloo

Baltic
Bar

Map p130 (www.balticrestaurant.co.uk; 74 Blackfriars Rd, SE1; ⏰noon-midnight Mon-Sat, to 10.30pm Sun; ⊖Southwark) This stylish Eastern European bar specialises – not surprisingly – in vodkas; some 60-plus,

Globe History

The original Globe – known as the 'Wooden O' after its circular shape and roofless centre – was erected in 1599. Rival to the **Rose Theatre** (p132), all was well but did not end well when the Globe burned to the ground within two hours during a performance of Shakespeare's *Henry VIII* in 1613 (a stage cannon ignited the thatched roof). A tiled replacement was speedily rebuilt only to be closed in 1642 by Puritans, who saw the theatre as the devil's workshop, and it was dismantled two years later – not to reappear again for more than three and a half centuries. Thatch was banned in London after the Great Fire of 1666 and it is the only example in all of the city.

including bar-infused concoctions, served straight in frozen glasses or long in fantastic cocktails.

King's Arms
Pub

Map p130 (www.windmilltaverns.com; 25 Roupell St, SE1; ⏰11am-11pm Mon-Fri, noon-midnight Sat, noon-10.30pm Sun; ⊖Waterloo, Southwark) Relaxed and charming when not crowded, this award-winning neighbourhood boozer at the corner of a terraced Waterloo backstreet was a funeral parlour in a previous life. The large traditional bar area, serving up a good selection of ales and bitters, gives way to a fantastically odd conservatory bedecked with junk-store eclectica of local interest.

Bankside & Southwark

Anchor Bankside
Pub

Map p130 (34 Park St, SE1; ⏰11am-11pm Sun-Wed, to midnight Thu-Sat; ⊖London Bridge) Firmly anchored in many guidebooks (including this one) – but with good reason – this riverside boozer dates to the early 17th century (subsequently rebuilt

THE SOUTH BANK ENTERTAINMENT

JON ARNOLD/GETTY IMAGES ©

after the Great Fire and again in the 19th century). Trips to the terrace are rewarded with superb views across the Thames but brace for a constant deluge of drinkers.

Borough & Bermondsey

George Inn   Pub

Map p130 (www.nationaltrust.org.uk/george-inn; 77 Borough High St, SE1; ☺11am-11pm; ⊖London Bridge) This magnificent old boozer is London's last surviving galleried coaching inn, dating from 1676 and mentioned in Dickens' *Little Dorrit*. It is thought to be on the site of the Tabard Inn, from where the pilgrims in Chaucer's *Canterbury Tales* set out (well lubricated, we suspect) on the road to Canterbury in Kent.

Woolpack   Pub

Map p130 (www.woolpackbar.com; 98 Bermondsey St; ☺11am-11pm Mon-Sat, to 10.30pm Sun; ⊖London Bridge) This lovely free house (a pub that doesn't belong to a brewery) is a crowd-pleaser: the decor is lovely – dark-wood panels downstairs, sumptuous Victorian wallpaper upstairs – the garden spacious, and it shows football and rugby games.

Rake   Pub

Map p130 (www.uttobeer.co.uk; 14 Winchester Walk, SE1; ☺noon-11pm Mon-Sat, to 8pm Sun; ⊖London Bridge) The tiny-but-perfectly-formed Rake offers more than 100 beers at any one time. The selection of bitters, real ales, lagers and ciders (with one-third pint measures) changes constantly. The bamboo-decorated decking outside is especially popular.

⭐ Entertainment

The South Bank of London is home to some heavy hitters when it comes to London's theatre scene. Music and performing arts are big generally at the Southbank Centre.

National Theatre   Theatre

Map p130 (☎020-7452 3000; www.nationaltheatre.org.uk; South Bank, SE1; ⊖Waterloo) England's flagship theatre – now in its sixth decade – showcases a mix of classic and contemporary plays performed by excellent casts in three theatres (Olivier, Lyttelton and Cottesloe). Outstanding artistic director Nicholas Hytner has over-

138

seen a golden decade at the theatre, with landmark productions such as *War Horse*.

Southbank Centre   Concert Hall

Map p130 (☎020-7960 4200; www.southbank-centre.co.uk; Belvedere Rd, SE1; ⊖Waterloo) The overhauled **Royal Festival Hall** Map p130 (☎020-7960 4242; admission £6-60) is London's premier concert venue and seats 3000. It's one of the best places for catching world and classical music artists. The sound is fantastic, the programming impeccable and there are frequent free gigs in the wonderfully expansive foyer.

Shakespeare's Globe   Theatre

Map p130 (☎020-7401 9919; www.shakespeares-globe.com; 21 New Globe Walk, SE1; seats £15-42, standing £5; ⊖St Paul's, London Bridge) This authentic Shakespearean theatre is a wooden O without a roof over the central stage area, and although there are covered wooden bench seats in tiers around the stage, many people (there's room for 700) do as 17th-century 'groundlings' did, standing in front of the stage.

BFI Southbank   Cinema

Map p130 (☎020-7928 3232; www.bfi.org.uk; Belvedere Rd, SE1; tickets £9; ⊙11am-11pm; ⊖Waterloo) Tucked almost out of sight under the arches of Waterloo Bridge is the British Film Institute, containing four cinemas that screen thousands of films each year (mostly arthouse), a gallery devoted to the moving image and the mediatheque, where you watch film and TV highlights from the BFI National Archive.

Old Vic   Theatre

Map p130 (☎0844 871 7628; www.oldvictheatre.com; The Cut, SE1; ⊖Waterloo) Never has there been a London theatre with a more famous artistic director. American actor Kevin Spacey took the theatrical helm 10 years ago, looking after this glorious theatre's programme. The Old Vic does both new and classic plays, and its cast and directors are consistently high-profile.

Kensington & Hyde Park

The area from Hyde Park to Chelsea is high-class territory. But it's not just about multimillion-pound properties, Qatari tycoons and exclusive shopping. The area serves up some of the capital's highlight attractions, particularly museums, and its communities are among the most cosmopolitan in London. Many of the restaurants are to die for.

Thanks to Prince Albert and the 1851 Great Exhibition, South Kensington is first and foremost 'museumland', with three of London's most magnificent standing cheek-by-jowl: the Natural History Museum, the Science Museum and the Victoria & Albert Museum.

Splendid Hyde Park and Kensington Gardens – one delightfully big sprawling mass of green – buffers more sedate Knightsbridge and Kensington from the energy, bright lights and havoc of the West End. Exclusive hotels and expensive shopping tend to keep this area the preserve of the wealthy, but literally everyone and their best friend seems to be in Harrods.

Victoria & Albert Museum (p146)

Kensington & Hyde Park Highlights

Victoria & Albert Museum (p146)

The extraordinary Victoria & Albert Museum of applied art is a true classic, and riveting for anyone interested in art or design. Within its vast Cromwell Rd premises the museum contains a staggering 145 galleries embracing everything from ancient Chinese ceramics to the Sony Walkman. The collection is, without question, the best of its kind in the world.

Shopping Around Knightsbridge & Chelsea (p163)

You need to put aside some time for quality shopping in Knightsbridge and Chelsea. Start with two of Britain's most famous department stores – the glitzy but incomparable Harrods (p163) and the rather chic Harvey Nichols (p163) – before rolling down Sloane St o Brompton Rd for fashion must-haves in luxurious boutiques. Harrods

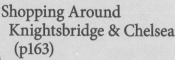

TRAVELPIX LTD/GETTY IMAGES ®

Science Museum (p150)

The fantastic collection in this museum is not just here for bad-weather days, even though some kids make an instant beeline for the ground floor shop's voice changers, bouncy globes and alien babies, and pretty much stay put. There's an astonishing range of exhibits, from Stephenson's steam engine, the Rocket (1829), to another rocket (the Nazi V-2), early computers (including the hefty Pegasus from 1959) and much more.

Albert Memorial (p155)

London boasts some stupendous relics from its Victorian heyday, but perhaps none is as extravagant or ostentatious as this highly ornate Kensington monument. Capturing the ambitious zeal of the Victorian age and the imperial authority of the 19th-century monarchy, the memorial defines a bygone age. Join a tour to examine the allegorical detail in its bombastic stonework.

Natural History Museum (p158)

This is a must for anyone with an interest in the natural world, or those with kids in tow. From its roaring T-Rex to the restful Wildlife Garden, the museum is an enthusiastic celebration of the natural world. The building itself is a stunning piece of architecture, while the Central Hall, with its astonishing Diplodocus skeleton, will simply blow you away.

Kensington & Hyde Park Walk

Embark on this leisurely two-mile walk around central London's enormous green lung starting at Hyde Park Corner tube station. The walk takes in the main part of the park and gardens, and ends up not far from Notting Hill station.

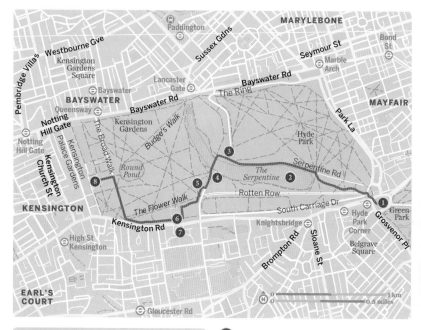

WALK FACTS

- **Start** Hyde Park Corner
- **Finish** Kensington Palace
- **Distance** 2.5 miles
- **Duration** 1½ hours

① Hyde Park Corner

Amid a swirl of traffic, climb monumental Wellington Arch (p151) for superb views. In the same square is the tasteful wall of eucalypt-green granite of the Australian and New Zealand War Memorials. To the east stands the Royal Air Force Bomber Command Memorial (2012) and to the north magnificent Apsley House (p151).

② The Serpentine

This L-shaped lake, once fed with waters from the underground River Westbourne, hosted the 2012 Olympic triathlon and marathon swimming events. Keep to the northern side and consider renting a paddle boat or taking the Serpentine solar shuttle boat to the Diana, Princess of Wales Memorial Fountain.

③ Serpentine Sackler Gallery

This new 880-sq-m gallery (p154), which opened in 2013 inside the Magazine (1805), a former Palladian villa–style gunpowder depot, aims to 'present the stars of tomorrow' in the arts. The original building has been augmented with an undulating extension designed by Pritzker Prize–winning architect Zaha Hadid.

④ Diana, Princess of Wales Memorial Fountain

This Cornish granite memorial fountain (p156), dubbed 'a moat without a castle', sits on a perfectly manicured lawn. Water flows from the highest point in both directions into a small pool at the bottom. Bathing is forbidden, but you can dip your feet.

⑤ Serpentine Gallery

This former teahouse is now one of the city's best contemporary art galleries (p154) and houses interesting exhibitions. A leading architect who has never built in the UK is annually commissioned to build a new 'Summer Pavilion' next door (open May to October).

⑥ Albert Memorial

The Albert Memorial (p155) is an astonishing chunk of Victoriana, completed when the British Empire spanned the globe. Commissioned by Queen Victoria in honour of her late husband, the extravagant memorial was restored at great expense at the end of the last millennium.

⑦ Royal Albert Hall

Opposite the Albert Memorial, this famous concert hall (p155) is a further monument to Queen Victoria's beloved husband. It has seen more big names and significant performances in its time than most others, including the choral version of Blake's *Jerusalem,* held to celebrate the granting of the vote to all women in 1928.

⑧ Kensington Palace

Princess Diana's restored former residence is now home to her son, Prince William, and his family. Stop off at this royal residence (p155) and take a look at the permanent and temporary exhibitions, and the stunning interiors, before relaxing on one of the many stretches of grass on offer in Kensington Gardens (p154).

⭐ The Best...

PLACES TO EAT

Zuma Decidedly stylish Japanese dining experience in Knightsbridge. (p159)

Gordon Ramsay A glorious culinary experience, earning three Michelin stars for over a decade. (p160)

Min Jiang London's best Chinese – with views. (p159)

Dinner by Heston Blumenthal Winning celebration of British cuisine with both traditional and modern accents. (p160)

Launceston Place Fantastic looks, outstanding food. (p159)

PLACES TO DRINK

Buddha Bar Chichi Chinese cocktail bar for a post-shopping sundowner. (p161)

606 Club Snap your fingers to some of the finest jazz sounds in London. (p162)

MUSEUMS

Victoria & Albert Museum Unique array of decorative arts and design in an awe-inspiring setting. (p146)

Natural History Museum A major hit with kids and adults alike in a beautiful building. (p158)

Science Museum Inventions, gadgets, eye-opening facts and figures, plus an amazing shop. (p150)

Kensington Palace (p155)
STUART BLACK/GETTY IMAGES ©

Don't Miss
Victoria & Albert Museum

The Museum of Manufactures, as the V&A was known when it opened in 1852, specialises in decorative art and design, with some two million objects reaching back 3000 years, from Britain and around the globe. It was part of Prince Albert's legacy to the nation in the aftermath of the successful Great Exhibition of 1851, and its original aims – which still hold today – were the 'improvement of public taste in design' and 'applications of fine art to objects of utility'. Free one-hour guided tours leave the main reception area at 10.30am, 12.30pm, 1.30pm and 3.30pm.

V&A

Map p152

www.vam.ac.uk

Cromwell Rd, SW7

admission free

🕐 10am-5.45pm Sat-Thu, to 10pm Fri

🚇 South Kensington

Level 1

The TT Tsui China collection (rooms 44 and 47e) displays lovely pieces, including a beautifully lithe wooden statue of the goddess Guanyin seated in *lalitasana* pose from AD 1200 and exquisite Tang dynasty porcelain. More than 400 objects from the Islamic Middle East are within the Islamic Middle East Gallery (room 42), including ceramics, textiles, carpets, glass and woodwork from the 8th century up to the years before WWI. Visit room 48a for the celebrated Raphael cartoons.

Level 2

The British Galleries, featuring every aspect of British design from 1500 to 1900, are divided between levels 2 (1500–1760) and 4 (1760–1900).

Level 3

The Jewellery Gallery (rooms 91–93) is outstanding, including pieces of exquisite intricacy, from early Egyptian, Greek and Roman jewellery to dazzling tiaras and contemporary designs. Design Since 1946 (room 76) celebrates design classics from a Le Corbusier chaise longue to Sony credit-card radio from 1985 and Nike 'Air Max' shoes from 1992.

Level 4

The Architecture Gallery (rooms 127 to 128a) vividly describes architectural styles via models and videos, while the brightly illuminated Contemporary Glass Gallery (room 131) is quite spectacular.

1 THE CAST COURTS

Question: in what single space can you see Trajan's *Column*, Michelangelo's *David* and many more classical and medieval works? Answer: the V&A's Cast Courts. This extraordinary collection of over 300 plaster casts is one of the wonders of the V&A, an exhilarating spectacle that has inspired and baffled visitors since it first opened in 1873.

2 THE ARDABIL CARPET

The Ardabil carpet, woven in Iran in 1539–40, is a masterpiece of weaving and design. It lies at the centre of the V&A's Islamic Middle East Gallery. To see the carpet in its full glory you must wait for the 10 minutes every half-hour when the light level rises, bringing the subtle colours and intricate design into full view.

3 THE ASCENSION RELIEF

The V&A has an outstanding collection of Renaissance sculpture. One of its greatest treasures is the Ascension relief, made by Donatello around 1428–30; its surface is carved with a miraculously light touch.

4 TIPU'S TIGER

Of the two million objects in the V&A, Tipu's Tiger is the best loved and most weird. Made in India in about 1793–4, it is an automaton, housing an organ inside a wooden tiger. The tiger crouches over the rigid body of an English officer, sinking his fangs into the man's cravat.

5 CHINESE TEAPOT

The V&A was founded in the 1850s to educate designers, manufacturers and the public in the principles of good design. An object that epitomises this lofty aim is the white porcelain teapot made in Dehua in China in the late 17th century. A slightly squashed globe of pure white porcelain, with a perfect circle as a handle, it anticipates modernism by more than two centuries.

Victoria & Albert Museum

HALF-DAY HIGHLIGHTS TOUR

The art- and design-packed V&A is vast: we have devised an easy-to-follow tour of the museum highlights to help cover some signature pieces while also allowing you to appreciate some of the grandeur of the museum architecture.

Enter the V&A by the Grand Entrance off Cromwell Rd and immediately turn left to explore the Islamic Middle East Gallery and to discover the sumptuous silk-and-wool **Ardabil Carpet ❶**. Among the pieces from South Asia in the adjacent gallery is the terrifying automated **Tipu's Tiger ❷**. Continue to the outstanding **Fashion Room ❸** with its displays of clothing styles through the ages. The magnificent gallery opposite, which houses the Raphael Cartoons, offers a shortcut via stairs on its far side to Level 2 and the Britain 1500–1760 Gallery; turn left in the gallery to

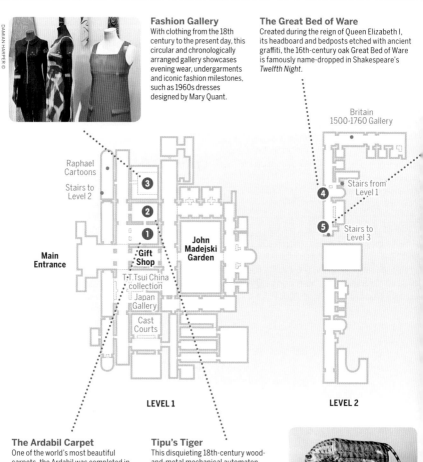

Fashion Gallery
With clothing from the 18th century to the present day, this circular and chronologically arranged gallery showcases evening wear, undergarments and iconic fashion milestones, such as 1960s dresses designed by Mary Quant.

The Great Bed of Ware
Created during the reign of Queen Elizabeth I, its headboard and bedposts etched with ancient graffiti, the 16th-century oak Great Bed of Ware is famously name-dropped in Shakespeare's *Twelfth Night*.

Britain 1500-1760 Gallery

Raphael Cartoons

Stairs to Level 2

❸

❷

❶

John Madejski Garden

Main Entrance

Gift Shop

T·T·Tsui China collection

Japan Gallery

Cast Courts

LEVEL 1

❹ Stairs from Level 1

❺ Stairs to Level 3

LEVEL 2

The Ardabil Carpet
One of the world's most beautiful carpets, the Ardabil was completed in 1540, one of a pair commissioned by Shah Tahmasp, ruler of Iran. The piece is most astonishing for the artistry of the detailing and the subtlety of design.

Tipu's Tiger
This disquieting 18th-century wood-and-metal mechanical automaton depicts a European being savaged by a tiger. When a handle is turned, an organ hidden within the feline mimics the cries of the dying man, whose arm also rises.

INDIAN SCHOOL / GETTY IMAGES ©

DAMIAN HARPER ©

find the **Great Bed of Ware** ④, beyond which rests the exquisitely crafted artistry of **Henry VIII's writing box** ⑤. Head up the stairs into the Metalware Gallery on Level 3 for the **Hereford Screen** ⑥. Continue through the Ironwork and Sculpture Galleries and through the Leighton Corridor to the glittering **Jewellery Gallery** ⑦, from where a succession of galleries bordering the John Madejski Garden lead you to the **Design Since 1946** ⑧ gallery, opposite the 20th Century Gallery (at the end of which are stairs and a lift to the rest of the museum).

Henry VIII's Writing Box
This exquisitely ornate walnut and oak 16th-century writing box has been added to over the centuries, but the original decorative motifs are superb, including Henry's coat of arms, flanked by Venus (holding Cupid) and Mars.

Design Since 1946
Weigh up some innovative classics that defined much of the late 20th century, when mobile phones were seriously chunky and portable audio cassette players were the latest must-have gadget.

DAMIAN HARPER ©

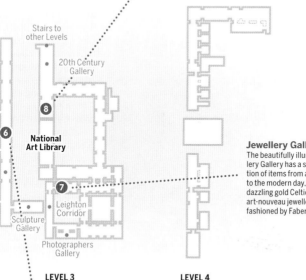

Stairs to other Levels

20th Century Gallery

Stairs from level 2

⑧

⑥

National Art Library

Ironwork Gallery

⑦

Leighton Corridor

Sculpture Gallery

Photographers Gallery

LEVEL 3

LEVEL 4

Jewellery Gallery
The beautifully illuminated Jewellery Gallery has a stunning collection of items from ancient Greece to the modern day, including a dazzling gold Celtic breastplate, art-nouveau jewellery and animals fashioned by Fabergé.

DAMIAN HARPER ©

The Hereford Screen
Designed by Sir George Gilbert Scott, this awe-inspiring choir screen is a labour of love, originally fashioned for Hereford Cathedral. An almighty conception of wood, iron, copper, brass and hardstone, there were few parts of the V&A that could support its great mass.

Discover Kensington & Hyde Park

🔁 Getting There & Away

○ **Underground** Kensington and Hyde Park are connected to the rest of London via stations at South Kensington, Sloane Square, Victoria, Knightsbridge and Hyde Park Corner. The main lines are Circle, District, Piccadilly and Victoria.

○ **Bus** Handy routes include 74 from South Kensington to Knightsbridge and Hyde Park Corner; 52 from Victoria to High St Kensington; 360 from South Kensington to Sloane Square and Pimlico; and 11 from Fulham Broadway to the King's Road, Sloane Square and Victoria.

○ **Bicycle** The Barclays Cycle Hire Scheme (p285) is very handy for pedal-powering your way in, out and around the neighbourhood.

Diana, Princess of Wales Memorial Fountain (p156)
PHILIP GAME/GETTY IMAGES ©

◉ Sights

Knightsbridge, Kensington & Hyde Park

Victoria & Albert Museum   Museum
See p146.

Science Museum   Museum
Map p152 (www.sciencemuseum.org.uk; Exhibition Rd, SW7; ⊙10am-6pm; ⊖South Kensington) **FREE** With seven floors of interactive and educational exhibits, this scientifically spellbinding museum will mesmerise adults and children alike.

The **Energy Hall,** on the ground floor, displays machines of the Industrial Revolution, including Stephenson's innovative rocket (1829). Nostalgic adults will delight in the **Apollo 10 command module** in the **Making the Modern World Gallery**.

Computing on the 2nd floor displays some intriguing devices, from Charles Babbage's radical analytical engine to hulking valve-based computers such as hefty Pegasus from 1959.

The 3rd-floor **Flight Gallery** (free tours 1pm most days) is a favourite place for children, with its gliders, hot-air balloon and aircraft, including the Gipsy Moth, which Amy Johnson flew to Australia in 1930. There are also fascinating insights into the pre-Wright brothers era of flight attempts, including Henson's ambitiously named Aerial Steam Carriage of 1847. This floor also features a **Red Arrows 3D flight simulation theatre** (adult/child £6/5) and **Fly 360 degree flight simulator capsules** (£12 per capsule).

Launchpad on the same floor is stuffed with hands-on gadgets exploring physics and the properties of liquids.

The hi-tech **Wellcome Wing** has an **IMAX Cinema** (adult/child £10/8) that shows the usual crop of travelogues, space adventures and dinosaur attacks in stunning 3D.

If you've kids under the age of six, pop down to the basement and the **Garden**, where there's a fun-filled play zone, including a water-play area, besieged by tots in red waterproof smocks.

Wellington Arch   Museum

Map p152 (www.english-heritage.org.uk; Hyde Park Corner, W1; adult/child 5-15 £4/2.40, with Apsley House £8.20/4.90; ⏰10am-5pm Wed-Sun Apr-Oct, 10am-4pm Wed-Sun Nov-Mar; 📶; Ⓔ Hyde Park Corner) Dominating the green space enclosed by the Hyde Park Corner roundabout, this imposing neoclassical arch from 1826 originally faced the Hyde Park Screen, but was shunted here in 1882 for road widening. The same year saw the removal of the disproportionately large equestrian statue of the duke crowning it, making space for Europe's largest bronze sculpture: *Peace Descending on the Quadriga of War* (1912), three years in the casting.

Until the 1960s part of the monument served as a tiny police station but it was restored and opened up to the public as a three-floor exhibition space; today it contains the Quadriga Gallery (for temporary exhibitions) and an exhibition tracing the history of the arch. The open-air balconies (accessible by lift) afford unforgettable views of Hyde Park, Buckingham Palace and the Houses of Parliament

Apsley House   Historic Home

Map p152 (www.english-heritage.org.uk; 149 Piccadilly, W1; adult/child £6.30/3.80, with Wellington Arch £8.20/4.90; ⏰11am-5pm Wed-Sun Apr-Oct, to 4pm Wed-Sun Nov-Mar; Ⓔ Hyde Park Corner) This stunning house, containing exhibits about the Duke of Wellington, was once the first building to appear when entering London from the west and was therefore known as 'No 1 London'.

Still one of London's finest, Apsley House was designed by Robert Adam for Baron Apsley in the late 18th century, but later sold to the first Duke of Wellington, who lived here until he died in 1852.

Though some of the duke's descendants still live in a flat here, 10 of its rooms are open to the public. Wellington memorabilia, including his death mask, fills the basement gallery, while there's an astonishing collection of china and silver, including a stunning Egyptian service, a divorce present from Napoleon to Josephine (she declined it).

The stairwell is dominated by Antonio Canova's staggering 3.4m-high statue of a fig-leafed Napoleon with titanic shoulders, adjudged by the subject as 'too athletic'. The 1st-floor Wellington Gallery contains paintings by Velasquez, Rubens, Van Dyck, Brueghel and Murillo and Goya.

Hyde Park   Park

Map p152 (⏰5.30am-midnight; Ⓔ Marble Arch, Hyde Park Corner, Queensway) London's largest royal park spreads itself over 142 hectares of neatly manicured gardens, wild expanses of overgrown grass and magnificent trees.

It was the first royal park to open to the public in the early 17th century, the famous venue of the Great Exhibition in 1851, and it became an enormous potato bed during WWII.

Life Guards on Parade

Catch the Queen's Life Guard (Household Cavalry) departing for Horse Guards Parade at 10.28am (9.28am on Sunday) from **Hyde Park Barracks** (Map p152; Knightsbridge, SW1; Ⓔ Knightsbridge) for the daily Changing of the Guard at **Horse Guards Parade** (p74), performing a ritual that dates back to 1660. They ride via Hyde Park Corner, Constitution Hill and the Mall.

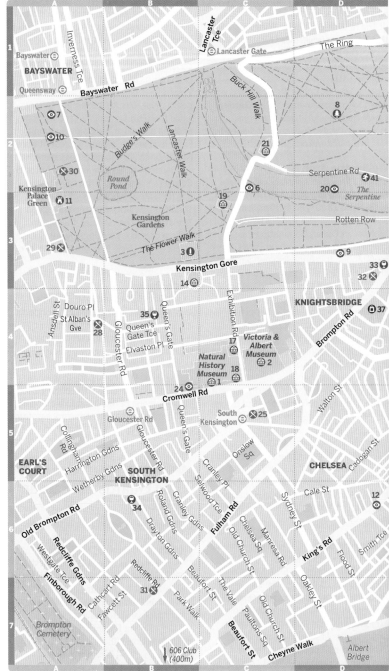

Bayswater

BAYSWATER

Queensway

Inverness Tce

⊙7

⊙10

Bayswater Rd

Budge's Walk

Lancaster Walk

Round Pond

Kensington Palace Green ⊞11

30

Lancaster Tce

Lancaster Gate

Buck Hill Walk

The Ring

8

21

19

⊙6

Kensington Gardens

The Flower Walk

29

Serpentine Rd 41

20 ⊙

The Serpentine

Rotten Row

3

Kensington Gore

9

33

32

14

KNIGHTSBRIDGE

37

Ansdell St

Douro Pl

St Alban's Gve

28

Gloucester Rd

35

Queen's Gate Tce

Queen's Gate

Elvaston Pl

Exhibition Rd

17

Victoria & Albert Museum 2

Brompton Rd

Natural History Museum

18

1

24 ⊙

Cromwell Rd

Queen's Gate

Walton St

Gloucester Rd

South Kensington

25

CHELSEA

Cadogan St

EARL'S COURT

Collingham Rd

Harrington Gdns

Wetherby Gdns

Gloucester Rd

SOUTH KENSINGTON

Onslow Sq

Cranley Pl

Cale St

12

34

Roland Gdns

Cranley Gdns

Drayton Gdns

Selwood Tce

Fulham Rd

Old Church St

Chelsea Sq

Sydney St

King's Rd

Flood St

Smith Tce

Old Brompton Rd

Redcliffe Gdns

Westgate Tce

Finborough Rd

Cathcart Rd

Fawcett St

Redcliffe Rd

31

Park Walk

Beaufort St

The Vale

Paultons Sq

Old Church St

Oakley St

Manresa Rd

Brompton Cemetery

606 Club (400m)

Beaufort St

Cheyne Walk

Albert Bridge

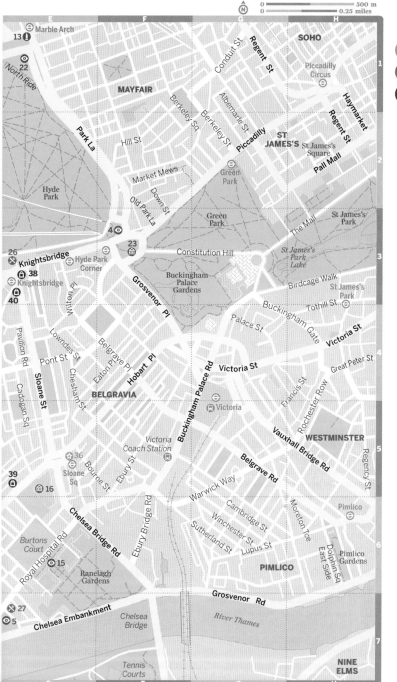

0   500 m
0   0.25 miles

SOHO

Marble Arch
13

22
North Ride

MAYFAIR

Conduit St
Regent St

Piccadilly
Circus

Haymarket

Albemarle St

Berkeley Sq
Berkeley St

Regent St

Hill St

Piccadilly

**ST
JAMES'S**
St James's
Square

Pall Mall

Park La

Market Mews

**Green
Park**

Down St

Old Park La

Green
Park

**Hyde
Park**

The Mall
St James's
Park

4

23

Constitution Hill

St James's
Park
Lake

26
Knightsbridge

38
Hyde Park
Corner

Grosvenor Pl

Buckingham
Palace
Gardens

Birdcage Walk
St James's
Park

Knightsbridge
40

Buckingham Gate
Tothill St

Pavilion Rd

Wilton Pl

Palace St

Victoria St

Lowndes St
Pont St
Chesham St

Belgrave Pl
Eaton Pl
Hobart Pl

Buckingham Palace Rd

Victoria St

Great Peter St

Sloane St

Cadogan Sq

BELGRAVIA

Francis St

Rochester Row

Victoria

Vauxhall Bridge Rd

WESTMINSTER

36

39

16

Sloane
Sq

Bourne St

Ebury St

Victoria
Coach Station

Belgrave Rd

Regency St

Warwick Way

Cambridge St

Moreton Tce

Pimlico

Chelsea Bridge Rd

Ebury Bridge Rd

Winchester St
Sutherland St
Lupus St

Dolphin Sq
East Side

Pimlico
Gardens

PIMLICO

Burtons
Court

Royal Hospital Rd

15

Ranelagh
Gardens

Grosvenor Rd

27
5

Chelsea Embankment

Chelsea
Bridge

River Thames

Tennis
Courts

**NINE
ELMS**

153

Kensington & Hyde Park

Hyde Park is separated from Kensington Gardens by the L-shaped Serpentine, a small lake that hosted the Olympic triathlon and marathon swimming events in 2012. Rent a paddle boat from the **Serpentine boathouse** Map p152 (☎020-7262 1330; adult/child per 30min £10/4, per 1hr £12/5) The **Serpentine solar shuttle boat** Map p152 (☎020-7262 1330; www.solarshuttle.co.uk; adult/child £5/3) harnesses solar power to ferry you from the boathouse to the Princess Diana Memorial Fountain in Kensington Gardens.

Serpentine Gallery   Art Gallery
Map p152 (www.serpentinegallery.org; ◷10am-6pm; ☎; ◉Lancaster Gate or Knightsbridge) FREE Resembling an unprepossessing 1930s tearoom in the midst of leafy Kensington Gardens, this is one of London's most important contemporary art galleries. Damien Hirst, Andreas Gursky, Louise Bourgeois, Gabriel Orozco, Tomoko Takahashi and Jeff Koons have all exhibited here.

Readings, talks and open-air cinema screenings take place here as well. Admission to the gallery is free but a £1 donation is appreciated. Situated just over the Serpentine Bridge is the flashy new **Serpentine Sackler Gallery**.

Kensington Gardens   Gardens
Map p152 (◷dawn-dusk; ◉High St Kensington) Immediately west of Hyde Park and across the Serpentine lake, these picturesque 275-acre gardens are technically part of Kensington Palace. The **Diana, Princess of Wales Memorial Playground** Map p152 (Kensington Gardens; ◉Queensway), in the northwest corner of the gardens, has some pretty ambitious attractions for children. Next to the playground stands the delightful **Elfin Oak**, a 900-year-old tree stump carved with elves, gnomes, witches and small creatures. George

Frampton's celebrated **Peter Pan** statue is close to the lake.

Kensington Palace   Palace

Map p152 (www.hrp.org.uk/kensingtonpalace; Kensington Gardens, W8; adult/child £14.50/ free; ⏰10am-6pm; ⊖High St Kensington) Built in 1605 the Kensington Palace became the favourite royal residence under William and Mary of Orange in 1689, and it remained so until George III became king and relocated to Bucking-ham Palace.

It still has private apartments where various members of the extended royal family, including Prince William and his family, live. In popular imagination it's most associated with three intriguing princesses: Victoria (who was born here in 1819 and lived here with her domineering mother until her accession to the throne), Margaret (sister of the current queen, who lived here until her death in 2002) and, of course, Diana. More than a million bouquets were left outside the gates following her death in 1997.

Venue for evenings of music and dance, the beautiful **Cupola Room** in the **King's State Apartments** is arranged with gilded statues and a gorgeous painted ceiling. The **Drawing Room** is beyond, where the king and courtiers would entertain themselves with cards. The **King's Grand Staircase** is a dizzying feast of trompe l'oeil while the **King's Gallery** displays some of the royal art collection. Queen Mary entertained her visitors in the **Queen's Apartments**.

Albert Memorial   Monument

Map p152 (☎020-7936 2568; www.royalparks. org.uk/parks/kensington-gardens/kensington-gardens-attractions/the-albert-memorial; tours adult/concession £6/5; ⏰tours 2pm & 3pm 1st Sun of month Mar-Dec; ⊖Knightsbridge, Gloucester Rd) FREE This splendid Victorian confection on the southern edge of Ken-sington Gardens, facing the Royal Albert Hall, is as ostentatious as the subject, Queen Victoria's German husband Albert (1819–61), was humble. Albert explicitly

insisted he did not want a monument; ignoring the good prince's wishes, the Lord Mayor instructed George Gilbert Scott to build the 53m-high, gaudy Gothic memorial in 1872.

An eye-opening blend of mosaic, gold leaf, marble and Victorian bombast, the renovated monument is topped with a crucifix. The 4.25m-tall gilded statue of the prince, surrounded by 187 figures representing the continents (Asia, Europe, Africa and America), the arts, industry and science, was erected in 1876. The 64m-long *Frieze of Parnassus* along the base portrays hundreds of eminent Victorians, many of them long forgotten even by historians of the period.

Royal Albert Hall   Historic Building

Map p152 (☎box office 0845 4015045; www. royalalberthall.com; Kensington Gore, SW7; 📶; ⊖South Kensington) This huge, domed, red-brick amphitheatre, adorned with a frieze

Speakers' Corner

The northeastern corner of Hyde Park, **Speakers' Corner** (Map p152; Park Lane; ⊖Marble Arch) is traditionally the spot for oratorical acrobatics and soapbox ranting. It's the only place in Britain where demonstrators can assemble without police permission, a concession granted in 1872 as a response to serious riots 17 years before. About 150,000 people had gathered to demonstrate against the Sunday Trading Bill, which forbade buying and selling on a Sunday, the only day working people had off, before Parliament only to be unexpectedly ambushed by police concealed within Marble Arch. If you've got something to get off your chest, do so on Sunday, although you'll mainly have fringe dwellers, religious fanatics and hecklers for company.

of Minton tiles, is Britain's most famous concert venue and home to the BBC's Promenade Concerts (the Proms) every summer. Book a one-hour front-of-house **guided tour** (☏0845 401 5045; adult/concession £11.50/9.50; ⏱hourly 10am-4.30pm), operating most days, from the box office at door 12. Check the website for dates for far less frequent 90-minute **backstage tours** (☏0845 401 5045; adult £16) and other tours.

Built in 1871, the hall was never intended as a concert venue but as a 'Hall of Arts and Sciences', so it spent the first 133 years of its existence tormenting everyone with shocking acoustics. The huge mushroom-like acoustic reflectors first dangled from the ceiling in 1969 and a further massive refurbishment was completed in 2004.

Diana, Princess of Wales Memorial Fountain   Memorial

Map p152 (Kensington Gardens, W2; ⊖Knightsbridge) This memorial fountain is dedicated to the late Princess of Wales, Diana. Envisaged by the designer Kathryn Gustafson as a 'moat without a castle' and draped 'like a necklace' around the southwestern edge of Hyde Park near the Serpentine Bridge, the circular double stream is composed of 545 pieces of Cornish granite, its waters drawn from a chalk aquifer located more than 100m below ground.

Marble Arch   Monument

Map p152 (⊖Marble Arch) Designed by John Nash in 1827, this huge white arch facing Speakers' Corner was moved here from its original spot in front of Buckingham Palace in 1851 because it was thought to be too unimposing an entrance to the royal manor. If you're feeling anarchic, walk through the central portal, a privilege reserved by (unenforced) law for the Royal Family and the ceremonial King's Troop Royal Horse Artillery.

Chelsea & Belgravia

King's Road
Street

Map p152 (⊖Sloane Sq) At the counter-cultural forefront of London fashion during the technicolour '60s and anarchic '70s, the King's Road today is more a stamping ground for the leisure-class shopping set. The last mohawk punks shuffled off sometime in the 1990s; today it's all Bang & Olufsen, Kurt Geiger and specialist shops.

In the 17th century Charles II fashioned a love nest here for himself and his mistress, Nell Gwyn, an orange-seller turned actress at the Drury Lane Theatre. Heading back to Hampton Court Palace at eventide, Charles would employ a farmer's track that inevitably came to be known as the King's Road.

Saatchi Gallery
Gallery

Map p152 (www.saatchi-gallery.co.uk; Duke of York's HQ, King's Rd, SW1; ⊙10am-6pm; ⊖Sloane Sq) FREE This enticing gallery hosts temporary exhibitions of experimental and thought-provoking work across a variety of media. The white and sanded bare-floorboard galleries are magnificently presented, but save some wonder for Gallery 15, where Richard Wilson's *20:50* is on permanent display. Mesmerising, impassive and ineffable, it's a riveting tour de force.

Chelsea Physic Garden
Garden

Map p152 (www.chelseaphysicgarden.co.uk; 66 Royal Hospital Rd, SW3; adult/child £9/6; ⊙11am-6pm Tue-Fri, to 10pm Wed Jul & Aug, 11am-6pm Sun Apr-Oct; 🗟; ⊖Sloane Sq) This walled pocket of botanical enchantment was established by the Apothecaries' Society in 1676 for students working on medicinal plants and healing. One of the oldest of its kind in Europe, the small grounds are a compendium of botany from carnivorous pitcher plants to rich yellow flag irises, a cork oak from Portugal, delightful ferns, rare trees and shrubs. Enter from Swan Walk.

157

JOHNNIE PAKINGTON/GETTY IMAGES ©

⭐ Don't Miss
Natural History Museum

This colossal building is infused with the irrepressible Victorian spirit of collecting, cataloguing and interpreting the natural world. The main museum building is as much a reason to visit as the world-famous collection within.

A highlight of the museum, the **Central Hall** resembles a cathedral nave – quite fitting for a time when the natural sciences were challenging the biblical tenets of Christian orthodoxy. Naturalist and first superintendent of the museum Richard Owen celebrated the building as a 'cathedral to nature'.

Your first impression as you enter is the dramatically over-arching skeleton of a Diplodocus (nicknamed Dippy), which inspires children to yank their parents to the fantastic **dinosaur gallery** in the Blue Zone, with its impressive overhead walkway passing Dromaeosaurus (a small and agile meat eater) before reaching the museum's star attraction: the roaring and shaking animatronic T-rex.

In the Green Zone, the **Mineral Gallery** is a breathtaking display of architectural perspective leading to the **Vault**, where you'll find the Aurora Collection of almost 300 coloured diamonds. The intriguing Treasures exhibition in the **Cadogan Gallery** houses a host of unrelated objects each telling its own unique story, from a chunk of moon rock to a dodo skeleton. The vast **Darwin Centre** focuses on taxonomy, showcasing 28 million insects and six million plants in a giant cocoon; glass windows allow you to watch scientists at work.

Sensational Butterflies Map p152 (adult/family £4.50/16; ☾10am-5.50pm mid-Apr–mid-Sep), a tent on the East Lawn, swarms with what must originally have been called 'flutter-bys'.

A slice of English countryside in SW7, the **Wildlife Garden** Map p152 (☾Apr-Oct) next to the West Lawn encompasses a range of British lowland habitats, including a meadow with farm gates and a bee tree where a colony of honey bees fills the air.

NEED TO KNOW

Map p152; www.nhm.ac.uk; Cromwell Rd, SW7; ☾10am-5.50pm; ⊖South Kensington

Royal Hospital Chelsea
Historic Buildings

Map p152 (www.chelsea-pensioners.co.uk; Royal Hospital Rd, SW3; ☺grounds 10am-noon & 2-4pm Mon-Sat, museum 10am-noon & 2-4pm Mon-Fri; ☏; ☻Sloane Sq) FREE Designed by Christopher Wren, this superb structure was built in 1692 to provide shelter for ex-servicemen. Since the reign of King William and Queen Mary it has housed hundreds of war veterans, known as Chelsea Pensioners. They're fondly regarded as national treasures, and cut striking figures in the dark-blue greatcoats (in winter) or scarlet frock coats (in summer) that they wear on ceremonial occasions. The museum contains a huge collection of war medals bequeathed by former residents and you'll get to peek at the hospital's Great Hall refectory, Octagon Porch, chapel and courtyards.

✖ Eating

Quality and cash being such easy bedfellows, you'll find some of London's finest establishments in the smart hotels and ritzy mews of Chelsea, Belgravia and Knightsbridge, but there's also a choice in all budget ranges. Chic and cosmopolitan South Kensington has always been reliable for pan-European options.

Knightsbridge, Kensington & Hyde Park

Daquise
Polish ££

Map p152 (☏020-7589 6117; http://daquise. co.uk; 20 Thurloe St, SW7; mains £15-22; ☺noon-11pm; ☻South Kensington) With an unassuming yet wholesome interior, this popular Polish restaurant welcomes diners with a heart-warming range of vodkas and a reasonably priced, regularly varying menu, where you can usually find the oft-seen *bigos*, a 'hunter's stew' of cabbage and pork, and an abundance of soups. The Monday to Saturday espresso lunch (£9) is attractively priced.

Orangery
Teahouse ££

Map p152 (☏020-3166 6112; www.hrp.org.uk/ kensingtonpalace/foodanddrink/orangery; Kensington Palace, Kensington Gardens, W8; tea £22.65, with Champagne £32.50; ☺10am-6pm Mar-Sep, to 5pm Oct-Feb; ☻Queensway, Notting Hill Gate, High St Kensington) ◢ The Orangery, housed in an 18th-century conservatory on the grounds of Kensington Palace, is lovely for lunch, especially if the sun is beaming. But the standout experience here is afternoon tea, for which you often need not book in advance.

Launceston Place
Modern British ££

Map p152 (☏020-7937 6912; www.launceston-place-restaurant.co.uk; 1a Launceston Pl, W8; 3-course lunch/Sun lunch/dinner £25/29.50/30; ☺closed lunch Mon; ◢; ☻Gloucester Rd, High St Kensington) This exceptionally handsome Michelin-starred restaurant hidden away on a picture-postcard Kensington street of Edwardian houses is super-chic. Prepared by Yorkshire chef Tim Allen, the food belongs within the acme of gastronomic pleasures, accompanied by an award-winning wine list. The adventurous will aim for the six-course tasting menu (£65).

Zuma
Japanese £££

Map p152 (☏020-7584 1010; www.zumarestaurant.com; 5 Raphael St, SW7; mains £15-75; ☺6-11pm daily & noon-2.30pm Mon-Fri, 12.30-3.30pm Sat & Sun; ☏; ☻Knightsbridge) A modern-day take on the traditional Japanese *izakaya* ('a place to stay and drink sake'), where drinking and eating harmonise, Zuma oozes style. Traditional Japanese materials combine with modern pronunciation for a highly contemporary feel. The private *kotatsu* rooms are the place for large dinner groups, or dine alongside the open-plan kitchen at the sushi counter.

Min Jiang
Chinese £££

Map p152 (☏020-7361 1988; www.minjiang. co.uk; 2-24 Kensington High St, 10th fl, Royal Garden Hotel, W8; mains £12-68; ☺noon-3pm & 6-10.30pm; ☻High St Kensington) Min Jiang serves up seafood, excellent wood-fired

Detour: Kew Gardens

As well as being a public garden and arboretum, **Kew Gardens** (www.kew.org.uk; Kew Rd; adult/child £16/free; 9.30am-6.30pm Apr-Aug, earlier closing other months; Kew Pier, Kew Bridge, Kew Gardens) is a pre-eminent research centre, maintaining its reputation as the most exhaustive botanical collection in the world.

After entering via Victoria Gate, you'll come almost immediately to a large pond overlooked by the enormous and iconic 700-glass-paned **Palm House**, a domed hothouse of metal and curved sheets of glass dating from 1848 and housing a splendid display of exotic tropical greenery; the aerial walkway offers a parrots'-eye view of the lush vegetation.

The beautiful **Temperate House** in the southeast of Kew Gardens (north of the pagoda) is the world's largest surviving Victorian glasshouse, an astonishing feat of architecture housing an equally sublime collection of plants. It is closed for much-needed restoration and will not open until 2018. Nearby **Evolution House** traces plant evolution over 3500 million years.

In the **Arboretum**, a short walk from Temperate House, a fascinating and much-enjoyed walkway takes you underground and then 18m up in the air into the tree canopy, for closer angles on tree anatomy.

Peking duck (half/whole £32/58) and sumptuously regal views over Kensington Gardens. The menu is diverse, with a sporadic accent on spice (the Min Jiang is a river in Sichuan, a province noted for its fiery cuisine).

Dinner by Heston Blumenthal   Modern British £££

Map p152 (020-7201 3833; www.dinner-byheston.com; Mandarin Oriental Hyde Park, 66 Knightsbridge, SW1; set lunch £36, mains £26-38; noon-2.30pm & 6.30-10.30pm; Knightsbridge) Sumptuously presented Dinner is a gastronomic tour de force, taking diners on a journey through British culinary history (with inventive modern inflections). Dishes carry historical dates to convey context, while the restaurant interior is a design triumph, from the glass-walled kitchen and its overhead clock mechanism to the large windows onto the park.

Chelsea & Belgravia

Penny Black   British ££

Map p152 (020-7349 9901; www.thepenny-black.com; 212 Fulham Rd, SW10; mains £12-30; noon-3pm & 6-11pm Tue-Sat, 10am-10.30pm Sun; West Brompton or Gloucester Rd) Led by head chef Jan Chanter, this contemporary and stylish restaurant is a stimulating blend of fresh, locally sourced ingredients, culinary excellence and highly appetising presentation. The beef Wellington and the Penny Black's other roasts are standout experiences and you can't go wrong with the seafood menu.

Gordon Ramsay   French £££

Map p152 (020-7352 4441; www.gordonramsay.com; 68 Royal Hospital Rd, SW3; 3-course lunch/dinner £55/95; noon-2.30pm & 6.30-11pm Mon-Fri; Sloane Sq) One of Britain's finest restaurants and still boasting three Michelin stars, this is hallowed turf for those who worship at the altar of gastronomy. It's true that it is a treat right from the taster to the truffles, but you won't get much time to savour it all. The blowout tasting Menu Prestige (£135) is seven superb courses of absolute perfection.

Drinking & Nightlife

Drayton Arms
Pub

Map p152 (www.thedraytonarmssw5.co.uk; 153 Old Brompton Rd, SW5; ⌚noon-11pm Mon-Sat, noon-10.30pm Sun; 🚌430, ⊖Gloucester Rd, South Kensington) This vast, comely Victorian corner boozer is delightful inside and out, with some bijou art-nouveau features (sinuous tendrils and curlicues above the windows and the doors), contemporary art on the walls, fabulous coffered ceiling and heated beer garden. The crowd is both hip and down-to-earth; great beer and wine selection.

Buddha Bar
Bar

Map p152 (www.buddhabarlondon.com; 145 Knightsbridge, SW1; cocktails from £10.50; ⌚noon-midnight Mon-Sat, noon-11.30pm Sun; 📶; ⊖Knightsbridge) When you've shopped your legs off in Knightsbridge, this serene Pan-Asian zone welcomes you into a world of Chinese bird-cage lanterns, subdued lighting, tucked-away corners and booths, perfect for sipping on a raspberry 'saketini' and chilling out. Live DJ nightly.

Queen's Arms
Pub

Map p152 (www.thequeensarmskensington.co.uk; 30 Queen's Gate Mews, SW7; ⌚noon-11pm Mon-Sat, noon-10.30pm Sun; ⊖Gloucester Rd) Just around the corner from the Royal Albert Hall, this godsend of a blue-grey painted pub in an adorable cobbled mews setting off bustling Queen's Gate beckons with a cosy interior and a right royal selection of draught ales and ciders.

Entertainment

Royal Albert Hall
Concert Hall

Map p152 (📞020-7589 8212; www.royalalberthall.com; Kensington Gore, SW7; ⊖South Kensington) This splendid Victorian concert hall hosts classical-music, rock and other performances, but is most famously the venue for the BBC-sponsored Proms. Booking is possible, but from mid-July to mid-September Proms punters also queue for £5 standing (or 'promenading') tickets that go on sale one hour before curtain-up. Otherwise the box office and prepaid ticket collection counter are both through door 12 (south side of the hall).

Royal Albert Hall

JOHNNIE PAKINGTON/GETTY IMAGES ©

Detour:
Notting Hill

PORTOBELLO ROAD MARKET

Like Camden and Spitalfields, **Portobello Road Market** (www.portobellomarket.org; Portobello Rd, W10; ⊗8am-6.30pm Mon-Wed, Fri & Sat, 8am-1pm Thu; ⊖Notting Hill Gate, Ladbroke Grove) is a worthy London attraction with the usual mix of street food, fruit and veg, antiques, colourful fashion, and trinkets you never thought you'd need. Although the shops along Portobello Rd open daily and the fruit and veg stalls (from Elgin Cres to Talbot Rd) only close on Sunday, the busiest day by far is Saturday, when antique dealers set up shop from Chepstow Villas to Elgin Cres. This is also when the fashion market (beneath Westway from Portobello Rd to Ladbroke Rd) is in full swing – although you can also browse for fashion on Friday and Sunday.

NOTTING HILL CARNIVAL

Every August, Notting Hill throws a big, long and loud party. Europe's leading street festival is a vibrantly colourful three-day celebration of Afro-Caribbean music, culture and food. Over a million people visit each year, taking part in the celebrations, thronging the streets and letting their hair down. The festival is a must if you want a spirited glimpse of multicultural London and its cross-pollination of music, food, clothing, language and heritage.

MUSEUM OF BRANDS, PACKAGING & ADVERTISING

This unexpected **museum** (www.museumofbrands.com; 2 Colville Mews, Lonsdale Rd, W11; adult/child £6.50/2.25; ⊗10am-6pm Tue-Sat, 11am-5pm Sun; ⊖Notting Hill Gate, Ladbroke Grove, Westbourne Park) is fairly low-tech but very eye-catching, with sponsored displays at the end of the gallery and exhibits showing the evolution of packaging of some well-known products including Johnson's Baby Powder and Guinness. It must be said, though, that it will largely be of interest to Britons; most others won't recognise most of the brands.

606 Club   Blues, Jazz

(☎020-7352 5953; www.606club.co.uk; 90 Lots Rd, SW10; music fee Sun-Thu £10, Fri & Sat £12; ⊗7pm-late Mon-Thu, 8pm-late Fri & Sat, 7-11.15pm Sun; ⊖Fulham Broadway) Named after its old address on King's Rd, which cast a spell over jazz lovers London-wide back in the '80s' this fantastic, tucked-away basement jazz club and restaurant gives centre stage to contemporary British-based jazz musicians nightly. Hidden behind a nondescript brick wall, the club frequently opens until 2am, although at weekends you have to dine to gain admission (booking advised). There's no entry charge as such but a 'music fee' will be added to your bill.

Royal Court Theatre   Theatre

Map p152 (☎020-7565 5000; www.royalcourt theatre.com; Sloane Sq, SW1; ⊖Sloane Sq) Equally renowned for staging innovative new plays and old classics, the Royal Court is among London's most progressive theatres and has continued to foster major writing talent across the UK. Tickets for concessions are £6 to £10, and £10 for everyone on Monday (four 10p standing tickets sold at the Jerwood Theatre Downstairs); tickets for under 26s are £8.

🔒 Shopping

Frequented by models and celebrities, and awash with new money (much from abroad) and Russian oligarchs, this well-heeled part of town is all about high fashion, glam shops, groomed shoppers and iconic top-end department stores. Even the charity shops along the chic King's Road resemble fashion boutiques.

Harrods
Department Store

Map p152 (www.harrods.com; 87 Brompton Rd, SW1; ⏱10am-8pm Mon-Sat, 11.30am-6pm Sun; ⊖Knightsbridge) Both garish and stylish at the same time, perennially crowded Harrods is an obligatory stop for London's tourists, from the cash strapped to the big, big spenders. The stock is astonishing and you'll swoon over the spectacular food hall.

High on kitsch, the Egyptian Elevator, with its ex-owner Mohammed Al Fayed's sphinxes, resembles something hauled in from an Indiana Jones epic film, while the memorial to Dodi and Diana merely adds surrealism.

Harvey Nichols
Department Store

Map p152 (www.harveynichols.com; 109-125 Knightsbridge, SW1; ⏱10am-8pm Mon-Sat, 11.30am-6pm Sun; ⊖Knightsbridge) At London's temple of high fashion, you'll find Chloé and Balenciaga bags, the city's best denim range, a massive make-up hall with exclusive lines, great jewellery and a fantastic restaurant called Fifth Floor.

John Sandoe Books
Books

Map p152 (www.johnsandoe.com; 10 Blacklands Tce; ⏱9.30am-6.30pm Mon-Sat, 11am-5pm Sun; ⊖Sloane Sq) The perfect antidote to impersonal book superstores, this atmospheric little bookshop is a treasure trove of literary gems and hidden surprises. In business for decades, loyal customers swear by it and the knowledgeable booksellers spill forth with well-read pointers.

Shanghai Tang
Clothing

Map p152 (www.shanghaitang.com; 6a/b Sloane St; ⏱10am-7pm Mon-Sat, noon-6pm Sun; ⊖Knightsbridge) Traditionally Chinese inspired and super-swish silk scarves, *cheongsam*s, elegant Chinese jackets, delicious tops, exquisite cardigans, gorgeous handbags and clutches from man-about-town David Tang, many served up in trademark neon vibrant colours.

Clerkenwell, Hoxton & Spitalfields

Come to this district for throbbing nightlife, hip shopping and innovative dining.

The three adjoining but very different districts are Clerkenwell, just north of the City; Shoreditch and its northern extension Hoxton, an area (roughly) between Old St tube station and just east of Shoreditch High St; and Spitalfields, centred on its eponymous market and Brick Lane, its main thoroughfare. This remains London's creative engine room and, for night owls, the place in town to wing to for wining, dining and a good time either side of midnight. There are sights and shops you'll want to explore by day, but they don't get too overrun so there's no compulsion to head out particularly early.

All three neighbourhoods have a glut of excellent cafes, restaurants, bars and clubs, but Shoreditch remains the centre of late-night gravity. Sunday is excellent for a leisurely stroll through Spitalfields.

Brick Lane (p174)
CHRIS MAREMAGNUM/GETTY IMAGES ©

Clerkenwell, Hoxton & Spitalfields Highlights

Geffrye Museum (p171)

An institution devoted to interiors may seem idiosyncratic, but this charming museum succeeds on all levels and affords a fascinating insight into the evolution of interiors in Britain. It's also housed in a beautiful old row of 18th-century almshouses, well worth seeing for themselves alone, along with a charming herb garden at the back.

Clubbing in Shoreditch (p176)

Nowhere in London can rival the creative maelstrom of the capital's coolest quarter. Prices may have risen over the past decade, but you can't beat an evening out in Shoreditch, where the most exciting of the capital's clubs – including XOYO (p177) and Cargo (p177) – rule.

Cargo

Shopping at Spitalfields Market (p179)

The market at Spitalfields has long been a London favourite – and even though (inevitably, given its position on some of London's prime real estate) the developers moved in and 'regenerated' part of the market, this place still has its fair share of excellent shopping, eating and atmosphere.

Brick Lane (p174)

Wander through wonderfully preserved Georgian Spitalfields, before emerging onto exuberant and cacophonous Brick Lane (p174) to explore Banglatown and the hip bars, shops and cafes of the Old Truman Brewery. Grab a cheap and filling spicy meal, peek into some of the many interesting shops or just soak up the atmosphere.

Drinking in a Local Pub (p176)

Serve up your poison according to taste in this well-stocked neighbourhood, from the historic, traditional pubs of Clerkenwell to the hip and fashionable bars of Shoreditch and Hoxton. Make a start with the Jerusalem Tavern (p176) and then see out the night taking your pick from some of London's coolest watering holes. Ye Olde Mitre (p176)

Spitalfields & Shoreditch Walk

This 2-mile walk takes you through one of London's most exciting and creative neighbourhoods. You can do it anytime, but for the best experience aim for Sunday mornings when two big markets are in full swing.

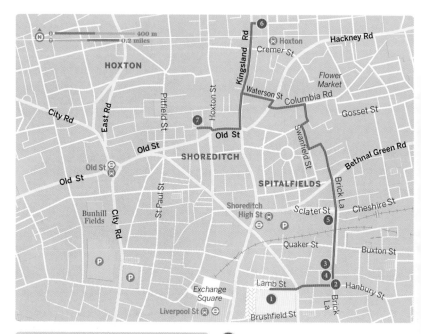

1 Spitalfields Market

One of London's most colourful and diverse markets (p178), this is a great weekend treat for clothing, records and food. Enter the old market building and get lost among the many stalls.

2 Brick Lane

From the market head east to Brick Lane. In 1550 this was just a country road leading to brickyards; by the 18th century it had been paved and lined with houses and cottages inhabited by the Huguenot silk weavers. Today the southern part of this vibrant street (p174) is full of touristy curry houses.

3 Old Truman Brewery

This was the biggest brewery in London by the mid-18th century, and the Director's House on the left dates from 1740. Next to the 19th-century Vat House is the 1830 Engineer's House and a row of former stables. The brewery shut down over 20 years ago and is now part of Sunday UpMarket.

4 Sunday UpMarket

From 10am to 5pm on Sundays, this market is relatively uncrowded, with wonderful clothes, music and crafts from young designers. The excellent food hall (at the Brick Lane end) is a tempting array of global grub, from Ethiopian veggie dishes to Japanese delicacies.

5 Brick Lane Market

On Sundays, around the Shoreditch tube station, you'll find good bargains on clothes, but the market (from 8am to 3pm Sundays) is good for furniture, household goods, bric-a-brac, secondhand clothes and cheap fashion. Saunter down Cheshire St for little boutiques featuring new designers and vintage collections.

6 Geffrye Museum

A small estate of Victorian houses, this fascinating museum (p171) is devoted to English interiors through the ages. Relax in the lovely glass cafe in the back, and have a look at the museum's aromatic herb garden.

7 Hoxton Square

End your walk by popping into Hoxton Sq. Check out the small park where there's always something going on and join the crowds having a drink outside in good weather. The square was built on the 'Hogsden Fields' where the playwright Ben Jonson fought a duel with and killed a man in 1598.

 The Best...

PLACES TO EAT

Moro Excellent Moorish menu, still winning plaudits. (p175)

Leila's Shop Strong on rustic charm and thoughtfully prepared food. (p175)

St John For British cuisine, St John remains one of London's best. (p175)

Fifteen Where Jamie Oliver trains the next big thing. (p175)

Paesan Italian *cucina povera* (cooking of the poor) is anything but that. (p174)

PLACES TO DRINK

Jerusalem Tavern Tiny but delightful, with beers from a Norfolk brewery. (p176)

Book Club A modern temple to good times, with great offbeat events. (p176)

Golden Heart Fun pub drawing an arty, trendy clientele. (p178)

Ye Olde Mitre Drink where Queen Elizabeth (the first one) danced. (p176)

PLACES TO DANCE

Fabric Hip Clerkenwell club for hedonists, with bars on three floors. (p176)

Cargo Creative music menu and trendy Shoreditch locale. (p177)

XOYO Diverse music menu and an eclectic crowd of dancers. (p177)

Brick Lane (p174)

Discover Clerkenwell, Hoxton & Spitalfields

Getting There & Away

o **Underground** Farringdon and Barbican are the stop-off points for Clerkenwell, on the Circle, Hammersmith & City and Metropolitan Lines. Old St is on the Bank branch of the Northern Line. Liverpool St, on the Central Line, gives you access to the City and the West End, as well as Bethnal Green and Stratford in the east.

o **Overground** Shoreditch High St and Hoxton are handy stops on the overground, running north to Dalston and Highbury & Islington, and south to Wapping.

o **Bus** Clerkenwell and Old St are connected with Oxford St by the 55 and with Waterloo by the 243. The 38 runs up Rosebery Ave, handy for Exmouth Market, on its way from Victoria to Islington. The 8 and 242 zip through the city and up Shoreditch High St.

Charterhouse
LONELY PLANET/GETTY IMAGES ©

⊙ Sights

Clerkenwell

Charterhouse Historic Building
Map p172 (www.thecharterhouse.org; Charterhouse Sq, EC1; tours £10; ⊙ guided tours 2.15pm Wed Apr-Aug; ⊖ Barbican or Farringdon) You need to book well in advance to visit this former Carthusian monastery, where the centrepiece is a Tudor hall with a restored hammerbeam roof. Its incredibly popular two-hour guided tours begin at the 14th-century gatehouse on Charterhouse Sq, before going through to the Preachers' Court, the Master's Court, the Great Hall and the Great Chamber, where Queen Elizabeth I stayed on numerous occasions. Tickets must be pre-booked either online or by post – most tours take place between April and August, although there are dates throughout the year.

St John's Gate Historic Building
Map p172 (St John's Lane; guided tours suggested donation £5; ⊙ priory church 10am-3pm Mon-Sat, guided tours 11am & 2.30pm Tue, Fri & Sat; ⊖ Farringdon) FREE This surprisingly out-of-place medieval gate cutting across St John's Lane is no modern folly, but the real deal. During the 12th century, the crusading Knights of St John of Jerusalem (a religious and military order with a focus on providing care to the sick) established a priory on this site that originally covered around 4 hectares.

Inside is the small **Museum of the Order of St John** Map p172 (www.museumstjohn.org.uk; St John's Lane, EC1; ⊙ 10am-5pm Mon-Sat) FREE, which covers the history of the order (including rare examples of the knights' armour), as well as the foundation of St

John Ambulance, set up in the 19th century to promote first aid and revive the order's ethos of caring for the sick. A guided tour will take you through the gate, the restored church, the sumptuous 1902 Chapter Hall and the council chamber that are still used by the order to this day.

Shoreditch

Geffrye Museum Museum

Map p172 (www.geffrye-museum.org.uk; 136 Kingsland Rd, E2; ☉10am-5pm Tue-Sat, noon-5pm Sun; ⊖Hoxton or Old St) FREE This series of beautiful 18th-century ivy-clad almshouses, with an extensive and well-presented herb garden, contains a museum devoted to domestic interiors, with each room of the main building furnished to show how the homes of the relatively affluent middle class would have looked from Elizabethan times right through to the end of the 19th century. A postmodernist extension completed in 1998 contains several 20th-century rooms (a flat from the 1930s, a room in the contemporary style of the 1950s and a 1990s converted warehouse complete with IKEA furniture) as well as a gallery for temporary exhibits, a shop and a restaurant. The garden is also organised by era, mirroring the museum's exploration of domesticity through the centuries.

Spitalfields

Dennis Severs' House Museum

Map p172 (☎020 7247 4013; www.dennissevers house.co.uk; 8 Folgate St, E1; ⊖Liverpool St) FREE This quirky Georgian house is named after the late American eccentric who restored and turned it into what he called a 'still-life drama'. Severs was an artist, and lived in the house (in a similar way to the original inhabitants) until his death in 1999.

Visitors today find they have entered the home of a 'family' of Huguenot silk weavers, who were common in the Spitalfields area in the 18th century. However, while they see the restored Georgian interiors, with meals and drinks half-abandoned and rumpled sheets, and while they smell cooking and hear creaking floorboards, their 'hosts' always remain just out of reach. Each of the 10 rooms re-creates a specific time in the house's history from 1724 to 1914; from the cellar to the bedrooms, the interiors demonstrate both the original function and design of the rooms, as well as the highs and lows of the area's history.

Bookings are essential for the Monday and Wednesday evening 'Silent Night' tours by candlelight (£14; 6pm to 9pm), but you can just show up on Sunday (£10; noon to 4pm) or the first and third Monday (£7; noon to 2pm) of each month.

Georgian Spitalfields

Crowded around its eponymous market and the marvellous Christ Church, Spitalfields is a layer cake of immigration from all over the world. Waves of French Huguenots, Jews, Irish and, more recently, Indian and Bangladeshi immigrants have made Spitalfields home, and it remains one of the capital's most multicultural areas. A walk down Brick Lane is the best way to get a sense of today's Bangladeshi community, but to get a taste of what Georgian Spitalfields was like, branch off to Princelet, Fournier, Elder and Wilkes Sts. Having fled persecution in France, the Huguenots set up shop here from the late 1600s, practising their trade of silk weaving. The attics of these grand town houses were once filled with clattering looms and the area became famous for the quality of its silk – even providing the material for Queen Victoria's coronation gown. To see inside one of these wonderful old buildings, visit **Dennis Severs' House** (above).

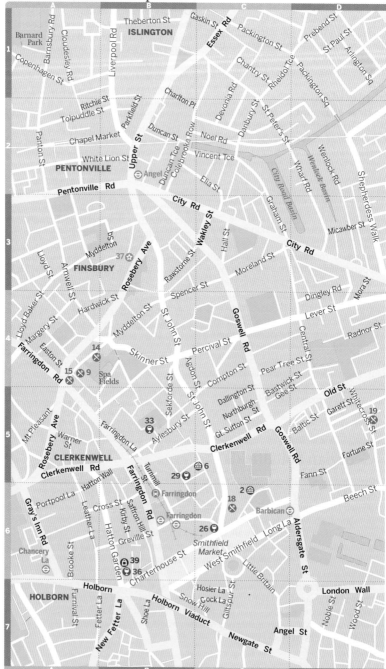

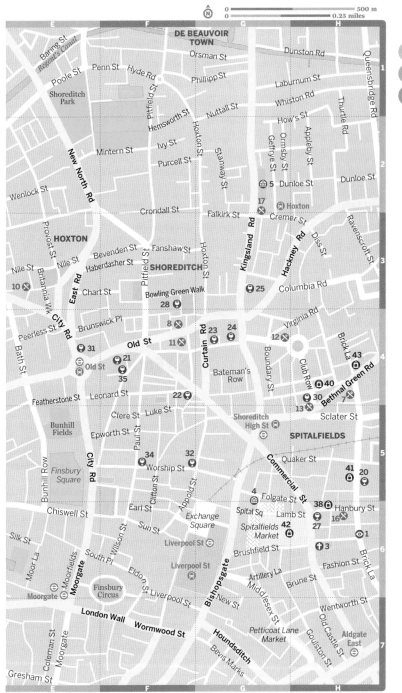

0 m 500 m
0 0.25 miles

Ⓝ

Baring St
Regent's Canal
Poole St
Penn St
Hyde Rd
Shoreditch Park
Pitfield St
Hemsworth St
Mintern St
Ivy St
Purcell St
New North Rd
Wenlock St
Provost St
HOXTON
Nile St
Nile St
Britannia Wk
Bevenden St
Haberdasher St
East Rd
Chart St
Brunswick Pl
City Rd
Peerless St
Bath St
Featherstone St
Leonard St
Clere St
Luke St
Bunhill Fields
Epworth St
Paul St
City Rd
Bunhill Row
Finsbury Square
Chiswell St
Earl St
Sun St
Silk St
Clifton St
Appold St
Worship St
Moor La
Moorfields
South Pl
Wilson St
Eldon St
Moorgate
Finsbury Circus
Liverpool St
London Wall
Wormwood St
Coleman St
Moorgate
Gresham St

Orsman St
Phillipp St
Penn St
Hyde Rd
Nuttall St
Stanway St
Hoxton St
Crondall St
Falkirk St
Fanshaw St
Pitfield St
SHOREDITCH
Bowling Green Walk
Hoxton St
Old St
Curtain Rd
Bateman's Row
Leonard St

Dunston Rd
Laburnum St
Whiston Rd
How's St
Ormsby St
Gefrye St
Appleby St
Thurtle Rd
Queensbridge Rd
Dunloe St
Dunloe St
Cremer St
Hackney Rd
Diss St
Ravenscroft St
Columbia Rd
Virginia Rd
Boundary St
Club Row
Brick La
Bethnal Green Rd
Sclater St
Shoreditch High St
SPITALFIELDS
Quaker St
Commercial St
Folgate St
Spital Sq
Lamb St
Spitalfields Market
Hanbury St
Brushfield St
Liverpool St
Bishopsgate
Liverpool St
Brune St
Artillery La
Middlesex St
New St
Fashion St
Brick La
Wentworth St
Old Castle St
Petticoat Lane Market
Houndsditch
Aldgate East
Bevis Marks

10 ☒
31 ☒
Old St
21
35
22
34
32
28
8 ☒
11 ☒
23
24
12 ☒
40
30
13 ☒
7 ☒
43
Hoxton
17 ☒
5
25
4
38
16 ☒
42
27
3
1
41
20

CLERKENWELL, HOXTON & SPITALFIELDS

Clerkenwell, Hoxton & Spitalfields

Brick Lane Street
Map p172 (◎ Shoreditch High St or Liverpool St) Full of noise, colour and life, Brick Lane is a vibrant mix of history and modernity, and a palimpsest of cultures. Today it is the centrepiece of a thriving Bengali community in an area nicknamed Banglatown. The southern part of the lane is one long procession of curry houses intermingled with fabric shops and South Asian supermarkets.

Christ Church Spitalfields Church
Map p172 (www.christchurchspitalfields.org; Commercial St, E1; ◎ 11am-4pm Tue, 1-4pm Sun; ◎ Shoreditch High St or Liverpool St) Opposite Spitalfields Market, on the corner of Commercial and Fournier Sts, is this restored church, where many of the area's weavers worshipped. The magnificent English baroque structure, with a tall spire sitting on a portico of four great Tuscan columns, was designed by Nicholas Hawksmoor and completed in 1729.

✖ Eating

As well as a wealth of fantastic cafes and restaurants, this area also hosts a number of food markets where you can grab a real variety of dishes and cuisines, from deliciously moist chocolate brownies to fiery Thai curries and overflowing burritos. Places to check out include **Exmouth Market** (Map p172; ◎ noon-3pm Thu & Fri; ◎ Farringdon or Angel), **Whitecross St Market** (Map p172; ◎ 11am-3pm Mon-Fri; ◎ Old St) and **Brick Lane** and the surrounding streets.

Clerkenwell

Paesan Italian £
Map p172 (☎ 020-7837 7139; http://paesanlondon.co; 2 Exmouth Market; mains £8-12; ◎ noon-3pm & 5-11pm Mon-Sat, noon-4pm Sun) This new kid on the block at Exmouth Market serves up sharing-sized dishes of cucina povera, a kind of Tuscan peasant food that is more refined than stick-to-the-ribs. Try the pappardelle pasta with rabbit ragout or the polpettone (meatballs) with salsa verde.

Moro
Fusion ££

Map p172 (☏020-7833 8336; www.moro.co.uk; 34-36 Exmouth Market, EC1; mains £16.50-21; ⊙noon-2.30pm & 6-10.30pm Mon-Sat, 12.30-2.45pm Sun; ⊖Farringdon or Angel) Moro serves Moorish cuisine, a fusion of Spanish, Portuguese and Moroccan flavours. The restaurant is always full and buzzing, and the food is divine. Reservations are essential but you can often turn up without a booking and perch at the bar for some tapas, wine and desserts.

St John
British £££

Map p172 (☏020-7251 0848; www.stjohnrestaurant.com; 26 St John St, EC1; mains £17-23; ⊙noon-3pm & 6-11pm Mon-Sat, 1-3pm Sun; ⊖Farringdon) This London classic is wonderfully simple – its light bar and cafe area giving way to a surprisingly small dining room where 'nose to tail' eating is served up courtesy of celebrity chef Fergus Henderson.

Shoreditch & Hoxton

Leila's Shop
Cafe £

Map p172 (17 Calvert Ave, E2; dishes £5-9; ⊙10am-6pm Wed-Sun; ⊖Shoreditch High St) Tucked away on up-and-coming Calvert Ave, Leila's Shop feels like a bohemian country kitchen. For breakfast, go for the eggs and ham, which come beautifully cooked in their own little frying pan. Sandwiches are freshly made with superior produce, and there's homemade lemonade and great coffee.

Fifteen
Italian ££

Map p172 (☏020-3375 1515; www.fifteen.net; 15 Westland Pl, N1; breakfast £2-8.50, trattoria £6-11, restaurant £11-25; ⊙noon-3pm & 6-10pm; 🛜; ⊖Old St) Jamie Oliver's nonprofit restaurant teams young chefs from disadvantaged backgrounds with experienced professionals, creating an ambitious and interesting Italian menu. The ground-floor trattoria is a relaxed venue, while the underground dining room is more formal.

Les Trois Garçons
Modern French £££

Map p172 (☏020-7613 1924; www.lestroisgarcons.com; 1 Club Row, E1; mains £15-27; ⊙noon-2pm Thu & Fri, 6-9.30pm Mon-Thu, 6-10.30pm Fri & Sat; ⊖Shoreditch High St) The name may prepare you for the French menu, but nothing on Earth could prepare you for the camp decor inside this made-over Victorian pub. A virtual menagerie of stuffed or bronze animals fills every surface, while chandeliers dangle between a set of suspended handbags.

The Pho Mile

Kingsland Rd has become famous for its string of Vietnamese cafes and restaurants, many of which are BYO and serve authentic and great-value cuisine.

Sông Quê (Map p172; www.songque.co.uk; 134 Kingsland Rd, E2; mains £6-9; ⊙noon-3pm & 5.30-11pm Mon-Fri, noon-11pm Sat & Sun; ⊖Hoxton) With the kind of demand for seats that most London restaurants can only dream of, this perennial favourite always has a line of people waiting for a table. Service is frenetic, but the food is great and good value.

Cây Tre (Map p172; ☏020-7729 8662; http://caytre.co.uk; 301 Old St, EC1; mains £7-9; ⊙noon-11pm Mon-Thu, to 11.30pm Fri & Sat, to 10.30pm Sun; ⊖Old St) Serves up all the classics to a mix of Vietnamese diners and Hoxton scenesters in a simple but nicely decorated and tightly packed space. Across the road its cafe, **Kêu** (Map p172; 332 Old St, EC1; baguettes £4.50; ⊙8am-8pm), offers up lip-smacking baguettes to eat in or takeaway, as well as soups, salads and specials.

Spitalfields

Brick Lane Beigel Bake · Bagels £

Map p172 (159 Brick Lane, E2; £1-4; ⏱24hr;
🚇Shoreditch High St or Liverpool St) You won't
find fresher (or cheaper) bagels anywhere
in London than at this bakery and delica-
tessen; just ask any taxi driver (it's their
favourite nosherie).

Rosa's · Thai ££

Map p172 (www.rosaslondon.com; 12 Hanbury
St, E1; mains £7-12.50; ⏱noon-10.30pm;
🚇Shoreditch High St or Liverpool St) Red-
fronted Rosa's is a cosy and simple Thai
restaurant, over two floors, just off Commercial St. Go for its signature pumpkin
curry, one of the super-fresh and zingy
salads or delicious chargrills.

Poppies · Fish & Chips £

Map p172 (www.poppiesfishandchips.co.uk;
6-8 Hanbury St, E1; mains £6-11; ⏱11am-11pm,
to 10.30pm Sun; 📶; 🚇Shoreditch High St
or Liverpool St) Glorious re-creation of a
1950s East End chippy, complete with
waitresses wearing pinnies and hairnets,
and retro memorabilia. As well as the
usual fishy suspects, it also does jellied
eels, homemade tartar sauce and mushy
peas.

🍷 Drinking & Nightlife

Clerkenwell

Jerusalem Tavern · Pub

Map p172 (www.stpetersbrewery.co.uk; 55
Britton St, EC1; ⏱11am-11pm Mon-Fri; 📶;
🚇Farringdon) Starting life as one of the
first London coffee houses in 1703, with
the 18th-century decor of tile mosaics
still visible, the JT is an absolute stunner,
though sadly it's both massively popular
and tiny, so come early to get a seat.

Fabric · Club

Map p172 (www.fabriclondon.com; 77a Charterhouse St, EC1; admission £8-18; ⏱10pm-6am
Fri, 11pm-8am Sat, 11pm-6am Sun; 🚇Farringdon)
This most impressive of superclubs is
still the first stop on the London scene for
many international clubbers. The crowd is
hip and well dressed without overkill, and
the music – electro, techno, house, drum
and bass and dubstep – is as superb as
you'd expect from London's top-rated
club.

Ye Olde Mitre · Pub

Map p172 (1 Ely Ct, EC1; ⏱11am-11pm Mon-Fri;
📶; 🚇Chancery Lane or Farringdon) A delightfully cosy historic pub, tucked away in a
backstreet off Hatton Garden (look for a
Fullers sign above a low archway on the
left), Ye Olde Mitre was built for the serv-
ants of Ely Palace. There's still a memento
of Elizabeth I – the stump of a cherry tree
around which she once danced.

Three Kings · Pub

Map p172 (7 Clerkenwell Close, EC1; ⏱noon-
11pm Mon-Fri, 5.30-11pm Sat; 📶; 🚇Farringdon)
Down-to-earth and welcoming pub,
attracting a friendly bunch of relaxed
locals for its quirky decor, great music
and good times.

Shoreditch & Hoxton

Book Club · Bar

Map p172 (☎020-7684 8618; www.wearetbc.
com; 100 Leonard St; ⏱8am-midnight Mon-Wed,
8am-2am Thu & Fri, 10am-2am Sat & Sun; 📶;
🚇Old St) This former Victorian warehouse
has been transformed into an innovative temple to good times. Spacious and
whitewashed with large windows upstairs
and a basement bar below, it hosts a real
variety of offbeat events, such as spoken
word, dance lessons and life drawing, as
well as a varied program of DJ nights.

DreamBagsJaguarShoes · DJ Bar

Map p172 (www.jaguarshoes.com; 32-36 Kingsland Rd, E2; ⏱noon-1am; 🚇Old St or Hoxton)
The bar is named after the two shops
whose two-floor space it now occupies,
and this nonchalance is a typical example
of the we-couldn't-care-less Shoreditch
chic. The small interior is filled with sofas
and Formica-topped tables, and art exhibitions deck the walls.

The Cocktail Hour

While mojitos and caipirinhas are these days two-a-penny in Shoreditch bars, there are some places that take their shaking far more seriously. Here is a list of our favourites. It's worth booking ahead at all of them.

Worship St Whistling Shop (Map p172; 📞 020-7247 0015; www.whistlingshop.com; 63 Worship St, EC2; 🕐 noon-1am Mon-Thu, to 2am Fri & Sat; 🚇 Old St) A 'Victorian' drinking den that takes cocktails to a molecular level, the Whistling Shop (as Victorians called a place selling illicit booze) serves expertly crafted and highly unusual concoctions using potions conjured up in its on-site lab.

Happiness Forgets (Map p172; 📞 020-7613 0325; www.happinessforgets.com; 8-9 Hoxton Sq, N1; 🕐 5-11pm Mon-Sat; 🚉 Hoxton, 🚇 Old St) The menu promises you mixed drinks and mischief at this low-lit, basement bar with good-value cocktails in a relaxed and intimate setting.

Nightjar (Map p172; 📞 020-7253 4101; www.barnightjar.com; 129 City Rd, EC1; 🕐 6pm-1.30am Tue & Wed, to 3.30am Thu-Sat; 🚇 Old St) Slick, wood-panelled speakeasy offering nightly live music. The well-executed cocktails are divided into four eras: before and during prohibition, postwar and Nightjar signatures.

Calloh Callay (Map p172; 📞 020-7739 4781; www.calloohcallaybar.com; 65 Rivington St, EC2; 🕐 6pm-midnight Sun-Wed, to 1am Thu-Sat; 🚇 Old St) Given it's inspired by *Jabberwocky*, Lewis Carroll's nonsense poem, this bar's eccentric decor doesn't come as a surprise. Try the Ale of Two Cities, which comes in a half-pint beer mug.

Loungelover (Map p172; 📞 020-7012 1234; www.lestroisgarcons.com; 1 Whitby St, E1; 🕐 6pm-midnight Sun-Thu, to 1am Fri & Sat; 🛜) The drinks and the look are both faultless at this Shoreditch institution, where it's all about the superb cocktails and the junk-shop chic of the decor.

Cargo — Club

Map p172 (www.cargo-london.com; 83 Rivington St, EC2; admission free-£16; 🕐 6pm-1am Mon-Thu, to 3am Fri & Sat, to midnight Sun; 🚇 Old St) Cargo is one of London's most eclectic clubs. Under its brick railway arches you'll find a dance-floor room, bar and outside terrace. The music policy is innovative and varied, with plenty of up-and-coming bands also on the menu.

XOYO — Club

Map p172 (www.xoyo.co.uk; 32-37 Cowper St, EC2; 🕐 hours vary; 🚇 Old St) Run by a group of music professionals, this lofty venue plays host to a finely chosen selection of gigs and club nights, as well as exhibiting art. The varied program – expect indie bands, hip hop, electro, dubstep and much in between – attracts a mix of clubbers.

Queen of Hoxton — Bar

Map p172 (www.queenofhoxton.com; 1-5 Curtain Rd, EC2; 🕐 5pm-midnight Mon-Wed, 5pm-2am Thu & Fri, 6pm-2am Sat; 🛜; 🚇 Liverpool St) Industrial-chic bar with a games room, basement and varied music nights, though the real draw card is the rooftop bar, with flowers, fairy lights and even a fish pond, with fantastic views across the city.

Aquarium — Club

Map p172 (www.clubaquarium.co.uk; 256-264 Old St, EC1; 🕐 hours vary; 🚇 Old St) The real attraction at this big and brash club is the swimming pool and Jacuzzi (towels provided) and the often very-late opening hours (selected nights until 9am). DJs play mainly house and techno to a

RICHARD I'ANSON/GETTY IMAGES ©

CLERKENWELL, HOXTON & SPITALFIELDS ENTERTAINMENT

mainstream, dressed-up crowd. Trainers are not welcome here.

Spitalfields

Golden Heart
Pub

Map p172 (110 Commercial St, E1; ⊙11am-11pm Mon-Sat, noon-10.30pm Sun; ⊖Liverpool St) It's an unsurprisingly trendy Hoxton crowd that mixes in the surprisingly untrendy interior of this brilliant Spitalfields boozer. It's famous as the watering hole for the cream of London's art crowd, but land-lady/celebrity Sandra keeps them all in line.

93 Feet East
Club

Map p172 (www.93feeteast.co.uk; 150 Brick Lane, E2; ⊙5-11pm Mon-Thu, to 1am Fri & Sat, 3-10.30pm Sun; ⊖Liverpool St or Shoreditch High St) This great and longstanding venue has a courtyard, three big rooms and an outdoor terrace that gets crowded on sunny afternoons, packed with a cool East London crowd.

⭐ Entertainment

Sadler's Wells
Dance

Map p172 (☎0844 412 4300; www.sadlerswells.com; Rosebery Ave, EC1; tickets £10-49; ⊖Angel) The theatre site dates from 1683 but was completely rebuilt in 1998; today it is the most eclectic and modern dance venue in town, with experimental dance shows of all genres and from all corners of the globe. The Lilian Baylis Studio stages smaller productions.

🛍 Shopping

This is a great area for discovering cool boutiques and market stalls for vintage clothes and up-and-coming designers. There are tonnes of shops off Brick Lane, especially in burgeoning Cheshire St, Hanbury St and the Old Truman Brewery on Dray Walk. Clerkenwell is mostly known for jewellery. For classic settings and unmounted stones, visit London's traditional jewellery and diamond trade area, Hatton Garden.

Spitalfields Market
Market

Map p172 (www.oldspitalfieldsmarket.com; Commercial St, btwn Brushfield & Lamb Sts, E1; ⊙10am-4pm Sun-Fri; ⊖Liverpool St) One of London's best markets, with traders hawking their wares here since the early 17th century. The covered market that you see today was built in the late 19th century, with the more modern development added in 2006. It is open six days a week, but Sundays are best and filled with fashion, jewellery, food and music stalls.

Rough Trade East
Music

Map p172 (www.roughtrade.com; Dray Walk, Old Truman Brewery, 91 Brick Lane, E1; ⊙8am-8pm Mon-Fri, 11am-7pm Sat & Sun; ⊖Liverpool St) This vast record store has an impressive selection of CDs and vinyl across all genres, as well as an interesting offering of books.

Tatty Devine
Jewellery

Map p172 (www.tattydevine.com; 236 Brick Lane, E2; ⊙11am-6pm Tue-Sun; ⊖Shoreditch High St) Hip and witty jewellery that's become the favourite of many young Londoners. Original designs feature all manner of fauna-and-flora inspired necklaces, as well as creations sporting moustaches, dinosaurs and bunting. Perspex name necklaces (made to order; £27.50) are also a treat.

Absolute Vintage
Vintage

Map p172 (www.absolutevintage.co.uk; 15 Hanbury St, E1; ⊙11am-7pm; ⊖Liverpool St or Shoreditch High St) Check out the mammoth vintage shoe collection here – there are colours and sizes for all, with footwear ranging from designer vintage to something out of your grandma's storage. Clothes for men and women line the back of the shop.

Labour & Wait
Homewares

Map p172 (www.labourandwait.co.uk; 85 Redchurch St, E2; ⊙11am-6pm Tue-Sun; ⊖Liverpool St or Shoreditch High St) Dedicated to simple and functional, yet scrumptiously stylish, traditional British homewares, Labour & Wait specialises in items by independent manufacturers who make their products the old-fashioned way. There are school tumblers, enamel coffee pots, luxurious lambswool blankets, elegant ostrich-feather dusters and even kitchen sinks.

The East End & Docklands

Traditional but fast-changing, this is an area of stimulating, multicultural neighbourhoods.
Despite immigrants settling here unbroken for several centuries, the East End remains home to London's best known denizen, the cockney. Because of its immigrant communities, however, it's also a diverse area to eat, drink and explore.

There may be few standout sights but exploration really pays dividends in these unique neighbourhoods. South of the East End is Docklands, once the hub of the British Empire then later a post-industrial wasteland. After massive regeneration it captures a vision of London's future as well as its history.

The extension of London Overground lines has made East London much easier to travel around in. The three main areas to target are the Queen Elizabeth Olympic Park (and neighbouring Hackney), Docklands itself (and adjoining waterside Limehouse and Wapping) and Whitechapel (from which Bethnal Green is just a short hop away).

Shadwell Basin, Docklands

East End & Docklands Highlights

Queen Elizabeth Olympic Park (p187)

The main draw of Queen Elizabeth Olympic Park is the Olympic Stadium and the striking Aquatics Centre. The award-winning Velodrome (aka the 'Pringle') has been praised for its aesthetic qualities, as well as its sustainable credentials and functional appeal. The 114m spiralling red structure is Anish Kapoor's ArcelorMittal Orbit, offering a vast panorama from its viewing platform.

1

2

Whitechapel Gallery (p186)

It's not surprising you'll find one of the city's most ambitious and eventful art galleries in one of London's most diverse and culturally vibrant neighbourhoods and thoroughfares. With cutting-edge exhibits, and the attention it gives to both luminaries and up-and-coming names in international art, this is a great place to check the pulse of contemporary art.

ERIC NATHAN/GETTY IMAGES ©

Docklands Skyline (p189)

PAUL SHEARS/GETTY IMAGES ©

You'd never guess it from the ultra-modern skyscrapers dominating the Isle of Dogs and Canary Wharf, but from the 16th century until the mid-20th century this was the centre of the world's greatest port and the hub of the British Empire. Since the late 1980s, the Docklands has been regenerated from its post-industrial decline into a top financial centre. Learn more about this area's fascinating (and powerful) past on a visit to the Museum of London Docklands.

BENJAMIN HOWELL/GETTY IMAGES ©

Columbia Road Flower Market (p195)

London's markets are perfect for catching the character of this vibrant city, in all its many facets and moods, and locals simply love to trawl through them. It may be a colourful celebration of flowers and plants, but a visit to Columbia Road Flower Market is also fun and perfect for seeing locals in their element.

Victoria Park (p187)

Around a quarter of London is gorgeous parkland, and it's not just the big royal parks that deserve attention. Often overlooked by visitors, this 86-hectare park – affectionately known as 'Vicky Park' to locals – is highly popular with Londoners who flock here in fine weather.

East End Walk

This easy stroll offers insight into the old and new of the East End, taking you through historic streets, over Regent's Canal, and through green parkland to Hackney Wick and the impressive Queen Elizabeth Olympic Park.

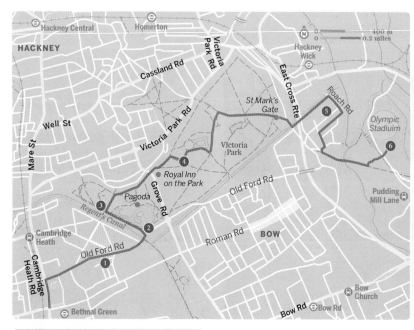

WALK FACTS

- **Start** Bethnal Green tube station
- **Finish** Queen Elizabeth Olympic Park
- **Distance** 3 miles
- **Duration** Two hours

1 Cyprus St

Exit the tube station at the Museum of Childhood and head north on Cambridge Heath Rd. Take the first right and continue until you can take a right into Cyprus Pl. The surrounding area here was heavily bombed during WWII and the tower blocks you can see if you raise your eyes skyward are a product of postwar redevelopment.

But beautifully preserved Cyprus St gives a taste of what Victorian Bethnal Green would have looked like. Continue left down Cyprus St and back onto Old Ford Rd.

2 Victoria Park

Just over marvellous Regent's Canal lies Victoria Park (p187), designed in the 1840s to improve East Londoners' quality of life. The park is a glorious place for a wander, with several lakes and immense expanses of greenery to explore.

3 Dogs of Alcibiades

Take the path down to the road around the lake and head left to the Dogs of Alcibiades howling on plinths, replicas of originals that stood here from 1912. Have a look at the newly rebuilt lakeside **pagoda**, part of the park's recent £12-million revamp.

④ Burdett-Coutts Memorial Fountain

Turn right here and then again at the end of the road and continue to the grand Royal Inn on the Park. Cross the road into the eastern section of the park and take a right towards the recently restored Burdett-Coutts Memorial Fountain (1862), a gift of the eponymous Angela, once the richest woman in England and a prominent philanthropist.

⑤ Hackney Wick

From here, carry on to the east lake and exit through St Mark's Gate at the park's northeastern tip. Head under the East Cross Bridge and then along the canal towpath. In the shadow of the Olympic Satdium, Hackney Wick is home to a warren of warehouses and a growing community of artists. Stop off at the Counter Cafe (p191) or Formans (p191) for views of the stadium, and check out their latest art exhibits.

⑥ Queen Elizabeth Olympic Park

From here you're a mere shot-put from the Queen Elizabeth Olympic Park (p187), which has helped welcome in a whole new era for the East End. Even if you missed the games the park is definitely worth a visit.

⭐ The Best...

PLACES TO EAT

Empress Inventive menu. (p191)

Formans Seafood and Olympic views. (p191)

Tayyabs Busy Punjabi restaurant. (p190)

Fish House Probably the best fish and chips in London. (p191)

Viajante Innovative fine dining. (p191)

PLACES TO DRINK

Dove Freehouse Range of brews. (p192)

Palm Tree East London boozer straight out of Central Casting. (p193)

Grapes Supercosy; bags of history. (p193)

Carpenter's Arms Good-looking pub with a notorious history. (p192)

Royal Inn on the Park A solid all-rounder facing Vicky Park. (p193)

PLACES FOR EAST END HISTORY

Museum of London Docklands Dockside history and lore. (p189)

Ragged School Museum Displays of Victorian teaching methods. (p187)

V&A Museum of Childhood The culture of childhood. (p187)

Ragged School Museum (p187)
NEIL SETCHFIELD/GETTY IMAGES ©

Discover the East End & Docklands

⟨⊥⟩ Getting There & Away

o **Underground** The Central Line runs from the West End and the City to Bethnal Green, Mile End and Stratford.

o **Overground** From Camden and Highbury, the overground links to Hackney, Hackney Wick and Stratford. A separate branch connects Dalston as well as Whitechapel and Wapping.

o **DLR** From Tower Gateway or Bank, the DLR provides a scenic link to Limehouse and Docklands, and with Stratford Domestic and International stations.

o **Bus** The 55 from Oxford St is a handy route to Hackney, as is the 38 from Victoria via Islington. The 277 runs from Hackney to the Docklands, via Victoria Park.

o **Train** A quick ride to London Fields, Cambridge Heath or Stratford from Liverpool St. The fast link from St Pancras is seven minutes to Stratford International.

Victoria Park
JEREMY VICKERS PHOTOGRAPHY/GETTY IMAGES ©

⊙ Sights

Whitechapel

Whitechapel Gallery   Gallery

Map p188 (📞020-7522 7888; www.whitechapelgallery.org; 77-82 Whitechapel High St, E1; ⊙11am-6pm Wed-Sun, to 9pm Thu; ⊖Aldgate East) FREE
This ground-breaking gallery, which moved into its main art nouveau building in 1899, extended into the library next door in 2009, doubling its exhibition space to 10 galleries. Founded by the Victorian philanthropist Canon Samuel Barnett at the end of the 19th century to bring art to the people of East London, it has made its name by putting on exhibitions by both established and emerging artists, cartoonists and architects, including Jackson Pollock (his first UK show), Gary Hume, Robert Crumb, Mies van der Rohe and Picasso (whose *Guernica* was exhibited here in 1939). The gallery's ambitiously themed shows change every couple of months, and there's also live music, poetry readings, talks and films.

Whitechapel Bell Foundry   Historic Building

Map p188 (www.whitechapelbellfoundry.co.uk; 32-34 Whitechapel Rd, E1; tours per person £12; ⊙tours 10am, 1.30pm & 4pm selected Sat, shop 9am-5pm Mon-Fri; ⊖Aldgate East, Whitechapel) The Whitechapel Bell Foundry has been standing on this site since 1738, although an earlier foundry nearby is known to have been in business in 1570. Both Big Ben (1858) and the Liberty Bell (1752) in Philadelphia were cast here, as was the 23-tonne bell rung at the 2012 Olympic opening ceremony. The foundry also cast a new bell for New York City's Trinity Church, damaged in the terrorist attacks of 11 September 2001.

Whitechapel Road
Street

Map p188 (◉Whitechapel) The East End's main thoroughfare, Whitechapel Rd hums with the babble of Asian, African and Middle Eastern languages, its busy shops and market stalls selling everything from Indian snacks to Nigerian fabrics and Turkish jewellery, as the East End's many ethnic groupings rub up against each other more or less comfortably.

Bethnal Green & Hackney

V&A Museum of Childhood
Museum

Map p188 (www.vam.ac.uk/moc; cnr Cambridge Heath & Old Ford Rds, E2; ◷10am-5.45pm; ♿; ◉Bethnal Green) FREE Housed in a renovated Victorian-era building moved from South Kensington in 1866, this branch of the Victoria & Albert Museum is aimed at both kids (with activity rooms and interactive exhibits, including a dressing-up box and sandpit) and nostalgic grown-ups who come to admire the antique toys.

Mile End & Victoria Park

Victoria Park
Park

Map p188 (www.towerhamlets.gov.uk; ◷dawn-dusk; ☐277 or 425, ◉Mile End) The 'Regent's Park of the East End', Victoria Park is an 86-hectare leafy expanse opened in 1845 – the first public park in the East End that came about after a local MP presented Queen Victoria with a petition of 30,000 signatures. In the early 20th century it was known as the Speaker's Corner of the East End.

Ragged School Museum
Museum

Map p188 (www.raggedschoolmuseum.org.uk; 46-50 Copperfield Rd, E3; ◷10am-5pm Wed & Thu, 2-5pm 1st Sun of month; ◉Mile End) FREE Both adults and children are charmed by this combination of mock Victorian schoolroom – with hard wooden benches and desks, slates, chalk, inkwells and abacuses – re-created East End kitchen and social history museum below. 'Ragged' was a Victorian term used to refer to the torn, dirty and dishevelled clothes worn by pupils.

Hackney Wick & Stratford

Queen Elizabeth Olympic Park
Park

(http://noordinarypark.co.uk; ◉Stratford) Creating world-class sporting facilities for the 2012 Games was, of course, at the forefront of the development, but this was well balanced with the aim of regenerating this area for generations to come. More than 30 new bridges were built to crisscross the River Lea. Waterways in and around the park were upgraded, with waste cleared and contaminated soil cleaned on a massive scale.

Most of the main venues – the Olympic Stadium, the Aquatics Centre and the Velodrome – are in the more manicured southern end. The north of the park has been given over to wetlands, which provide a much wilder environment than the gardens and landscaping of the southern half. Set to open to the public in phases, the developments to transform the park into its promised legacy will take at least another 25 years to complete.

Wapping & Limehouse

Wapping
Neighbourhood

Map p188 (◉Wapping) Wapping's towering warehouses, built at the beginning of the 19th century, still give an atmospheric picture of an area once notorious for slave traders, drunk sailors and prostitutes. Although there's nothing to actually mark it, down on the riverside below Wapping New Stairs (near the marine police station) was **Execution Dock** Map p188 (Wapping New Stairs, E1; ☐100, underground rail Wapping), where convicted pirates were hanged and their bodies chained to a post at low tide, to be left until three tides had washed over their heads.

Limehouse
Neighbourhood

Map p188 (®DLR Limehouse or Westferry) There isn't much to Limehouse, although it became the centre of London's Chinese community – its first Chinatown – after some 300 sailors settled here in 1890. It gets a mention in Oscar Wilde's *The Picture of Dorian Gray* (1891), when the protagonist passes by this way in search

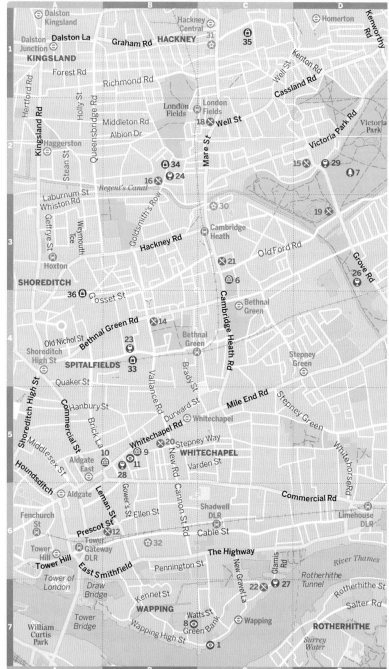

of opium. The most notable attraction here is **St Anne's, Limehouse** Map p188 (www.stanneslimehouse.org; cnr Commercial Rd & Three Colt St, E1), Nicholas Hawksmoor's earliest church (1725).

Docklands

Museum of London Docklands
Museum

Map p188 (www.museumoflondon.org.uk/docklands; Hertsmere Rd, West India Quay, E17; adult/student & under 16yr/senior £5/free/£3; ⏱10am-6pm; 🚆DLR West India Quay) Housed in a converted warehouse dating from 1802, this museum offers a comprehensive overview of the entire history of the Thames from the arrival of the Romans in AD 43. Well organised with knowledgable and helpful staff, it's at its best when dealing with specifics such as the docks during WWII, as well as their controversial transformation into the Docklands during the 1980s.

The tour begins on the 3rd floor (take the lift to the top) with the Roman settlement of Londinium and works its way downwards through the ages. Keep an eye out for the scale model of old London Bridge. Other highlights include Sailortown, a re-creation of the cobbled streets, bars and lodging houses of a mid-19th-century dockside community and nearby Chinatown, and more detailed galleries such as London, Sugar & Slavery, which examines the capital's role in the transatlantic slave trade.

🍴 Eating

The East End's multiculturalism has ensured that its ethnic cuisine stretches far and wide, with some fantastic low-key eateries serving authentic and value-for-money fare. But the area's gentrification has introduced a slew of gastropubs and more upmarket restaurants. Places to head if you want to sniff out your own favourites include Columbia Rd, Broadway Market and the streets just to the north of Victoria Park (known to some as Hackney Village).

THE EAST END & DOCKLANDS EATING

Map labels:

0 — 500 m
0 — 0.25 miles

Hackney Wick
East Cross Rte
Roach Rd
13
17
Olympic Stadium
4
Old Ford Rd
Roman Rd
Tredegar Rd
Fairfield Rd
King Edward VII (1.7km)
Bow Rd
Bow Church
Bow Rd
Mile End
Hamlets Way
Bow Common La
Mile End Park
5
Burdett Rd
Devons Rd
LIMEHOUSE
2
East India Dock Rd
25
Narrow St
Westferry DLR
Westferry Rd
West India Quay DLR
3
Canary Wharf
Canary Wharf DLR
Heron Quay's DLR
Marsh Wall
CANARY WHARF
7

189

The East End

Whitechapel

Tayyabs
Indian, Pakistani £

Map p188 (📞020-7247 9543; www.tayyabs.
co.uk; 83-89 Fieldgate St, E1; mains £6.50-12;
⊙noon-11.30pm; ⊖Whitechapel) This buzzing (OK, crowded) Punjabi restaurant
is in another league to the eateries on
Brick Lane. *Seekh* kebabs, masala fish
and other starters served on sizzling hot
plates are delicious, as are accompani-
ments such as dhal, naan and raita. Daily
specials are also available. Expect a long
queue (even with a booking).

Café Spice Namasté
Indian ££

Map p188 (📞020-7488 9242; www.cafespice.
co.uk; 16 Prescot St, E1; mains £14-19, 2-course
set lunch £15.95; ⊙noon-midnight Mon-Fri,
6.30pm-midnight Sat; 🚉DLR Tower Gateway,
⊖Tower Hill) Chef Cyrus Todiwala has
taken an old magistrate's court just a
10-minute walk from Tower Hill and decorated it in carnival colours; the service
and atmosphere are as bright as the
walls. The Parsi and Goan menu is famous
for its superlative *dhansaak* (lamb stew
with rice and lentils; £15.95) but just as
good are the tandoori dishes and the
Goan king-prawn curry.

Bethnal Green & Hackney

E Pellici
Cafe £

Map p188 (332 Bethnal Green Rd, E2; dishes
£5-7.80; ⊙7am-4pm Mon-Sat; 🚌8, ⊖Bethnal
Green) There aren't many reasons to rec-
ommend a stroll down Bethnal Green Rd,
but stepping into this diminutive Anglo-
Italian cafe is one of them. You're likely to
be met by a warmer-than-average greet-
ing as you squeeze onto a table among
an amiable collection of East Enders.
Opened in 1900, the wood-panelled cafe
is bedecked with museum-quality original
fittings.

Green Papaya
Vietnamese £

Map p188 (191 Mare St, E8; mains £6.50-8.50;
⊙5-11pm Tue-Sun; 🚌55 or 277, 🚉London
Fields) This simple but friendly neighbourhood restaurant has been serving up high-
quality Vietnamese food to Hackney diners
for a dozen years. The extensive menu is
strong on vegetarian and seafood dishes.

F. Cooke
British £

Map p188 (9 Broadway Market, E8; mains £3-4;
⊙10am-7pm; 🚌55, 🚉Cambridge Heath) If you
want a glimpse of what eating out was like
in Broadway Market before the street was

gentrified, head to the F. Cooke pie and mash shop. This family business has been going strong since 1900, and the shop still has the original signage and tiles, along with plenty of family photographs hung around the walls and sawdust on the floor.

Viajante — Fusion £££

Map p188 (www.viajante.co.uk; Patriot Sq, E2; tasting menu lunch £28-70, dinner £65-90, Corner Room mains £10-12; ☺noon-2pm Fri-Sun & 6-9.30pm Wed-Sun; ☎; ⊖Bethnal Green) Chef Nuno Mendes' heads this Michelin-starred restaurant and produces inventive, beautifully put together dishes with an exciting fusion of flavours. The elegant dining room is stylish and modern with the original Edwardian features kept intact. The open kitchen lets you take a peak at what you'll get for your tasting menus.

Mile End & Victoria Park

Pavilion — Cafe £

Map p188 (www.the-pavilion-cafe.com; cnr Old Ford & Grove Rds, E3; mains £4.50-8; ☺8.30am-5pm; ☐277, ⊖Mile End, then) Superb cafe overlooking an ornamental lake in Victoria Park, serving breakfasts and lunches made with locally sourced ingredients and excellent coffee.

Empress — Modern European ££

Map p188 (☎020-8533 5123; www.empresse9.co.uk; 130 Lauriston Rd, E9; mains £12-17; ☺noon-3.15pm & 6-10.15 Mon-Fri, 10am-3.15pm & 6-10.15pm Sat, noon-9.30pm Sun; ☐277, ⊖Mile End, then) This pretty pub conversion on the western edge of Victoria Park belts out excellent Modern European cuisine under the watchful eye of chef Elliott Lidstone, with such fine assemblages as snails and bone marrow and braised pork shoulder with spelt and fennel. It serves an excellent weekend brunch. Special bargain nights include Monday £10 dinner and some Tuesdays' three-course Frugal Feast (£20). Well considered wine list.

Fish House — Fish ££

Map p188 (www.fishhouse.co.uk; 126-128 Lauriston Rd, E9; mains £8.50-12.50; ☺noon-10pm; ⊖Mile End, then ☐277) The freshest of fresh fish and crustaceans are dispensed from both a busy takeaway section and a cheerful sit-down restaurant. The lobster bisque and Colchester oysters are always good, while the generous fish pie bursting with goodies from the briny deep is exceptional.

Hackney Wick & Stratford

Counter Cafe — Cafe £

Map p188 (www.thecountercafe.co.uk; 7 Roach Rd, E3; dishes £4.50-8; ☺7.30am-5pm Mon-Fri, 9am-5pm Sat & Sun; ☎; ⊖Hackney Wick) Directly overlooking the Olympic Stadium, this friendly local cafe serves up fantastic coffee and breakfasts, sandwiches and pies. The mismatched, thrift-store furniture, painting-clad walls and relaxed atmosphere make this a favourite with the local artist community.

Formans — British ££

Map p188 (☎020-8525 2365; www.formans.co.uk; Stour Rd, Fish Island, E3; mains £11.50-20; ☺7-11pm Thu & Fri, 10am-2pm & 7-11pm Sat, noon-5pm Sun; ☎; ⊖Hackney) This diminutive restaurant, with unrivalled views over the Olympic Stadium, serves a fantastic variety of smoked salmon made in-house as well as an interesting range of dishes with ingredients sourced from within the British Isles.

Wapping & Limehouse

Wapping Food — Modern European ££

Map p188 (☎020-7680 2080; www.thewappingproject.com; The Wapping Project, Wapping Hydraulic Power Station, Wapping Wall, E1; mains £14-21; ☺6.30-10.30pm Mon-Fri, 10am-4pm & 7-10.30pm Sat, 10am-4pm Sun; ☎; ⊖Wapping) Stylish dining room set among the innards of a disused power station, creating a spectacular and unexpectedly romantic atmosphere. The high-quality, seasonal menu changes daily but might include gems such as guinea fowl wrapped in pancetta, or onglet with beetroot and horseradish.

Docklands

Gun
Gastropub £££

(📞020-7515 5222; www.thegundocklands.com; 27 Coldharbour, E14; mains £15-27; ⏰11am-midnight Mon-Sat, til 11pm Sun; 🛜; 🚇Canary Wharf) Set at the end of a pretty, cobbled street, this riverside pub has been seriously dolled up, but still manages to ooze history. Previously a local dockers pub, dating from the early 18th century, it is claimed that Lord Nelson had secret assignations with Lady Emma Hamilton here (hence the naming of the toilets).

🍷 Drinking & Nightlife

Whitechapel

Rhythm Factory
Club

Map p188 (www.rhythmfactory.co.uk; 16-18 Whitechapel Rd, E1; ⏰opening hours vary; 🚇Aldgate East) Perennially hip and popular, the Rhythm Factory is a club and venue

hosting a variety of bands and DJs of all genres that keep the up-for-it crowd happy until late.

Bethnal Green & Hackney

Dove Freehouse
Pub

Map p188 (www.dovepubs.com; 24-28 Broadway Market, E8; ⏰noon-11pm Sun-Fri, 11am-11pm Sat; 🛜; 🚌55, 🚆Cambridge Heath) This pub attracts at any time with its rambling series of rooms and Belgian beers such as Trappist, wheat and fruit-flavoured beers. Drinkers spill out onto the street in warmer weather, or hunker down in the back room with board games when it's chilly.

Carpenter's Arms
Pub

Map p188 (www.carpentersarmsfreehouse. com; 73 Cheshire St, E2; ⏰4-11.30pm Mon-Wed, noon-11.30pm Thu & Sun, til 12.30am Fri & Sat; 🛜; 🚆Bethnal Green, 🚇Shoreditch High St) After a browse in the shops along Cheshire St, you'll probably end up outside this gorgeous corner pub. Once notorious – the pub was owned in the '60s by the Kray brothers, who gave it over to

Left: Broadway Market (p195); **Below:** Columbia Road Flower Market (p195)

(LEFT) ORIEN HARVEY/GETTY IMAGES ©; (BELOW) SCOTT R BARBOUR/GETTY IMAGES ©

their mother – it has been well restored to a trendy, yet cosy pub combining traditional pub architecture with contemporary touches.

Mile End & Victoria Park

Palm Tree   Pub
Map p188 (127 Grove Rd, E3; ⊙noon-midnight Mon-Thu, to 2am Fri & Sat, to 1am Sun; 🚌277, ⊖Mile End) The Palm, the quintessential East End pub on the Regent's Canal, is loved by locals, students and trendies alike, with its comforting gold-flock wall-paper, photos of also-ran crooners and a handful of different guest ales every week. There's live music Friday to Sunday from around 9.30pm.

Royal Inn on the Park   Pub
Map p188 (www.royalinnonthepark.com; 111 Lauriston Rd, E9; ⊙noon-11pm; 🛜; 🚌277, ⊖Mile End, then) On the northern border of Victoria Park, this excellent place has a half-dozen real ales and Czech lagers on tap, outside seating to the front and a recently made-over garden at the back.

Hackney Wick & Stratford

King Edward VII   Pub
(www.kingeddie.co.uk; 47 Broadway, E15; ⊙noon-11pm Sun-Wed, noon-midnight Thu-Sat; ⊖Stratford) Built in the 19th century this lovely old boozer is a series of handsome rooms set around a central bar. The front bar and saloon are the most convivial, and there's a little leafy courtyard at the back. A decent selection of ales and wine, and some great pub grub, make this a real highlight of the area.

Wapping & Limehouse

The Grapes   Pub
Map p188 (www.thegrapes.co.uk; 76 Narrow St, E14; ⊙noon-3pm & 5.30-11pm Mon-Wed, noon-11pm Thu-Sun; DRL Limehouse) One of Lime-house's renowned historic pubs – there's apparently been a drinking house here since 1583 – the Grapes is tiny, especially the riverside terrace, which can only really comfortably fit about a half-dozen close

The Grapes (p193)

LONELY PLANET/GETTY IMAGES ©

friends, but it's cosy inside and exudes plenty of old-world charm.

Prospect of Whitby
Pub

Map p188 (57 Wapping Wall, E1; ☺noon-11pm Sun-Thu, to midnight Fri & Sat; 🛜; ⊖Wapping) Once known as the Devil's Tavern, the Whitby is said to date from 1520, making it the oldest riverside pub in London. It's firmly on the tourist trail now, but there's a smallish terrace at the front and the side overlooking the Thames, a decent restaurant upstairs and open fires in winter.

⭐ Entertainment

Wilton's
Theatre

Map p188 (☏020-7702 2789; www.wiltons.org. uk; 1 Graces Alley, E1; tour £6; ☺tour 3pm & 6pm Mon, Mahogany Bar 5-11pm Mon-Fri; 🚆DLR Tower Gateway, ⊖Tower Hill) A gloriously atmospheric example of one of London's Victorian public-house music halls, Wilton's hosts a real variety of shows, from comedy and classical music to literary theatre and opera. You can also take

a one-hour guided tour of the building to hear more about its fascinating history.

Bistrotheque
Cabaret, Bar

Map p188 (☏020-8983 7900; www.bistrotheque. com; 23-27 Wadeston St, E2; ☺5.30pm-midnight Mon-Fri, 11am-midnight Sat, 11am-11pm Sun; 🚆Cambridge Heath, ⊖Bethnal Green) This converted warehouse offers hilarious transvestite lip-synching in its ground-floor Cabaret Room and high-quality dining in its stylish whitewashed restaurant above. It's also worth coming just for the Napoleon bar, a moody, slightly decadent room with dark walls (the oak panels came from a stately home in Northumberland) and plush seating; the drinks are expertly mixed and the bar staff always friendly.

Hackney Empire
Theatre

Map p188 (☏020-8985 2424; www.hackneyem-pire.co.uk; 291 Mare St, E8; ☺performance times vary; 🚌38 or 277, 🚆Hackney Central) The programming at this renovated Edwardian Music Hall (1901) is eclectic to say the least and certainly defines 'something for everyone' – from hard-edged political theatre to opera and comedy. The Empire is definitely one of the best places to catch a pantomime at Christmas.

🔒 Shopping

The boutiques and galleries lining Columbia Rd (which are usually open at the weekend only) and the shops along Broadway Market and Cheshire St are part of London's up-and-coming independent retail scenes. If you're after something a little more mainstream, Westfield Stratford City, currently Europe's largest urban shopping centre, can't fail to satisfy. There's also a shopping mall beneath the Canary Wharf skyscrapers, with similar shops, bars and restaurants.

Columbia Road Flower Market
Market

Map p188 (Columbia Rd, E2; ⊙8am-3pm Sun; ⊖Old St) A real explosion of colour and life, this weekly market sells a beautiful array of flowers, pot plants, bulbs, seeds and everything you might need for the garden. A lot of fun, even if you don't buy anything, the market gets really packed so go as early as you can, or later on, when the vendors sell off the cut flowers cheaply.

Broadway Market
Market

Map p188 (www.broadwaymarket.co.uk; London Fields, E8; ⊙9am-5pm Sat; ⊖Bethnal Green) There's been a market down this pretty street since the late 19th century, the focus of which has become artisan food, arty knick-knacks, books, records and vintage clothing. A great place on a Saturday.

Beyond Retro
Vintage

Map p188 (www.beyondretro.com; 110-112 Cheshire St, E2; ⊙10am-7pm Mon-Wed, Fri & Sat, til 8pm Thu, 11.30am-6pm Sun; ⏚Bethnal Green, ⊖Shoreditch High St) East London branch of a West End **shop** (p92) with huge selection of vintage clothes, including wigs, shoes, jackets and lingerie, expertly slung together in a lofty warehouse.

Burberry Outlet Shop
Fashion

Map p188 (29-31 Chatham Pl, E9; ⊙10am-6pm Mon-Sat, 11am-7pm Sun; ⏚55, ⊖Hackney Central) This outlet shop stocks seconds from the reborn-as-trendy Brit brand's current and last season's collections. Prices are around 30% lower than those in the main shopping centres.

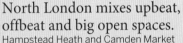

Hampstead & North London

North London mixes upbeat, offbeat and big open spaces. Hampstead Heath and Camden Market should top your list; Camden is a major sight and its energy is intoxicating, while Hampstead Heath will offer you a glorious day out and an insight into how North Londoners spend their weekend.

You could spend an eternity here exploring the sights and nightlife, so you'll have to pick and choose carefully.

Because this part of London is predominantly residential, it is at its busiest at the weekend. Most sights are relatively quiet during the week, with the possible exceptions of the British Library and the Wellcome Collection.

North London is largely a wealthy area, full of 20- or 30-somethings, young families and celebrities (especially in Primrose Hill). The nightlife is excellent with great pubs in Hampstead or Islington and fab live music in Camden.

Regent's Park (p205)
SIMONE BECCHETTI/GETTY IMAGES ©

Hampstead & North London Highlights

British Library (p202)

Bibliophiles will have a field day discovering the treasures of this incredibly rich library and marvelling at the accumulated wisdom stored within its walls. An impressive shrine to the written word and the nation's principal copyright library, there's not only one copy of every British and Irish publication here but, for antiquarians and historians, a rare wealth of ancient manuscripts, maps and documents.

1

2 ## Highgate Cemetery (p200)

London's Victorian cemeteries can be extraordinarily interesting places. Highgate Cemetery – the king of kings in the Victorian Valhalla roll-call – is fascinating whether you're a name hunter, an architecture buff, a photographer or just someone in search of the ruins-reclaimed-by-nature look. If you're a communist, you'll probably ignore all of the above and simply come to lay flowers at the grave of Karl Marx.

MARK THOMAS/GETTY IMAGES ©

Kenwood House (p208)

There's no better conclusion to a walk across Hampstead Heath on a sunny day than arriving at this sublime house. Kenwood House is a magnificent piece of stately villa architecture. Transformed by Robert Adam in the 18th century, the house's beautiful exterior also contains a breathtaking art collection and a gorgeous library. The setting in Hampstead Heath is stunning.

3

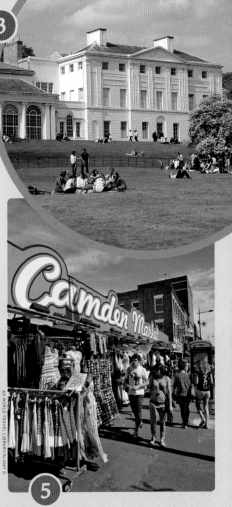

4

Parliament Hill (p208)

London's heath land is a chance to escape the urban jungle for a while, or at least view it from a pleasantly buffered distance. Few views of London are as choice as the one unfolding from Parliament Hill in epic Hampstead Heath. Our advice is to prepare a simple picnic, throw a blanket on the grass and enjoy the panorama.

5

Camden Market (p208)

London's scattered markets are a must for those on the hunt for shopping ideas and a confluence of goods from all over the place. This famous North London market has an astonishing variety of goods, from vintage clothing and antiques to musical instruments, food and more. And when you have had your fill of picking through the stalls, there are fantastic pubs, canal views and knockout live-music venues nearby.

Hampstead Heath Walk

Sprawling Hampstead Heath, with its rolling woodlands and meadows, feels a million miles away from metropolitan London. Covering 320 hectares it is home to some 180 bird species, a rich array of flora (including 800 trees) and expansive views.

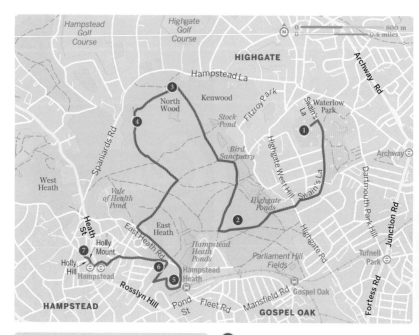

WALK FACTS

- **Start** Highgate Cemetery
- **Finish** Holly Bush pub
- **Distance** 6 miles
- **Duration** Three hours

❶ Highgate Cemetery

The final resting place of Karl Marx, George Eliot and other notables, this supreme cemetery is divided into Eastern and Western sections. There are some magnificent images of nature relentlessly taking over neo-Gothic headstones in the east but to visit the overgrown, atmospheric West Cemetery, you'll need to join a tour.

❷ Parliament Hill

From the cemetery head down Swain's Lane to the roundabout with Highgate West Hill, and climb up to Parliament Hill (p208) – a Hampstead Heath high point – for some all-inclusive views south over town. Have a picnic lunch before continuing your walk.

❸ Kenwood House

Traverse the heath to this magnificent neoclassical 18th-century mansion (p208), a glorious sweep of perfectly landscaped gardens leading down to a picturesque lake – the setting for summer concerts. It contains a magnificent art collection, with paintings by Rembrandt, Constable, Turner and others.

4 Henry Moore & Barbara Hepworth Sculptures

London is dotted with works of art by Moore and Hepworth, and not far from Kenwood House are two of their sculptures that complement their open-air setting. The tall *Monolith (Empyrean)* by Hepworth is carved from blue Corrib limestone and dates from 1953; *Two Piece Reclining Figure No 5* by Moore is cast in bronze.

5 Keats House

Cross the heath to this elegant Regency house on Wentworth Pl, once home to the golden boy of the Romantic poets. Keats wrote *Ode to a Nightingale* while sitting under a plum tree (now vanished, but a new tree has been planted) in the garden here in 1819.

6 No 2 Willow Road

Architecture fans will want to swing past this modernist property, the central house in a block of three, designed by Ernö Goldfinger in 1939. Entry to the then path-breaking property is by guided tour until 3pm (after which nonguided viewing is allowed).

7 Holly Bush

This beautiful pub at 22 Holly Mount is a fitting conclusion to your journey, with an antique Victorian interior, a secluded hilltop location, open fires in winter and a knack for making you stay longer than you had intended. Set above Heath St, it's accessible via Holly Bush Steps, a small set of steps going up from Holly Mount.

⭐ The Best...

PLACES TO EAT

Ottolenghi Mediterranean sensation. (p210)

Towpath Mediterranean on Regent's Canal. (p211)

Mangal Ocakbasi Turkish budget meat feast. (p211)

Market Excellent British food. (p209)

Trullo Exquisite, pizza-less, Italian fare (p210)

PLACES TO DRINK

Garden Gate Packed with old English charm. (p215)

Bar Pepito Spanish bodega. (p213)

Spaniard's Inn Watering hole of the famous and infamous. (p215)

Edinboro Castle Laid-back pub with a great garden. (p214)

Holly Bush Classic English pub.

PARKS & GARDENS

Hampstead Heath London's famous heathland; astonishing views. (p208)

Regent's Park Vast John Nash–designed expanse of green. (p205)

Hampstead Heath (p208)
OLIVER STREWE/GETTY IMAGES ©

⭐ Don't Miss
British Library

In 1998 the British Library moved to its current premises between King's Cross and Euston stations. At a cost of £500 million, it was Britain's most expensive building. Colin St John Wilson's exterior of straight lines of red brick, which Prince Charles reckoned was akin to a 'secret police building', is not one that is universally loved. But even those who don't like the building from the outside will be won over by the spectacularly cool and spacious interior.

Map p206

www.bl.uk

96 Euston Rd, NW1

Ritblat Gallery free; special exhibition cost varies

🕒9.30am-6pm Mon & Wed-Fri, to 8pm Tue, to 5pm Sat, 11am-5pm Sun

⊖King's Cross/St Pancras

King's Library

Central King's Library holds the 85,000-volume collection of King George III, displayed in the eerily beautiful 17m-high glass-walled tower.

The collection is considered one of the most significant of the Enlightenment period, and was bequeathed to the nation by the king's son, George IV, in 1823. The volumes were kept at the British Museum, but after a bomb fell on the collection during WWII, they were moved to the Bodleian Library in Oxford and only moved back to London in 1998, when the new British Library opened.

Sir John Ritblat Gallery

The highlight of a visit to the British Library is the Sir John Ritblat Gallery, where the most precious and high-profile documents are kept. The collection spans almost three millennia of history and contains manuscripts, religious texts, maps, music scores, autographs, diaries and more.

Rare texts from all the main religions are represented, including the *Codex Sinaiticus*, the first complete text of the New Testament; a Gutenberg *Bible* (1455), the first Western book printed using movable type; and stunningly illustrated Jain sacred texts.

There are historical documents, including two of four remaining copies of the *Magna Carta* (1215), the charter credited with setting out the basis of human rights in English law. Not so important, but poignant, is Captain Scott's final diary including an account of explorer Lawrence Oates' death.

Literature is well represented, with an 11th-century copy of *Beowulf*, Shakespeare's *First Folio* (1623) and manuscripts by some of Britain's best-known authors, including Lewis Carroll, Jane Austen and Thomas Hardy.

Music fans will love the Beatles' earliest handwritten lyrics and original scores by Handel, Mozart and Beethoven.

The Philatelic Exhibition

Based on collections established in the 19th century and consisting of more than 80,000 items, including postage and revenue stamps and postal stationery from almost every country and periods.

Tours

There are **guided tours** (☎01937 546 546; **adult/child £8/6.50; one hour**) of the library's public areas daily at 10.30am (11.30am on Sunday) and 3pm. Tours on Sunday include a visit to one of the reading rooms. Other tours, including tours of the conservation studios, are also regularly available. Bookings are recommended.

One for the Books

The British Library, containing upwards of 14 million volumes, is the nation's principal copyright library: it stocks one copy of every British and Irish publication as well as historic manuscripts, books and maps from the British Museum. Along with its excellent permanent collections, the British Library has regular temporary exhibitions of various authors, genres and themes, all connected to its records.

Library Cafes

All the catering at the British Library comes courtesy of the wonderful Peyton & Byrne, the progeny of Irish chef Oliver Peyton. There are three main outfits: the 1st floor **restaurant** (mains £5-10; ⏱9.30am-5pm Mon-Fri, to 4pm Sat; 📶), with spectacular views of the King's Library Tower; the **cafe** (⏱9.30am-7.30pm Mon-Thu, to 5.30pm Fri, to 4.30pm Sat & Sun; 📶) on the ground floor, which serves hot drinks, pastries and sandwiches; and the **Espresso Bar** (⏱8am-7pm Mon-Fri, 9am-5.30pm Sat, 10am-4pm Sun).

Discover Hampstead & North London

Getting There & Away

o **Underground** Northern Line stops include Camden, Hampstead, Highgate and Angel.

o **Overground** The Overground crosses North London from east to west and is useful for areas such as Dalston that are not connected to the tube. The new East London Overground line runs through the east and on to South London.

o **Bus** There is a good network of buses in North London connecting various neighbourhoods to each other and to the centre of town.

Canal barges, Regent's Park
PHILIP GAME/GETTY IMAGES ©

⊙ Sights

North London is a collection of small neighbourhoods, ancient villages that were slowly drawn into London as the metropolis expanded. King's Cross has historically been a blight on the capital's landscape, but the opening of the beautiful St Pancras International train terminal and the massive urban renewal behind the station has made this part of town more attractive.

King's Cross & Euston

British Library   Library
See p202.

Wellcome Collection   Museum
Map p212 (www.wellcomecollection.org; 183 Euston Rd, NW1; ⊙10am-6pm Tue, Wed, Fri & Sat, 10am-10pm Thu, 11am-6pm Sun; ⊕Euston Sq) **FREE** Focusing on the interface of art, science and medicine, this clever museum is surprisingly fascinating. There are interactive displays where you can scan your face and watch it stretched into the statistical average; wacky modern sculptures inspired by various medical conditions; and downright creepy things, such as an actual cross-section of a body and enlargements of parasites (fleas, body lice, scabies) at terrifying proportions.

The Wellcome Collection styles itself as a 'destination for the incurably curious', a pretty accurate tag for an institution that seeks to explore the links between medicine, science, life and art. It's a serious topic but the genius of the museum is that it presents it in an accessible way. The heart of the permanent exhibition is Sir Henry Wellcome's collection

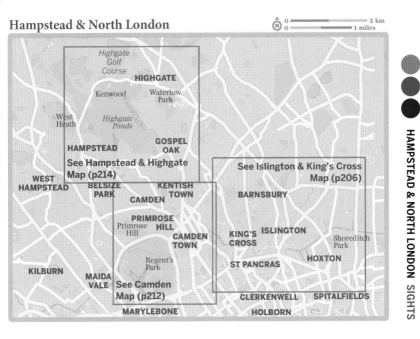

of objects from around the world. Wellcome (1853–1936), a pharmacist, entrepreneur and collector, was fascinated with medicine and amassed more than a million objects associated with life, birth, death and sickness from different civilisations.

London Canal Museum   Museum

Map p206 (www.canalmuseum.org.uk; 12-13 New Wharf Rd, N1; adult/child £4/2; ⏰10am-4.30pm Tue-Sun & bank holidays; ⊖King's Cross/ St Pancras) This quirky but fascinating museum is in an old ice warehouse dating from the 1860s. It traces the history of Regent's Canal and the ice business, a huge trade in late Victorian London, with 35,000 tonnes imported from Norway in 1899 alone.

Regent's Park

London Zoo   Zoo

Map p212 (www.londonzoo.co.uk; Outer Circle, Regent's Park, NW1; adult/child £25/19; ⏰10am-5.30pm Mar-Oct, to 4pm Nov-Feb; ⊖Camden Town) Established in 1828, these zoological gardens are among the oldest in the world, and are where the word 'zoo' origi-

nated. The emphasis nowadays is firmly placed on conservation, education and breeding, with fewer species and more spacious conditions. Highlights include **Tiger Territory**, **Penguin Beach**, **Gorilla Kingdom** and **Butterfly Paradise**. Feeding sessions or talks take place during the day.

Regent's Park   Park

Map p212 (www.royalparks.org.uk; ⏰5am-dusk; ⊖Regent's Park, Baker St) The most elaborate and ordered of London's many parks, this one was created around 1820 by John Nash, who planned to use it as an estate to build palaces for the aristocracy. Although the plan never quite came off, you can get some idea of what Nash might have achieved from the buildings along the Outer Circle.

Among its many attractions are the London Zoo, Regent's Canal along its northern side, an ornamental lake, an open-air theatre in Queen Mary's Gardens where Shakespeare's plays are performed during the summer months, ponds and colourful flowerbeds.

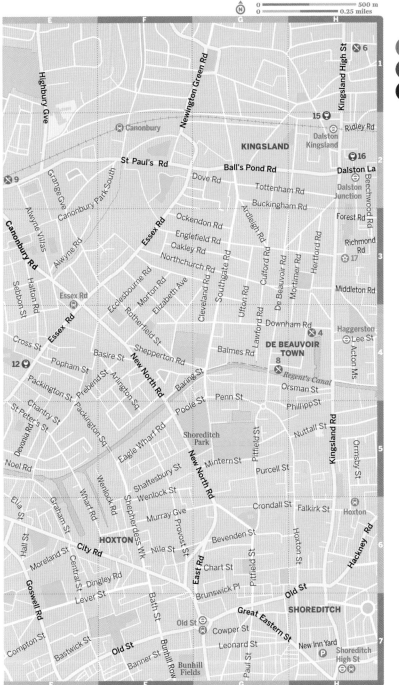

0   500 m
0   0.25 miles

Kingsland High St

◎6

15 ◎

Canonbury

Ridley Rd

Dalston
Kingsland

KINGSLAND

◎16

Newington Green Rd

St Paul's Rd

Ball's Pond Rd

Dalston La

Dove Rd

Dalston
Junction

◎9

Grange Gve

Tottenham Rd

Beechwood Rd

Forest Rd

Highbury Gve

Buckingham Rd

Canonbury Park South

Ardleigh Rd

Richmond
Rd

◎17

Ockendon Rd

Alwyne Villas

Englefield Rd

Middleton Rd

Canonbury Rd

Alwyne Rd

Essex Rd

Oakley Rd

Culford Rd

De Beauvoir Rd

Mortimer Rd

Hertford Rd

Northchurch Rd

Southgate Rd

Halton Rd

Ecclesbourne Rd

Cleveland Rd

Seabon St

Morton Rd

Elizabeth Ave

Essex Rd

Ufton Rd

Lawford Rd

Downham Rd

◎4

Haggerston
Lee St

Cross St

Rotherfield St

Balmes Rd

DE BEAUVOIR
TOWN

Acton Ms

Essex Rd

Shepperton Rd

8

Basire St

Baring St

Regent's Canal

12 ◎

Popham St

New North Rd

Orsman St

Packington St

Prebend St

Arlington Sq

Poole St

Penn St

Phillipp St

St Peter's St

Chantry St

Packington Sq

Eagle Wharf Rd

Shoreditch
Park

Pitfield St

Nuttall St

Kingsland Rd

Ormsby St

Devonia Rd

Mintern St

Noel Rd

Purcell St

Wharf Rd

Shaftesbury St

New North Rd

Ela St

Wenlock Rd

Wenlock St

Crondall St

Falkirk St

Hoxton

Hall St

Graham St

Shepherdess Wk

Murray Gve

Provost St

Bevenden St

Hoxton St

Hackney Rd

Moreland St

HOXTON

Nile St

East Rd

Chart St

Pitfield St

City Rd

Central St

Dingley Rd

Brunswick Pl

Old St

Goswell Rd

Lever St

Bath St

SHOREDITCH

Compton St

Old St

Banner St

Great Eastern St

Cowper St

Leonard St

New Inn Yard

Bastwick St

Paul St

Shoreditch
High St

Bunhill Row

Bunhill
Fields

Old St

Islington & King's Cross

Camden

Camden Market
Market

Map p212 (Camden High St, NW1; ⊙10am-6pm; ⊖Camden Town, Chalk Farm) Although – or perhaps because – it stopped being cutting-edge several thousand cheap leather jackets ago, Camden market gets a whopping 10 million visitors each year and is one of London's most popular attractions.

What started out as a collection of attractive craft stalls by Camden Lock on the Regent's Canal now extends in various shape or form most of the way from Camden Town tube station to Chalk Farm tube station. There are four main market areas – **Buck Street Market**, **Lock Market**, **Canal Market** and **Stables Market** – although they seem to blend into one with the crowds snaking along and the 'normal' shops lining the streets. You'll find a bit of everything: clothes (of variable quality) in profusion, bags, jewellery, arts and crafts, candles, incense and myriad decorative titbits.

There are dozens of food stalls at the Lock Market and the Stables Market, with virtually every type of cuisine on offer. Quality varies but is generally pretty good and affordable, and you can eat on the big communal tables or by the canal.

Hampstead & Highgate

Hampstead Heath
Park

Map p214 (☐Gospel Oak, Hampstead Heath, ⊖Hampstead) Sprawling Hampstead Heath, with its rolling woodlands and meadows, feels a million miles away – despite being approximately four – from London proper. It covers 320 hectares, most of it woods, hills and meadows, and is home to about 180 bird species, 23 species of butterflies, grass snakes, bats and a rich array of flora. It's a wonderful place for a ramble, especially to the top of **Parliament Hill** (Map p214), which offers expansive views across the city. Those of a more artistic bent should make a beeline for **Kenwood House** (Map p214; www.english-heritage.org.uk; Hampstead Lane, NW3; ☐Gospel Oak, Hampstead Heath) but stop to admire the **sculptures by Henry Moore and Barbara Hepworth** (Map p214) along the way.

 Eating

With its historic pubs, smart cafes, market stalls and gastronomic restaurants, North London is not a place where you'll be left without options. Islington has the most gourmet addresses; elsewhere you'll find a large choice running from Austrian and Greek to Russian and Turkish.

King's Cross & Euston

Karpo
Modern British ££

Map p206 (www.karpo.co.uk; 23-27 Euston Rd, NW1; mains £10-16; ◷7am-11pm; 🛜📶; 🚇King's Cross/St Pancras) There is something utterly refreshing about Karpo, with its bright, modern space, its 'living wall', gracious service and delicious, seasonal menu served round the clock. It all looks effortless. Expect plenty of revitalised British classics such as Jerusalem artichokes, purple sprouting broccoli, cod and lamb.

Caravan
Mediterranean ££

Map p206 (📞020-7101 7661; www.caravankingscross.co.uk; Granary Bldg, 1 Granary Sq, N1C; mains £7-15; ◷8am-10.30pm Mon-Thu, 8am-midnight Fri, 10am-midnight Sat, 10am-4pm Sun; 🛜📶; 🚇King's Cross/St Pancras) In the freshly renovated Granary Building on the edge of Regent's Canal, Caravan dishes out tasty fusion Mediterranean food. You can opt for several small plates to share as meze or tapas or stick to main-sized plates.

Camden

Dirty Burger
Burgers £

Map p214 (www.eatdirtyburger.com; Sanderson Cl, 79 Highgate Rd, NW5; burger £5.50; ◷7am-midnight Mon-Thu, 7am-1am Fri, 9am-1am Sat, 9am-11pm Sun; 🚉Gospel Oak, 🚇Kentish Town) The beauty of this place, a chic shack rather than a restaurant, is its simplicity: apart from sausages and bacon until 11am, Dirty Burger does nothing but burgers. And what burgers – thick, juicy, horribly messy, with mustard, gherkin and cheese.

Manna
Vegetarian ££

Map p212 (📞020-7722 8082; www.mannav.com; 4 Erskine Rd, NW3; mains £14-20; ◷6.30-10.30pm Tue-Fri, noon-3pm & 6.30-10.30pm Sat, noon-3pm Sun; 📶; 🚇Chalk Farm) Tucked away on a side street in Primrose Hill, this little place does a brisk trade in inventive vegetarian cooking. The menu features such mouthwatering dishes as green korma, wild garlic and pea risotto cake and superb desserts.

Market
Modern British ££

Map p212 (📞020-7267 9700; www.market-restaurant.co.uk; 43 Parkway, NW1; 2-course lunch £10, mains £10-14; ◷noon-2.30pm & 6-10.30pm Mon-Sat, 1-3.30pm Sun; 🚇Camden Town) This fabulous restaurant is an ode to great, simple British food with a hint of European thrown in. The light and airy space with bare brick walls, steel tables and basic wooden chairs reflects this simplicity.

York & Albany
Brasserie ££

Map p212 (www.gordonramsay.com/yorkandalbany; 127-129 Parkway, NW1; mains £14-24, 2-/3-course menu £19/22; ◷7-11am, noon-3pm & 6-11pm Mon-Sat, 7am-9pm Sun; 📶; 🚇Camden Town) Part of chef Gordon Ramsay's culinary empire, this chic brasserie, serves classics with a Mediterranean twist such as roast leg of rabbit with potatoes and lemony anchovies, and confit lamb shoulder with soft polenta. You can eat at the bar, in the lounge or in the more formal dining room.

Walking along Regent's Canal

The canals that were once a trade lifeline for the capital have now become a favourite escape for Londoners, providing a quiet walk away from traffic and crowds. For visitors, an added advantage of Regent's Canal towpath is that it provides an easy (and delightful) shortcut across North London.

You can, for instance, walk from Little Venice to Camden in less than an hour; on the way, you'll pass Regent's Park, London Zoo, well-heeled Primrose Hill, beautiful villas designed by architect John Nash as well as redevelopments of old industrial buildings into trendy blocks of flats. Allow 15 to 20 minutes between Camden and Regent's Park, and 25 to 30 minutes between Regent's Park and Little Venice.

Hampstead & Highgate

Wells Tavern   Gastropub ££

Map p214 (📞020-7794 3785; www.thewell-shampstead.co.uk; 30 Well Walk, NW3; mains £12-17; ⏰noon-3pm & 7-10pm; 🚇Hampstead) This popular gastropub, with a surprisingly modern interior (given its traditional exterior), is a real blessing in good-restaurant-deprived Hampstead. The menu is proper posh English pub grub – Cumberland sausages, mash and onion gravy, or just a full roast with all the trimmings.

Gaucho Grill   Argentine £££

Map p214 (📞020-7431 8222; www.gauchorestaurants.co.uk; 64 Heath St , NW3; mains £15-52; ⏰noon-11pm Mon-Sat, from 10am Sun; 🚇Hampstead) Carnivores, rejoice: this is one of the finest places for steak in London. There are several branches of this Argentinian grill across the capital but this one has the advantage of being less busy than its counterparts, thanks to its residential setting.

Islington

Trullo   Italian ££

Map p206 (📞020-7226 2733; www.trullorestaurant.com; 300-302 St Paul's Rd, N1; mains £8.50-25; ⏰12.30-3pm & 6-10.30pm Mon-Sat, 12.30-3pm Sun; 🚇Highbury & Islington) The great thing about Trullo is that it gives pride of place to Italian food that doesn't feature pasta or pizza. There are some exquisite pasta dishes, it must be said, but the star attraction is the charcoal grill, which churns out succulent T-bone steaks or tasty pork chops with baked borlotti beans or polenta.

Ottolenghi   Mediterranean ££

Map p206 (📞020-7288 1454; www.ottolenghi.co.uk; 287 Upper St, N1; mains £9-12; ⏰8am-11pm Mon-Sat, 9am-7pm Sun; 🍴; 🚇Highbury & Islington, Angel) This is the pick of Upper Street's many eating options – a brilliantly bright, white space that's worth a trip merely to see the beautiful cakes in the deli. But get a table at this temple to good food

Left: Food stalls at Camden Lock Market (p208); **Below:** Cupcakes at Ottolenghi, Islington

(LEFT) JON ARNOLD/JAI/CORBIS ©; (BELOW) MAISANT LUDOVIC/HEMIS.FR/GETTY IMAGES ©

to really appreciate the exquisite fusion Mediterranean cuisine.

Dalston

Towpath
Cafe £

Map p206 (Regent's Canal towpath, N1, btwn Whitmore Bridge & Kingsland Rd Bridge; mains £3-10; ⊙8am-dusk Tue-Fri, 9am-dusk Sat & Sun, Mar-Nov only; Haggerston rail Bus 67, 149) One of London's most special places to eat – if the weather is fine, that is, since this is a cafe on the bank of Regent's Canal. It's a simple affair with four small units looking on to the canal – two serve for sitting 'inside' for shelter from possible drizzle, and the other two are the kitchen and bar.

Mangal Ocakbasi
Turkish £

Map p206 (www.mangal1.com; 10 Arcola St, E8; mains £7-12; ⊙noon-midnight; 🚇Dalston Kingsland, Dalston Junction) Mangal is the quintessential Turkish *ocakbasi* (open-hooded charcoal grill, the mother of all BBQs) restaurant: cramped and smoky and serving superb mezze, grilled lamb chops, quail and lip-smacking kebabs. It has been here for almost 20 years and is always busy. It's BYO.

Duke's Brew & Que
American ££

Map p206 (🕿020-3006 0795; www.dukes-brewandque.com; 33 Downham Rd, N1; mains £10.25-23.50; ⊙4-11pm Mon-Fri, 11am-11pm Sat & Sun; 🚇Haggerston) There aren't very many restaurants that smoke their meat but Duke's is one, and we whole-heartedly support the effort! The house speciality is ribs, pork or beef, smoked over hickory and various wood and lovingly barbecued until the meat falls off the bone. Wash it down with a beer from the nearby Beaver-town Brewery.

Camden

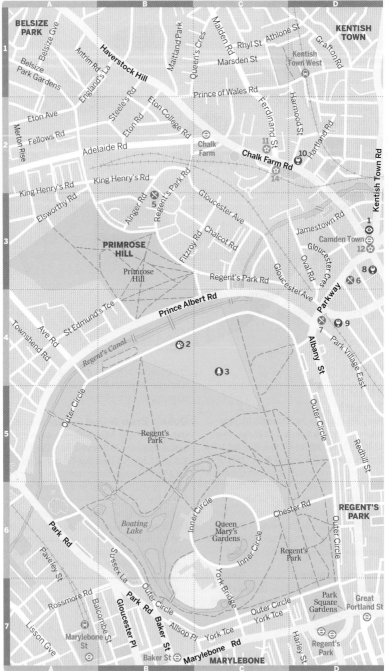

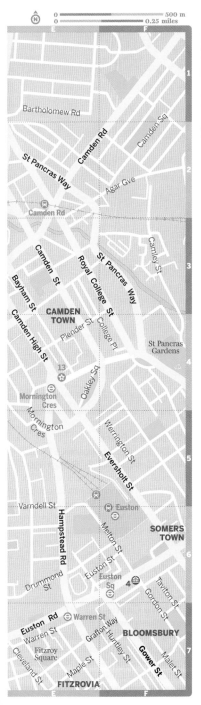

Camden

🍷 Drinking & Nightlife

Camden Town is one of North London's favoured drinking areas, with more bars and pubs pumping music than you can manage to crawl between. The hills of Hampstead are a real treat for old-pub aficionados, while painfully hip Dalston is currently London's coolest place to drink. As for King's Cross, there are new places opening all the time.

King's Cross

Bar Pepito   Wine Bar

Map p206 (www.camino.uk.com/pepito; 3 Varnishers Yard, The Regent Quarter, N1; ⏱5pm-midnight Mon-Fri, from 6pm Sat; ⊖King's Cross/St Pancras) This tiny, intimate *bodega* (Spanish wine bar) specialises in sherry, a wine from the region of Andalucía. Novices fear not: the staff are on hand to advise. They're also experts at food pairings (top-notch ham and cheese selections).

Big Chill House   DJ Bar

Map p206 (www.bigchill.net; 257-259 Pentonville Rd, N1; ⏱9am-midnight Mon-Thu, to 3am Fri & Sat, 11am-midnight Sun; 🛜; ⊖King's Cross/St Pancras) A three-floor space with a good selection of live music and DJs, and a great terrace for hanging out, this place

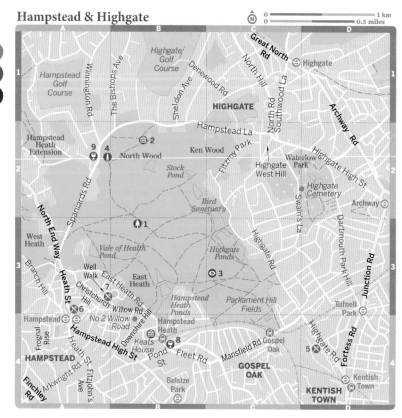

Hampstead & Highgate

is run by the same people behind the popular Big Chill festival and record label. The music choice is always varied and international, the sound system is fantastic and entry is free most nights.

6 St Chad's Place
Bar

Map p206 (www.6stchadsplace.com; 6 St Chad's Pl, WC1; ⏰8am-11pm Mon-Fri; ⊖King's Cross/ St Pancras) Once a mechanic's workshop, this Victorian warehouse has scrubbed up well to become one of the shining lights in King's Cross's regeneration. It is favoured by local business people for informal meetings during the day but the same customers enjoy good music and live DJs on Friday nights.

Camden

Edinboro Castle
Pub

Map p212 (www.edinborocastlepub.co.uk; 57 Mornington Tce, NW1; ⏰noon-11pm; 🛜; ⊖Camden Town) A reliable Camden boozer, the large and relaxed Edinboro has a refined Primrose Hill atmosphere. It boasts a full menu, gorgeous furniture designed for slumping and a fine bar. Where the pub comes into its own is in its huge beer garden, complete with BBQ and table football and adorned with fairy lights for long summer evenings.

Lock Tavern — Pub

Map p212 (www.lock-tavern.co.uk; 35 Chalk Farm Rd, NW1; ⏱noon-midnight Mon-Thu, to 1am Fri & Sat, to 11pm Sun; ⊖Chalk Farm) An institution in Camden, the black-clad Lock Tavern rocks for several reasons: it's cosy inside, has an ace roof terrace from where you can watch the market throngs, the food is good, the beer plentiful and it also has a roll-call of guest bands and DJs at the weekend to spice things up.

Black Cap — Gay

Map p212 (www.theblackcap.com; 171 Camden High St, NW1; ⏱noon-1am Sun-Tue, to 2am Wed & Thu, to 3am Fri & Sat; ⊖Camden Town) This friendly, sprawling place is Camden's premier gay venue, and attracts people from all over North London. There's a great outdoor terrace, the pleasantly pub-like upstairs Shufflewick bar and the downstairs club, where you'll find plenty of hilarious camp cabaret as well as decent dance music.

Hampstead & Highgate

Hampstead and Highgate are the places to go for historic, charming old pubs where Sunday lunch always seems to turn into an afternoon.

Garden Gate — Pub

Map p214 (www.thegardengatehampstead.co.uk; 14 South End Rd, NW3; ⏱noon-11pm Mon-Fri, 10.30am-midnight Sat, 10.30am-10.30pm Sun; ⏺⏸; ⏴Hampstead Heath) At the bottom of the heath hides this gem of a pub, a 19th-century cottage with a gorgeous beer garden. It serves Pimms and lemonade in summer and mulled wine in winter, both ideal after a long walk on the heath.

Spaniard's Inn — Pub

Map p214 (www.thespaniardshampstead.co.uk; Spaniards Rd, NW3; ⏱noon-11pm Mon-Fri, from 9am Sat, from 11am Sun; ⏸21) This marvellous tavern dates from 1585 and has more character than a West End musical. It was highwayman Dick Turpin's hang-out between robbing escapades, but it has also served as a watering hole for more savoury characters, such as Dickens, Shelley, Keats and Byron. There's a big, blissful garden that is crammed at weekends.

Islington

Bull — Pub

Map p206 (www.thebullislington.co.uk; 100 Upper St, N1; ⏱noon-midnight Sun-Wed, to 1am Thu-Sat; ⏺; ⊖Angel, Highbury & Islington) One of Islington's liveliest pubs, the Bull serves 27 kinds of draught lager, real ales, fruit beers, ciders and wheat beer, plus a large selection of bottled drinks and wine. The mezzanine is generally a little quieter than downstairs, although on weekend nights you'll generally struggle to find a seat.

Barrio North — DJ Bar

Map p206 (www.barrionorth.com; 45 Essex Rd, N1; ⏱Sun-Wed 5pm-midnight, to 1am Thu, to 3am Fri & Sat; ⊖Angel, Highbury & Islington) This cocktail/DJ bar is one of the most fun in Islington. The atmosphere, decor and music are a celebration of all things Latino with a hint of London and New York thrown in (if you can, grab a seat in the fairy-lit cut-out caravan). The cocktails are unrivalled with selections from across the Americas.

Dalston

Dalston Roof Park — Bar

Map p206 (www.bootstrapcompany.co.uk; Print House, 18 Ashwin St, E8; ⏱5-11pm Tue-Thu, 3pm-midnight Fri & Sat, 3-10pm Sun May-Sep; ⏸Dalston Kingsland, Dalston Junction) It is spaces like Dalston Roof Park that make you regret the fact that London ain't sunny year-round. Because when you sit in the colourful chairs, on the bright green Astroturf, looking over the Dalston skyline with a drink in your hand, it really is something. The bar puts on an excellent program of arts events and BBQs, too. Membership (£3) required.

Toro Y Moi performing at KOKO in Camden

DREW STEWART/ALAMY ©

Dalston Jazz Bar Cocktail Bar

Map p206 (4 Bradbury St, N16; ☺5pm-1am Mon-Thu, to 3am Fri & Sat, to midnight Sun; ☐76, 149, ☐Dalston Kingsland, Dalston Junction) Hidden just off the chaos of Kingsland High St, Dalston Jazz Bar is a cocktail place where the neighbourhood's hip and friendly inhabitants congregate for a bite to eat, plenty of drinking and a good old romp to hip-hop, R&B and reggae. Strangely, given the name, live jazz only features on Friday and Saturday nights.

⭐ Entertainment

North London is the capital's home of music, so you can be sure to find live music of some kind every night of the week. A number of venues such as KOKO and the Electric Ballroom are multi-purpose, with gigs in the first part of the evening (generally around 7 or 8pm), followed by club nights from 10pm. Check details with the venue before heading out.

Passing Clouds Club

Map p206 (www.passingclouds.org; 1 Richmond Rd, E8; ☺6pm-12.30am Mon-Thu, to 2.30am Fri & Sat, 2pm-12.30am Sun; ☐243, 76, ☐Dalston Junction, Dalston Kingsland) One of those little flickers of nightlife brilliance, Passing Clouds throws legendary parties that go until the early hours of the morning. The music is predominantly world oriented, with a lot of African influence and regular Afrobeat bands, and a reputable jam session on Sunday nights (from 9pm).

KOKO Concert Venue

Map p212 (www.koko.uk.com; 1a Camden High St, NW1; ☺7-11pm Sun-Thu, to 4am Fri & Sat; ☐Mornington Cres) Once the legendary Camden Palace, where Charlie Chaplin, the Goons and the Sex Pistols have all performed, KOKO is keeping its reputation as one of London's better gig venues. The theatre has a dance floor and decadent balconies, and attracts an indie crowd with Club NME on Friday. There are live bands almost every night of the week.

Electric Ballroom Concert Venue

Map p212 (www.electricballroom.co.uk; 184 Camden High St, NW1; club nights £7-15, gigs £10-40; ☐Camden Town) One of Camden's historic venues, the Electric Ballroom has been entertaining North Londoners since

1938. Many great bands and musicians have played here, from Blur to Paul McCartney, The Clash and U2. There are club nights on Fridays (Sin City: metal music) and Saturdays (Shake: a crowd pleaser of dance anthems from the 70s, 80s and 90s).

Proud Camden   Live Music
Map p212 (www.proudcamden.com; Horse Hospital, Stables Market, NW1; free-£15; ⏰11am-1.30am Wed, to 2.30am Thu-Sat; ⊖Camden Town, Chalk Farm) Camden's former Horse Hospital, which looked after horses injured pulling barges on nearby Grand Union Canal, is now one of Camden's great music venues. There are live bands, DJs and art exhibitions. It's fantastic in summer, when the terrace is open.

Barfly   Live Music
Map p212 (www.mamacolive.com/thebarfly; 49 Chalk Farm Rd, NW1; gigs from £8, club nights £3-5; ⏰7pm-3am Mon-Sat, to midnight Sun; ⊖Chalk Farm) This typically grungy, indie-rock Camden pub is well known for hosting small-time artists looking for their big break. The focus is on indie rock. The venue is small, so you'll feel like the band is just playing for you and your mates. There are club nights most nights of the week.

🔒 Shopping

Shopping in North London is all about vintage and second-hand clothes. Dalston rules in the vintage department; it is also a prime area for pop-up shops. Primrose Hill and Hampstead are the places to go for quality second-hand designer pieces.

Gill Wing   Gifts
Map p206 (www.gillwing.co.uk; 190 Upper St, N1; ⏰9am-6pm Mon-Sat, from 10am Sun; ⊖Highbury & Islington) Gill Wing's gift shop is a

staple of Upper St: it is basically impossible to walk past without doing a double-take at the sweet-shop-like window full of colourful glasses, cards, children's toys and other eclectic titbits. Short of ideas? Let the charming staff help you.

Harry Potter Shop   Children
Map p206 (departure concourse, King's Cross station, N1; ⏰10am-6pm; ⊖King's Cross/St Pancras) Harry Potter fans unite, this is your very own window into the world of the child wizard. Set up as a wand shop (wands from around £25), with wood panels and plenty of shelves and drawers, it also sells jumpers sporting the colours of Hogwarts' four houses and assorted merchandise. It's literally next to Platform 9¾ from where the Hogwarts Express leaves King's Cross to go to Hogwarts each term.

Annie's Vintage Costumes & Textiles   Vintage
Map p206 (www.anniesvintageclothing.co.uk; 12 Camden Passage, N1; ⏰11am-6pm; ⊖Angel) One of London's most enchanting vintage shops, Annie's has costumes to make you look like Greta Garbo.

Housmans   Books
Map p206 (www.housmans.com; 5 Caledonian Rd, N1; ⏰10am-6pm Mon-Sat, noon-6pm Sun; ⊖King's Cross/St Pancras) This long-standing, not-for-profit bookshop, where you'll find books that are unavailable on the shelves of the more mainstream stockists, is a good place to keep up to date with all sorts of progressive, political and social campaigns, and with your more radical reads.

Greenwich

Greenwich is packed with gorgeous architecture, parkland and standout museums. The divide between North and South London may remain, but growing numbers of North Londoners have warmed to South London's more affordable property prices, leafy charms and relaxed tempo. And nowhere typifies this atmosphere more successfully than Greenwich, with its eye-catching blend of stately, royal architecture, charming side streets, cottages and riverside pubs.

From a sightseeing perspective, there are some beautiful views from Greenwich Park's high point, and there's the world-famous Royal Observatory, the fabulous National Maritime Museum and the magnificent Old Royal Naval College. Greenwich Market is a must for those shopping and snacking.

Greenwich is one of the highlights of any visit to London, so allow a day to do it justice.

Old Royal Naval College (p229)
LINDA STEWARD/GETTY IMAGES ©

Greenwich Highlights

Royal Observatory (p224)

Time is a largely intangible and abstract concept, but it's fair to say that the closest you can get to touching it is by paying a visit to the Royal Observatory in Greenwich, and straddling hemispheres and time zones as you stand between the actual meridian line. Get here before 1pm on any day of the week to see the red time ball at the top of the Royal Observatory drop

Greenwich Park (p224)

By any standards Greenwich Park, designed by André Le Nôtre, the man responsible for the gardens at Versaille is a pretty special place. The panorami views of London from the top of the hil are spectacular and the entire place is wonderful for a long walk or a picnic when the weather's good. Don't miss the deer park in the southeast corner.

National Maritime Museum (p232)

With its handsome naval heritage and good-looking riverside perch, Greenwich is ideally suited for a definitive glance back at Britain's nautical history. Steer a course through the world's largest museum devoted to the sea and explore a simply riveting collection of artefacts.

Old Royal Naval College (p229)

A visit to Greenwich is not complete without a visit to this former naval hospital, designed by Christopher Wren at the end of the 17th century. The colourful details of the murals within the glorious Painted Hall can draw you into hours of exploration and discovery, while the chapel just opposite is outstanding. This is one of Greenwich's top sights, so don't rush through it.

Greenwich Market (p233)

Packed with stalls, Greenwich's famous market is perfect browsing territory for gift ideas, but it also serves up some excellent snacks three days a week, when you can savour flavours from around the world. Dotted around the perimeter of the market are some excellent shops, rounding out a highly appetising picture.

Greenwich Walk

This genteel and charming neighbourhood, magnificently placed by a bend in the Thames, has heaps to offer beyond its big-ticket sights. This itinerary links together more discreet attractions tucked away from the main drag.

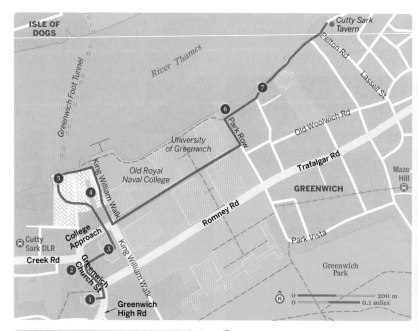

- **Start** St Alfege Church
- **Finish** Cutty Sark Tavern
- **Distance** One mile
- **Duration** 30 minutes

① St Alfege Church

Designed by Nicholas Hawksmoor in 1718 to replace a 12th-century Saxon church, this church features a restored mural by James Thornhill, a wood-panelled interior and a 'Tallis' keyboard with middle keyboard octaves from the Tudor period. St Alfege Passage is a lovely stone-paved alley running past the churchyard behind the church.

② Beehive

Wander down Greenwich Church St to join the Greenwich vinyl junkies at this funky meeting ground of old records and retro togs. Pop in to this fascinating shop (p233) and leave with a mod-print dress, vintage Bakelite telephone and/or a copy of Bowie's *Hunky Dory*.

③ Greenwich Market

Cross the road to dive into this lively and well-stocked market (p228). Rub shoulders with the crowds looking for gifts and souvenirs from the stalls, pick up tasty snacks or browse through the market's absorbing choice of shops.

4 Cutty Sark

One of Greenwich's icons, this historic clipper ship (p226) reopened in April 2012 after six years and £25 million of extensive renovations following a disastrous fire in 2007. Phoenix-like, it has re-emerged every bit as stunning as it once was.

5 Greenwich Foot Tunnel

Completed in 1902, the 370m-long Greenwich Foot Tunnel running under the Thames from the Isle of Dogs is fun to explore. The lifts down to the tunnel now run 24 hours a day but should they be out of order (again!) it's between 88 to 100 steps down and – shudder – up.

6 Trafalgar Tavern

Head south along King William Walk and cross the grounds of the Old Royal Naval College to this cavernous and historic pub (p230), with big windows onto the river. Dickens drank here (using it as the setting for the wedding breakfast scene in *Our Mutual Friend*) and prime ministers Gladstone and Disraeli dined on the pub's celebrated whitebait.

7 Walking by the River

A short walk east along the Thames puts Greenwich's riverside character into clear definition. This section of the Thames Path is most attractive closer to Greenwich, with fantastic views of Canary Wharf and the river. Do what locals do and have an evening drink at the Cutty Sark Tavern (p231).

✪ The Best...

PLACES TO EAT

Inside Smart restaurant with a deservedly popular Modern European menu. (p228)

Old Brewery Handy cafe by day, commendable restaurant by night. (p228)

Spread Eagle French delicacies in a former coaching inn (p230)

PLACES TO DRINK

Trafalgar Tavern Where the greats from the past sipped and supped. (p230)

Greenwich Union Good-looking, fantastic pub with a great range of microbrewery beers and a congenial interior. (p231)

Cutty Sark Tavern Riverside perch and decent beer at one convenient location. (p231)

SIGHTS

Greenwich Park Get lost in this lovely, immaculately groomed space. (p224)

Royal Observatory Stand between the Prime Meridian and plant a foot in both east and west. (p224)

National Maritime Museum Engrossing collection of artefacts from Britain's nautical heritage. (p232)

Old Royal Naval College Beautiful interior of decorative artwork and lavish design. (p229)

Old Royal Naval College (p229)
CHRIS LAURENS/GETTY IMAGES ©

Royal Observatory & Greenwich Park

One of London's favourite attractions and part of the National Maritime Museum, the Royal Observatory is where the study of the sea and the stars converge. The Prime Meridian charts its line through the grounds of the observatory, chosen quite arbitrarily in 1884, cleaving the globe into the eastern and western hemispheres. The observatory sits on a hill within leafy and regal Greenwich Park, London's oldest royal park, with its fabulous views, 72 hectares of trees and lush greenery.

Map p227

www.rmg.co.uk

Greenwich Park, SE10

adult/child £7/2.50

🕘10am-5pm

🚉DLR Cutty Sark

Flamsteed House

The excellent Royal Observatory is divided into two sections. The northern portion of the site, for which you must pay admission, is dedicated to horology. Charles II ordered the construction of the Christopher Wren–designed Flamsteed House – the original observatory building – in 1675; it contains the magnificent Octagon Room, where timepieces are housed. It also has absorbing galleries dedicated to timekeeping and longitude.

Outside Flamsteed House, the globe is decisively sliced into east and west, where visitors can straddle both hemispheres in the Meridian Courtyard, with one foot either side of the meridian line. Every day at 1pm the red time ball at the top of the Royal Observatory continues to drop as it has done since 1833.

Astronomy Centre

The southern half contains the highly informative (and free) Astronomy Centre, where you can touch the oldest object you will ever encounter: part of the Gibeon meteorite, a mere 4.5 billion years old! Other engaging exhibits include an orrery (mechanical model of the solar system, minus Uranus and Neptune) from 1780, astronomical documentaries, a first edition of Newton's seminal *Principia Mathematica* and the opportunity to view the Milky Way in multiple wavelengths.

Also here is the state-of-the-art **Peter Harrison Planetarium** Map p227 (adult/child £6.50/4.50), London's sole planetarium, with a digital laser projector that can cast entire heavens onto the inside of its roof.

Greenwich Park

Handsome host of the equestrian events during the 2012 Olympic Games, this 73-hectare park is one of London's loveliest expanses of green, with a rose garden, picturesque walks and astonishing views from the crown of the hill. The oldest enclosed royal park, it is partly the work of André Le Nôtre, the landscape architect who designed the gardens of Versailles. The park is rich in sights and facilities, including a teahouse near the Royal Observatory, a cafe behind the National Maritime Museum, a deer park, tennis courts in the southwest and a boating lake at the Queen's House end.

Ranger's House

The elegant **Wernher Collection** Map p227 (www.english-heritage.org.uk; Greenwich Park, Chesterfield Walk, SE10; adult/child £6.70/4; ⏱tours only at 11am & 2pm Sun-Wed Apr-Sep; 🚇Greenwich or DLR Cutty Sark)housed in a Georgian villa (1723) that was once home to the park's ranger contains some 700 works of art (medieval and Renaissance paintings, porcelain, silverware, tapestries) amassed by one Julius Wernher (1850–1912), a German-born railway engineer's son who struck it rich in the diamond fields of South Africa in the 19th century. The Spanish Renaissance jewellery collection is the best in Europe, and the rose garden out front defies description when in blossom in May/June.

Prime Meridian

The Greenwich Meridian was selected as the global Prime Meridian at the International Meridian Conference in Washington DC in 1884. Greenwich thereafter became the world's common zero for longitude and standard for time calculations, replacing the multiple meridians that had existed previously. Greenwich was assisted in its bid by the earlier US adoption of Greenwich Mean Time for its own national time zones. Furthermore, the majority of world trade already used sea charts that identified Greenwich as the Prime Meridian.

Discover Greenwich

⟷ Getting There & Away

○ **Underground, DLR & Train** Greenwich can be reached from the Cutty Sark DLR station; or via trains from Charing Cross or London Bridge to Greenwich.

○ **Walking** If coming from Docklands to Greenwich, consider walking under the river via the Greenwich Tunnel.

○ **Boat** Thames Clippers (p285) go to Greenwich from Millennium Pier.

○ **Bus** To reach the O2 arena by bus, board the 188 outside the Cutty Sark DLR station.

○ **Cable Car** Cross from O2 to Docklands via the **Emirates Air Line** (www.emiratesairline.co.uk; adult/child single £4.30/2.20, return £8.60/4.40, with Oyster or Travelcard single £3.20/1.60, return £6.40/3.20; ⏱7am-9pm Mon-Fri, from 8am Sat, from 9am Sun Apr-Sep, closes 1hr earlier Oct-Mar; 🚇DLR Royal Victoria, Ⓔ North Greenwich).

Tulip Staircase, Queen's House
VULTURE LABS/GETTY IMAGES ©

◉ Sights

Royal Observatory Historic Building
See p224.

Greenwich Park Park
See p224.

Queen's House Historic Building
Map p227 (www.rmg.co.uk/queens-house; Romney Rd, SE10; ⏱10am-5pm; 🚇DLR Cutty Sark) FREE
The first Palladian building built by architect Inigo Jones after he returned from Italy is far more enticing than the art collection it contains, even though it includes some Turners, Holbeins, Hogarths and Gainsboroughs. The ceremonial **Great Hall** is the principal room – a gorgeous cube shape, with an elaborately tiled floor dating to 1637.

The house was begun in 1616 for Anne of Denmark, wife of James I, but was not completed until 1638, when it became the home of Charles I and his queen, Henrietta Maria. The beautiful helix-shaped **Tulip Staircase** (named for the flowers on the wrought-iron balustrade; sadly no photos allowed) leads to a gallery on level 2, hung with paintings and portraits with a sea or seafaring theme from the National Maritime Museum's fine art collection. Look out for the strikingly modernist Sixty Degrees South by Herbert Barnard John Everett.

Cutty Sark Ship
Map p227 (www.cuttysark.org.uk; King William Walk, SE10; adult/child £12/6.50; ⏱10am-5pm; 🚇DLR Cutty Sark) This Greenwich landmark, the last of the great clipper ships to sail between China and England in the 19th century, finally

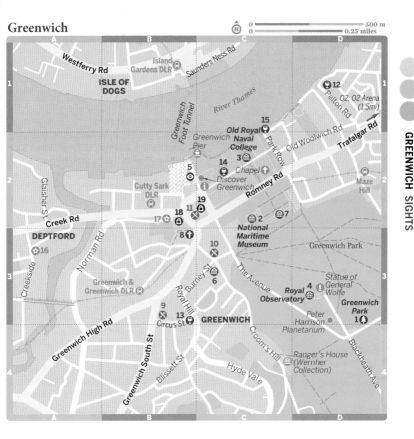

reopened in April 2012 after six years and £25 million of extensive renovations following a disastrous fire caused by a vacuum cleaner in 2007. All we can say is that it was worth the wait: the Cutty Sark is a stunner and a brilliant attraction.

The exhibition in the ship's hold tells her story as a tea clipper at the end of the 19th century (and then wool and mixed cargo). Launched in 1869 in Scotland, she made eight voyages to China in the 1870s, sailing out with a mixed cargo and coming back with a bounty of tea. There are films, interactive maps and plenty of illustrations and props to get an idea of what life on board was like.

On the top deck, you can visit the crew's cramped living quarters and the officer's plush cabins. Visits end in the basement gallery located underneath the ship: the hull, covered in golden Muntz metal plates, appears to be floating and is a breathtaking sight. There is also an intriguing collection of figureheads, one of the largest of its kind in the world.

Fan Museum   Museum
Map p227 (www.fan-museum.org; 12 Crooms Hill, SE10; adult/child £4/free; ⊙11am-5pm Tue-Sat, noon-5pm Sun; ⊠Greenwich, DLR Cutty Sark) The world's only museum entirely devoted to fans has a wonderful collection of ivory, tortoiseshell, peacock-feather and folded-fabric examples alongside kitsch battery-powered versions and huge ornamental Welsh fans. The setting, an 18th-century Georgian town house, also has a Japanese-style garden plus the **Orangery** Map p227 (half/full tea £5/6; ⊙3-5pm Tue & Sun), with lovely trompe l'œil murals and twice-weekly afternoon tea.

Greenwich

O2 Notable Building
(www.theo2.co.uk; Peninsula Sq, SE10; ⊖North
Greenwich) The 380m-wide circular O2,
on the Greenwich Peninsula just 10
minutes by bus from Greenwich itself,
cost £750 million to build in 2000 as the
Millennium Dome. Once the definitive
white elephant, it has finally found its
purpose as a multipurpose venue hosting
big-ticket concerts, sporting events (it
was the gymnastics and basketball venue
for the 2012 Olympics) and blockbuster
exhibitions. There are dozens of bars
and restaurants inside too. You can also
now climb to the top; **Up at the O2** (www.
theo2.co.uk/upattheo2; SE10; tickets from £22;
⊙hours vary) isn't exactly your thrill-
seeking destination but it's definitely
not for the faint-hearted. Equipped with
climbing suit and a harness, you'll scale
the famous white dome to arrive at a

viewing platform perched 52m above the
Thames with sweeping views of Canary
Wharf, the river, Greenwich and beyond.

✕ Eating

Greenwich Market Market £
Map p227 (www.shopgreenwich.co.uk/greenwich-
market; College Approach, SE10; ⊙10am-5.30pm
Tue-Sun; ☑; ⓡDLR Cutty Sark) Perfect for
snacking your way through a world atlas
of food while browsing the other market
stalls, come here for delicious food-to-go,
from Spanish tapas to Thai curries, sushi,
Polish dumplings, French crêpes, Brazilian
churros, smoked Louisiana sausages and
more; follow your nostrils and make your
pick, and wash it all down with a glass of
fresh farmhouse cider.

Tai Won Mein Chinese £
Map p227 (39 Greenwich Church St, SE10; mains
from £4.95; ⊙11.30am-11.30pm; ☑; ⓡDLR
Cutty Sark) The staff may be a bit jaded but
this great snack spot – the Cantonese
name just means 'Big Bowl of Noodles' –
serves epic portions of carbohydrate-rich
noodles to those overcoming Greenwich's
titanic sights.

Old Brewery Modern British ££
Map p227 (www.oldbrewerygreenwich.com;
Pepys Bldg, Old Royal Naval College, SE10; mains
cafe £7-12, restaurant £10.50-18.50; ⊙cafe
10am-5pm, restaurant 6-11pm; ☑; ⓡDLR Cutty
Sark) A working brewery with splendidly
burnished 1000L copper vats at one end
and a high ceiling lit with natural sunlight,
the Old Brewery is a cafe serving lovely
bistro fare by day and a restaurant by
night, serving a choice selection of fine
dishes carefully sourced from the best
seasonal ingredients.

Inside Modern European ££
Map p227 (☎020-8265 5060; www.insider-
estaurant.co.uk; 19 Greenwich South St, SE10;
mains £13.95-21.95, 2-/3-course set menu
£19.95/24.95; ⊙noon-2.30pm & 6.30-10.30pm
Tue-Sat, noon-3.30pm Sun; ⓡDLR Greenwich)
With white walls, modern art and linen
tablecloths, Inside is a relaxed kind of

DOUG MCKINLAY/GETTY IMAGES ©

Don't Miss
Old Royal Naval College

When Christopher Wren was commissioned by King William III and Queen Mary II to construct a naval hospital here in 1692, he conceived it in two halves to protect the river views from the Queen's House. Built on the site of the Old Palace of Placentia, where Henry VIII was born in 1491, the hospital was initially intended for those wounded in the victory over the French at La Hogue. In 1869 the building was converted to a Naval College; today it's home to the University of Greenwich and Trinity College of Music.

Designed as a dining hall for sailors, the **Painted Hall** (⊘10am-5pm) is one of Europe's greatest banquet rooms, dressed in decorative 'allegorical baroque' murals by artist James Thornhill. The magnificent ceiling mural above the Lower Hall is a feast, showing William and Mary enthroned amid symbols of the Virtues. Beneath William's feet grovels the defeated French king Louis XIV, furled flag in hand.

With its mix of ancient Greek and naval motifs, the beautiful **chapel** Map p227 (⊘10am-5pm Mon-Sat, from 12.30pm Sun) in the Queen Mary Building is decorated in an elaborate rococo style. The chapel is famed for its excellent acoustics and regularly hosts concerts, many of them free; check the website for details.

The **Discover Greenwich** Map p227 (www.ornc.org; The Pepys Building, King William Walk; ⊘10am-5pm) FREE exhibition delves into the history of Greenwich with models and hands-on exhibits, many aimed at children. It also contains artefacts from King Henry VIII's old palace, unearthed during a dig in 2005.

Daily **guided tours** (adult/child £5/free; ⊘noon & 2pm) of the college take you behind the scenes as well as to the main sights. Tours must be booked at the **Greenwich Tourist Office** Map p227 (www.visitgreenwich.org.uk/tourist-information-centre; Pepys House, 2 Cutty Sark Gardens, SE10; ⊘10am-5pm; 🚇DLR Cutty Sark).

NEED TO KNOW

Map p227; www.oldroyalnavalcollege.org; 2 Cutty Sark Gardens, SE10; ⊘10am-5pm; 🚇DLR Cutty Sark

place and one of Greenwich's best restaurants. The fine food hits the mark, ranging tastily and affordably from pumpkin and red lentil soup, to pan fried wild sea bass, and apple and rhubarb crumble.

Spread Eagle French £££
Map p227 (www.spreadeaglerestaurant.co.uk; 1-2 Stockwell St, SE10; mains £12-24, lunch/dinner 2-course set-menu £13.50/22.50; ⏰noon-3pm

---

Free Music in Greenwich

The **Trinity Laban Conservatoire of Music and Dance** (p233) offers regular free concerts in Greenwich: they're held in **St Alfege Church** (p222) at 1.10pm on Thursdays and at various times in the chapel of the Old Royal Naval College. Check the website for details.

& 6-10pm Tue-Sat, noon-5pm Sun; 🚊DLR Cutty Sark) Smart, French-inspired restaurant opposite the Greenwich Theatre in what was once the terminus for the coach service to/from London.

🍸 Drinking & Nightlife

The drinking options in Greenwich are top-notch, a mixture of superb, historic old pubs and trendy microbreweries. A must after a day's sightseeing, even if you're not staying in the area.

Trafalgar Tavern Pub
Map p227 (www.trafalgartavern.co.uk; 6 Park Row, SE10; ⏰noon-11pm Mon-Thu, to midnight Fri & Sat, to 10.30pm Sun; 🚊DLR Cutty Sark) Lapped by the tidal waters of the Thames, this elegant tavern with big windows looking onto the river is steeped in history. Dickens apparently knocked back a few here – and used it as the setting for the

Left: Glass-roofed visitors centre at the *Cutty Sark* (p226); **Below:** The Old Brewery

(LEFT) JOHN GAFFEN/ALAMY ©; (BELOW) LONELY PLANET/GETTY IMAGES ©

wedding breakfast scene in *Our Mutual Friend* – and prime ministers Gladstone and Disraeli used to dine on the pub's celebrated whitebait.

Cutty Sark Tavern
Pub

Map p227 (www.cuttysarktavern.co.uk; 4-6 Ballast Quay, SE10; ⏰11am-11pm Mon-Sat, noon-10.30 Sun; 🚉DLR Cutty Sark) Housed in a bow-windowed, wood-beamed Georgian building on the Thames, the Cutty Sark is one of the few independent pubs left in Greenwich. Half a dozen cask-conditioned ales on tap line the bar, with a riverside sitting-out area opposite. It's a 15-minute walk from the DLR station or hop on a bus along Trafalgar Rd and walk north.

Greenwich Union
Pub

Map p227 (www.greenwichunion.com; 56 Royal Hill, SE10; ⏰noon-11pm Mon-Sat, 11.30am-10.30pm Sun; 🚉DLR Cutty Sark) The award-winning Union plies six or seven local microbrewery beers, including raspberry and wheat varieties, and a strong list of ales, plus bottled international brews. It's a handsome place, with duffed up leather armchairs and a welcoming long, narrow aspect that leads to the conservatory and beer garden at the rear.

The Old Brewery
Bar

Map p227 (www.oldbrewerygreenwich.com; Pepys Bldg, Old Royal Naval College, SE10; ⏰11am-11pm Mon-Sat, noon-10.30pm Sun; 🚉DLR Cutty Sark) Situated within the grounds of the old Royal Naval College, the Old Brewery is run by the Meantime Brewery, selling its own brew draught Imperial Pale Ale (brewed on site), along with a heady range of over 50 beers, from Belgian Trappist ales to fruity and smoked beers. We love the 'bottle chandelier' inside and the courtyard for sunny days.

JANE SWEENEY/GETTY IMAGES ©

⭐ Don't Miss
National Maritime Museum

Narrating the long history of seafaring Britain, this is one of Greenwich's top attractions.

The exhibits are arranged thematically and highlights include **Miss Britain III** (the first boat to top 100mph on open water) from 1933, the 19m-long **golden state barge** built in 1732 for Frederick, Prince of Wales, and the huge **ship's propeller** installed on level 1. Families will love these, as well as the **ship simulator** and the **children's gallery** on the second floor where kids can let rip.

Adults are likely to prefer the fantastic (and slightly more serene) galleries. **Voyagers: Britons and the Sea** on the ground floor showcases some of the museum's incredible archives; **Traders: the East India Company and Asia** looks back on Britain's maritime trade with the East in the 19th century; while **Atlantic: Slavery, Trade, Empire** explores the triangular trade between Europe, Africa and America from the 1600s to the 1850s.

A new gallery, **Nelson, Navy, Nation 1688–1815**, focuses on the history of the Royal Navy during the conflict-ridden 18th century and features the coat in which Admiral Nelson was fatally wounded.

NEED TO KNOW

Map p227; www.rmg.co.uk/national-maritime-museum; Romney Rd, SE10; ⏰10am-5pm; 🚆DLR Cutty Sark

🌟 Entertainment

Early September sees Greenwich play host to London's largest comedy festival,

the **Greenwich Comedy Festival** (www.greenwichcomedyfestival.co.uk). Usually set in the Old Royal Naval College, at the time of writing the festival was looking for a new venue – check the website for updates.

Up the Creek
Comedy

Map p227 (www.up-the-creek.com; 302 Creek Rd, SE10; admission £4-16; ⌚7.30-11pm Thu & Sun, to 2am Fri & Sat; ⊠Greenwich, DLR Cutty Sark) Bizarrely enough, the hecklers can be funnier than the acts at this great club. Mischief, rowdiness and excellent comedy are the norm with open mic nights on Thursdays (www.theopenmic.co.uk; £4) and Sunday specials (www.sundayspecial.co.uk; £6). There's an after-party disco on Fridays and Saturdays.

O2 Arena
Live Music

(www.theo2.co.uk; Peninsula Sq, SE10; ⊖North Greenwich) One of the city's major concert venues, hosting all the big names – the Rolling Stones, Britney Spears, Prince and many others – inside the 20,000-capacity stadium. It's also a popular venue for sporting events (tennis, horseriding etc). Ticket prices start at £20.

Laban Theatre
Dance

Map p227 (www.trinitylaban.ac.uk; Creekside, SE8; admission £6-15; ⊠Deptford Bridge, DLR Greenwich) Home of the **Trinity Laban Conservatoire of Music and Dance** (www.trinitylaban.ac.uk), the Laban Theatre presents student dance performances, graduation shows and regular performances by the resident troupe, Transitions Dance Company. Its stunning £23 million home was designed by Herzog & de Meuron, who also designed the Tate Modern.

🔒 Shopping

Greenwich is a paradise for lovers of retro clothes stores and handicrafts.

Greenwich Market
Handicrafts

Map p227 (www.shopgreenwich.co.uk/greenwich-market; SE10; ⌚10am-5.30pm Tue-Sun) Greenwich may be one of the smallest of London's many markets but it holds its own when it comes to quality: on Tuesdays, Wednesdays, Fridays and weekends, stallholders tend to be small, independent artists, offering original prints, wholesome beauty products, funky jewellery and accessories, cool fashion pieces and so on.

Greenwich Architecture

Greenwich is home to an extraordinary interrelated cluster of classical buildings. All the great architects of the Enlightenment made their mark here, largely due to royal patronage. In the early 17th century, Inigo Jones built one of England's first classical Renaissance homes, the Queen's House, which still stands today. Charles II was particularly fond of the area and had Sir Christopher Wren build both the Royal Observatory and part of the Royal Naval College, which John Vanbrugh then completed in the early 17th century.

On Tuesdays, Thursdays and Fridays, it's vintage, antiques and collectables.

Beehive
Vintage

Map p227 (320-322 Creek Rd, SE10; ⌚10.30am-6pm Tue-Sun; ⊠DLR Cutty Sark) Funky meeting ground of old vinyl (Bowie, Rolling Stones, vintage soul) and retro togs (frocks, leather jackets and overcoats).

Emporium
Vintage, Music

Map p227 (330-332 Creek Rd, SE10; ⌚10.30am-6pm Wed-Sun; ⊠DLR Cutty Sark) This lovely vintage shop has glass cabinets crammed with costume jewellery and old perfume bottles, while gorgeous jackets and blazers intermingle on the racks. The men's offering is unusually good for vintage shops.

Arty Globe
Gifts, Souvenirs

Map p227 (www.artyglobe.com; 15 Greenwich Market; ⌚11am-6pm; ⊠DLR Cutty Sark) The unique fisheye-view drawings of areas of London (and other cities, including New York, Paris and Berlin) by architect Hartwig Braun are works of art and appear on the bags, placemats, notebooks, coasters, mugs and jigsaws available in this tiny shop. They make excellent gifts.

Oxford○
50km / 30mi
100km / 60mi
LONDON ✪
Windsor ○ ○**Hampton**
Ⓝ
English Channel

Day Trips

Hampton Court Palace (p236)

One of the best days out that London has to offer, this palace should not be missed by anyone with an interest in British history, Tudor architecture and/or delightful gardens.

Windsor (p240)

An affluent town dominated by the epicentre of British royalty – the Queen's principal residence – Windsor is a pleasant and very civilised place to explore.

Oxford (p241)

Though it's the world's oldest university town, Oxford has more to offer than just its prestigious colleges, including delightful architecture and world-class museums.

Bridge of Sighs, Hertford College, Oxford (p241)

⊛ Don't Miss
Hampton Court Palace

London's most spectacular Tudor palace, this
16th-century icon concocts an imposing sense of
history, from the huge kitchens and grand living
quarters to the spectacular gardens, complete
with a 300-year-old maze.

☎ 0844-482 7777

www.hrp.org.uk/
HamptonCourtPalace

Hampton Court Rd,
East Molesey KT8

adult/child
£17.60/8.80

🕐 10am-6pm late Ma
late Oct, to 4.30pm
late Oct-late Mar

🚢 from Westminster
Pier, Apr-Sep, 3hr,
🚉 Hampton Court

Entering the Palace

Passing through the magnificent Great Gatehouse (1521), you arrive first in the Base Court and then the Clock Court, named after the 16th-century astronomical clock that still shows the sun revolving round the earth. From these two courtyards you can follow any or all of the seven sets of rooms and exhibitions in the complex.

Henry VIII's Kitchens

Accessible immediately to the left after entering are the delightful Tudor kitchens, once used to rustle up meals for a royal household of some 1200 people. The kitchens have been fitted out to resemble how they might have looked in Henry VIII's day; don't miss the Great Wine Cellar, which handled the 300 barrels each of ale and wine consumed here annually in the mid-16th century.

Henry VIII's Apartments

The stairs inside Anne Boleyn's Gateway between the Base and Clock Courts lead up to Henry VIII's State Apartments, including the celebrated Great Hall, the largest single room in the palace, decorated with tapestries and what is considered the country's finest hammer-beam roof. Further along the corridor is the beautiful Chapel Royal, built in just nine months and still a place of worship after 450 years. An excellent view of the fan-vaulted ceiling is available from the Royal Pew.

William III's Apartments

West of the baroque colonnade designed by Christopher Wren in the Clock Court is the entrance to William III's Apartments; reach the 1st floor via the stunning King's Staircase, with murals (1700) by Antonio Verrio that flatter the king by comparing him to Alexander the Great. Highlights include the King's Presence Chamber, dominated by a throne backed with scarlet hangings; the King's Great Bedchamber, with a bed topped with ostrich plumes; and the King's Closet (where His Majesty's toilet has a velvet seat).

Mary II's Apartments

William's wife, Mary II, had the Queen's Apartments, accessible up the Queen's Staircase, decorated by William Kent. When Mary died in 1694, work on these was incomplete; they were finished during the reign of George II. The rooms are shown as they might have been when Queen Caroline used them for entertaining between 1716 and 1737. Compared with the King's Apartments, those for the queen seem austere, although the Queen's Audience Chamber has a 'canopy of state' as imposing as the king's throne.

Georgian Private Apartments

The Georgian Rooms were used by George II and Queen Caroline on the court's last visit to the palace in 1737. Do not miss the fabulous Tudor Wolsey Closet with its richly decorated early 16th-century ceiling and painted panels, commissioned by Henry VIII.

Gardens & Maze

Beyond the palace are the stunning gardens. In the restored 24-hectare Riverside Gardens, you'll find the Great Vine. Planted in 1768, it's still producing just under 320kg of grapes per year. No one should leave Hampton Court without losing themselves in the famous 800m-long maze, made of hornbeam and yew and planted in 1690.

Haunted Hampton Court

Arrested for treason and adultery and detained in the palace in 1541, Henry VIII's fifth wife, Catherine Howard, was dragged screaming down a gallery at the palace by her guards after she attempted to meet with the king and plead her innocence. Her ghost is said to do a repeat performance to this day in the Haunted Gallery leading to the Royal Pew.

Hampton Court Palace

A DAY AT THE PALACE

With so much to explore and seemingly infinite gardens, it can be tricky knowing where to begin. It helps to understand how the palace has grown over the centuries and how successive royal occupants embellished Hampton Court to suit their purposes and to reflect the style of the time.

As soon as he had his royal hands upon the palace from Cardinal Thomas Wolsey, Henry VIII began expanding the **Tudor architecture** ❶, adding the **Great Hall** ❷, the exquisite **Chapel Royal** ❸, the opulent Great Watching Chamber and the gigantic **kitchens** ❹. By 1540 it had become one of the grandest and most sophisticated palaces in Europe. James I kept things ticking over, while Charles I added a new tennis court and did some serious art-collecting – including acquiring **Mantegna's Triumphs of Caesar** ❺.

❼ The Maze
Around 150m north of the main bulding
Created from hornbeam and yew and planted in around 1700, the maze covers a third of an acre within the famous palace gardens. A must-see conclusion to Hampton Court, the maze takes the average visitor about 20 minutes to reach the centre.

Tudor Architecture
Dating to 1515, the heart of the palace serves as one of the finest examples of Tudor architecture in the nation. Cardinal Thomas Wolsey was responsible for transforming what was originally a grand medieval manor house into a stunning Tudor palace.

Tudor Kitchens
These vast kitchens were the engine room of the palace. With a staff of 200 people, there were six spit-rack-equipped fireplaces, with roast meat always on the menu (to the tune of 8200 sheep and 1240 oxen per year).

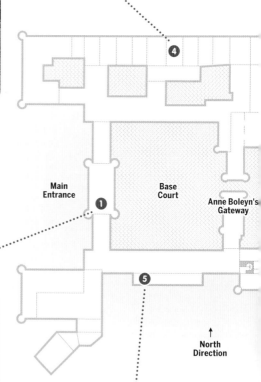

Main Entrance ❶

Base Court

Anne Boleyn's Gateway

❺

↑ North Direction

The Triumphs of Caesar
Acquired by Charles I in 1629, Italian artist Andrea Mantegna's nine-painting series *The Triumphs of Caesar* portray Julius Caesar returning to Rome in a triumphant procession, accompanied by the spoils of war.

After the Civil War, puritanical Oliver Cromwell warmed to his own regal proclivities, spending weekends in the comfort of the former Queen's bedroom and selling off Charles I's art collection. In the late 17th century, William and Mary employed Sir Christopher Wren for baroque extensions, chiefly the William III Apartments, reached by the **King's Staircase** ⑥. William III also commissioned the world-famous **maze** ⑦.

TOP TIPS

» Ask one of the red-tunic-garbed warders for anecdotes and information.

» Tag along with a themed tour led by costumed historians or join a Salacious Gossip Tour for scandalous royal stories.

» Grab one of the audio tours from the Information Centre.

The Great Hall
This grand dining hall is the defining room of the palace, displaying what is considered England's finest hammer-beam roof, 16th-century Flemish tapestries telling the story of Abraham, and some exquisite stained-glass windows.

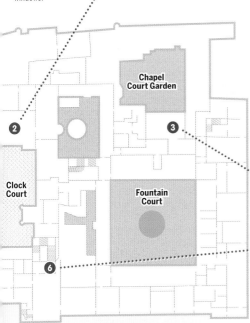

Chapel Royal
The blue-and-gold vaulted ceiling was originally intended for Christ Church, Oxford, but was installed here instead; the 18th-century oak reredos was carved by Grinling Gibbons. Books on display include a 1611 1st edition of the King James Bible, printed by Robert Barker.

The King's Staircase
One of five rooms at the palace painted by Antonio Verrio and a suitably bombastic prelude to the King's Apartments, the overblown King's Staircase adulates William III by elevating him above a cohort of Roman emperors.

OPEN FOR INSPECTION

The palace was opened to the public by Queen Victoria in 1838.

Windsor

With its romantic architecture and superb state rooms, Windsor Castle is one of Britain's premier tourist attractions. Since it is so close to central London and easily accessible by rail and road, it usually crawls with tourists.

Getting There & Away

Bus Green Line Buses (☎0871 200 2233; www.greenline.co.uk) 701 and 702 link Victoria coach station with Windsor (return from £9.50, one hour) at least hourly every day.

Train National Rail trains (☎0845 748 4950; www.nationalrail.co.uk) from Waterloo station go to Windsor Riverside station every 30 minutes, or hourly on Sunday (return from £8.50, one hour). Trains from Paddington go via Slough to Eton and Windsor Central station (return from £8.50, 30 to 45 minutes).

Need to Know

○ **Area code** ☎01753

○ **Location** 25 miles west of London

○ **Tourist office** (☎01753-743900; www.windsor.gov.uk; Thames St, Old Booking Hall, Windsor Royal Station; ☺9.30am-5.30pm Mon-Sat, 10am-4pm Sun May-Aug, 10am-5pm Mon-Sat, 10am-4pm Sun Sep-Apr)

◉ Sights

Windsor Castle   Castle

(www.royalcollection.org.uk; adult/child £17.75/10.60, when State Apartments closed £9.70/6.45; ☺9.45am-5.15pm Mar-Oct, 9.45am-4.15pm Nov-Feb) British monarchs have inhabited Windsor Castle for more than 900 years, and it is well known to be the Queen's favourite residence and the place she calls home after returning from her work 'week' (now just Tuesday and Wednesday) at the 'office' (Buckingham Palace). If the Queen is in residence, you'll see the Royal Standard (*not* the Union Flag) flying from the Round Tower.

A disastrous fire in 1992 nearly wiped out this incredible piece of English cultural heritage. Luckily damage, though severe, was limited and a £37 million restoration, completed in 1997 has returned the state apartments to their former glory.

Starting out as an earth and timber castle erected around 1080 by William the Conqueror and rebuilt in stone in 1170, this is one of the world's greatest surviving medieval castles, and its longevity and easy accessibility from London guarantee its popularity.

The castle precinct, covering more than five hectares, is divided into three wards. In the Upper Ward, the **State Apartments**, which are closed to the public at certain times (check the website), resound with history. The self-paced audioguide tour starts with the impossibly opulent **Grand Staircase** and weapons-filled **Grand Vestibule** (including the bullet that killed Admiral Nelson) and leads into the **Waterloo Chamber**, created to commemorate the battle of that name and filled with portraits of the great and the good by Sir Thomas Lawrence (1769–1830).

From here you move to the **King's Rooms** and **Queen's Rooms**. These are lessons in how the other half lives, with opulent furniture, tapestries and paintings by Canaletto, Dürer, Gainsborough, Van Dyck, Hogarth, Holbein, Rembrandt and Rubens. Next is the extraordinary **St George's Hall**, the room most damaged by the 1992 fire but now brought back to life, including its signature hammerbeam roof. (The fire actually broke out in what was a chapel next door and is now the **Lantern Lobby**). The tour ends in the **Garter Throne Room**.

Outside on the North Terrace you can't help noticing the queues that form for the impossibly intricate **Queen Mary's Dolls' House**, the 1924 work of architect Sir Edwin Lutyens on a scale of 1:12.

Moving westward through the Middle Ward and past the distinctive **Round Tower**, rebuilt in stone from the original

Norman keep in 1180, you enter the Lower Ward. Here one of Britain's finest examples of early English architecture, **St George's Chapel** (begun by Edward IV in 1475, but not completed until 1528), has a superb nave done in Perpendicular Gothic style, with gorgeous fan vaulting and a massive stained-glass West Window (1508).

South of the castle is beautiful **Windsor Great Park** (☉8am-dusk) covering an area of some 40 sq miles.

✖ Eating & Drinking

Gilbey's   Modern British ££
(✆01753-854921; www.gilbeygroup.com; 82-83 High St, Eton; mains from £16.50, 2-/3-course menu £19.50/25.50; ☉noon-2.30pm & 6-9.30pm; 📶) This little restaurant just beyond the bridge in Eton is one of the area's finest. Terracotta tiling and a sunny courtyard garden and conservatory give Gilbey's a continental cafe feel, complimented by a superb Modern British menu. Weekend afternoon tea is also offered.

Bel & the Dragon   British ££
(✆01753-866056; www.belandthedragon.co.uk; 1 Datchet Rd, Windsor; mains £9-28; ☉lunch & dinner; 📶♿) With a congenial and inviting publike feel, this homely but modern restaurant and bar in an old 11th-century house a short stroll from the Thames pulls out the stops: service is warm and welcoming and the seasonal seafood and roasts are crowd-pleasingly good, as are the afternoon teas.

Two Brewers   Pub
(34 Park St, Windsor; ☉11.30am-11pm Mon-Thu, 11.30am-11.30pm Fri-Sat, noon-10.30pm Sun) This 17th-century inn perched on the edge of Windsor Great Park is close to the castle's tradesmen's entrance and supposedly frequented by staff from the castle. Think low-beamed ceilings, dim lighting and royal photographs with irreverent captions on the wall.

Changing of the Guard

A must for any visitor to Windsor is the **changing of the guard** (☉11am Mon-Sat Apr-Jul, alternate days Aug-Mar), a fabulous spectacle of pomp and ceremony that draws large crowds to Lower Ward. If you're just interested in watching the marching bands and not within the castle grounds, find a spot along High St. The guards leave from Victoria Barracks on Sheet St at 10.45am and return an hour later.

Oxford

Victorian poet Matthew Arnold called Oxford 'that sweet city with her dreaming spires'. These days the spires co-exist with a flourishing commercial city that has some typical urban social problems. But for visitors, the superb architecture and the unique atmosphere of the more than three dozen colleges – synonymous with academic excellence – and their courtyards and gardens remain major attractions.

Getting There & Away

Bus Oxford Tube (✆01865-772250; www.oxfordtube.com) and Oxford Bus Company (✆785400; www.oxfordbus.co.uk) buses depart every 10 to 30 minutes round the clock from London's Victoria coach station (return from £16) and can be boarded at various other points in London, including Marble Arch, Notting Hill Gate and Shepherd's Bush. Journey time is an hour and 40 minutes.

Train There are two trains (✆0845 748 4950; www.nationalrail.co.uk) per hour from London's Paddington station (return from £23, one hour).

Oxford

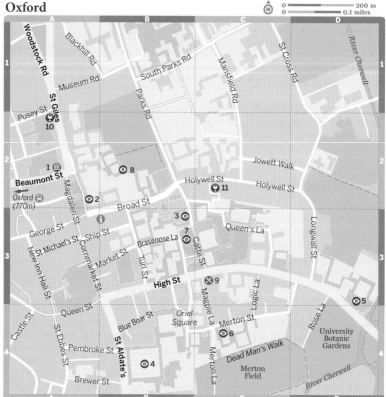

Oxford

⊙ Sights	(p242)
1 Ashmolean Museum	A2
2 Balliol College	A2
3 Bodleian Library	B3
4 Christ Church College	B4
5 Magdalen College	D3
6 Merton College	C4
7 Radcliffe Camera	B3
8 Trinity College	B2

⊗ Eating	(p243)
9 Quod	C3

⊕ Drinking & Nightlife	(p243)
10 Eagle & Child	A2
11 Turf Tavern	C2

Need to Know

○ **Area code** ☏01865

○ **Location** 59 miles northwest of London

○ **Tourist office** (Map p242; ☏252200; www.
visitoxfordandoxfordshire.com; 15-16 Broad St;
⊙9.30am-5pm Mon-Sat, 10am-3.30pm Sun,
closes 30 mins later in winter)

⊙ Sights

Christ Church
College
Notable Building

Map p242 (www.chch.ox.ac.uk; St Aldate's; adult/
child £8/6.50; ⊙9am-5pm Mon-Sat, 2-5pm
Sun) Founded in 1525 and now massively
popular with Harry Potter fans, having
appeared in several of the films, Christ

Church is the largest and grandest of all the 38 colleges. The main entrance is below Tom Tower (1681), designed by Christopher Wren and containing a 7-tonne bell called Great Tom. Visitors enter further down St Aldate's via the wrought-iron gates of the War Memorial Gardens and Broad Walk. The college chapel is Christ Church Cathedral, the smallest in the country.

Other Colleges   Notable Buildings

(www.ox.ac.uk/colleges) If time and opening hours permit (check website for details), consider visiting any of the following important colleges: **Magdalen College** Map p242 (www.magd.ox.ac.uk; High St; adult/child £5/4; ⏰noon-7pm), pronounced *maud-lin,* with huge grounds bordering the River Cherwell; **Merton College** Map p242 (www.merton.ox.ac.uk; Merton St; admission £2, guided tour £2; ⏰2-5pm Mon-Fri, 10am-5pm Sat & Sun, guided tour 45min), with a 14th-century library where JRR Tolkien wrote much of the *Lord of the Rings;* **Trinity College** Map p242 (www.trinity.ox.ac.uk; Broad St; adult/child £1.75/1; ⏰10am-noon & 2-4pm Sun-Fri, 2-4pm Sat), with an exquisitely carved chapel; and **Balliol College** Map p242 (www.balliol.ox.ac.uk; Broad St; adult/child £2/1; ⏰10am-5pm, dusk in winter), founded in 1263 and thought to be the oldest college in Oxford.

Bodleian Library   Library

Map p242 (www.bodley.ox.ac.uk; Broad St; Divinity School adult/child £1/free, audioguide £2.50, library tours £7, 30min tours £5, extended tour £13; ⏰9am-5pm Mon-Fri, to 4.30pm Sat, 11am-5pm Sun, library tours 10.30am, 11.30am, 1pm & 2pm Mon-Sat, 11.30am, 2pm & 3pm Sun) The early-17th-century Bodleian Library is one of the oldest public libraries in the world and one of just three copyright libraries in England. It is connected by tunnel with the Palladian-style **Radcliffe Camera** Map p242 (Radcliffe Sq; extended tours £13) (1749), which functions as a reading room for the Bodleian and supports Britain's third-largest dome. The very symbol of Oxford, the only way to see the inside of the Radcliffe Camera reading room is to join an extended 1½-hour tour (£13) of the Bodleian Library departing at 9.15am

on Wednesday and Saturday and 11.15am and 1.15pm most Sundays.

Ashmolean Museum   Museum

Map p242 (www.ashmolean.org; Beaumont St; ⏰10am-6pm Tue-Sun) FREE Britain's oldest public museum (1683) is second in reputation only to London's British Museum. It contains everything from Egyptian mummies and Chinese art to European and British paintings by the likes of Rembrandt and Michelangelo. New basement displays include such curiosities as the death mask of Oliver Cromwell, Lawrence of Arabia's Arab robes and the lantern Guy Fawkes was carrying when arrested on 5 November 1605.

✖️ Eating & Drinking

Quod   Modern British ££

Map p242 (📞01865-202505; www.quod.co.uk; 92-94 High St; mains £11.50-22; ⏰7am-11pm Mon-Sat, to 10.30pm Sun) Bright, buzzing and decked out with modern art, this place dishes up modern brasserie-style food to the masses. It's always bustling and, at worst, will tempt you to chill by the bar with a cocktail while you wait. The two-course set lunch (£12.95) is good value.

Turf Tavern   Pub

Map p242 (4-5 Bath Pl; ⏰11am-11pm) Hidden away down a narrow alleyway, this tiny medieval pub is one of the town's best loved and bills itself as 'an education in intoxication'. Serving 11 real ales, it's always packed with a mix of students, professionals and the lucky tourists who manage to find it.

Eagle & Child   Pub

Map p242 (49 St Giles; ⏰11am-11pm Mon-Thu, to midnight Fri & Sat, noon-10.30pm Sun) Affectionately known as the 'Bird & Baby', this atmospheric place, dating from 1650, was once the favourite haunt of Tolkien and CS Lewis. Its wood-panelled rooms and good selection of real ales still attract a mellow crowd.

London
In Focus

Shakespeare's Globe (p136)
MICHAEL DUNNING/GETTY IMAGES ©

London Today

St James's Park (p63)

> 66
> *London reaffirmed itself as a capital of dynamism and change*
> 99

belief systems
(% of population)

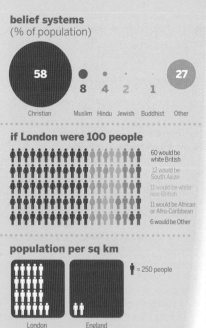

58 Christian 8 Muslim 4 Hindu 2 Jewish 1 Buddhist 27 Other

if London were 100 people

60 would be white British

12 would be South Asian

11 would be white non-British

11 would be African or Afro-Caribbean

6 would be Other

population per sq km

♦ ≈ 250 people

London   England

London vs the Rest?

As the economic downturn double-dips its way into the record books, the UK is increasingly a nation of two halves: London and the rest. Between 2007 and 2011, the London economy grew by a huge 12.4% against a backdrop of negative growth elsewhere. In most parts of the city, property prices have continued to gallop ahead; in 2013, the cost of a London home surged past £500,000, double the national average. London employment has been rosier than the rest of the nation since 2007 while average incomes are 30% higher than elsewhere in the UK.

The Olympic Effect

The UK's most painful recession ever was briefly forgotten during the ebullience of the 2012 Olympic Games in London, when Team GB seized their best gold-medal haul since the 1908 event. After seven years of planning, it was London's big moment in the global spotlight. The city was appraised, reappraised, examined

SYLVAIN SONNET/GETTY IMAGES ©

IN FOCUS LONDON TODAY

crisis. Many Londoners have called for greater efforts to promote integration of ethnic communities into British culture, but the subject remains a political minefield, especially since the terrorist bombings on the London Transport network in 2005. The 2013 murder of off-duty soldier Lee Rigby in Woolwich by two Islamist extremists only underscored those fears. Some Londoners insist immigrants should conform to a national credo, while others point the finger at UK foreign policy, insisting it is divisive.

and compared against a raft of expectations. Yet the £9 billion sporting event won almost universal media acclaim for its professionalism and spirit, with many hailing it as one of the best Olympic Games ever. The games left an area of East London with world-class sports facilities and gave added gloss (and brand new transport infrastructure) to one of the most visited cities in the world. London reaffirmed itself as a capital of dynamism and change.

Ethnicity & Multiculturalism

London is undergoing its most thorough ethnic transformation in its history. The 2011 census revealed that white Britons in London now constitute a minority (45%) for the first time in its 2000-year history. The figures coincided with a period of growing scepticism over the EU, exacerbated by the ongoing Eurozone

Austerity & Change

After the 2010 general election, the Conservative Party and Liberal Democrats were forced to forge the first coalition government since WWII. With an economy crippled by debt and overspend, a new Age of Austerity dawned. Some pundits linked the devastating London riots of 2011 with cutbacks and economic hardship, others blamed the erosion of social and personal responsibility in modern Britain. Despite the disorder and buoyed by popular support, Conservative Boris Johnson defied his critics and won a second term as mayor of London in 2012.

Moving Forwards

An ambitious redesign of London's transport options is either in the pipeline or already on the streets. The London Overground was expanded and a cable car over the River Thames now lashes together North Greenwich and the Royal Docks. Crossrail will bring high-frequency underground trains linking east and west London along two brand new lines costing £15.9 billion, due to commence operation in 2018.

247

History

Hampton Court Palace (p236)

EURASIA PRESS/GETTY IMA

The Romans are the real founders of London and the wall built around their settlement of Londinium still more or less demarcates the City of London. London has had a roller-coaster journey, experiencing conflict, apocalyptic plague, cataclysmic conflagrations and bombardment with the world's first space rockets (the V-2). But even when on its knees the city has always been able to get up and move on, constantly re-inventing itself.

The Romans

The empire-building Romans colonised Britain in AD 43, establishing the port of Londinium. They slung a wooden bridge over the Thames (near the site of today's London Bridge) and created a thriving colonial outpost before abandoning British soil for good in 410.

AD 43
The Romans invade Britain and establish the colony of Londinium on the north bank of the River Thames.

Saxon & Norman London

Saxon settlers, who colonised the southeast of England from the 5th century onwards, established themselves outside the city walls due west of Londinium in Lundenwic. Saxon London grew into a prosperous town segmented into 20 wards, each with its own alderman and resident colonies of German merchants and French vintners. But Viking raids finally broke the weakening Saxon leadership, which was forced to accept the Danish leader Canute as king of England in 1016. With the death of Canute's brutal son Harthacanute in 1042, the throne passed to the Saxon Edward the Confessor, who went on to found a palace and an abbey at Westminster.

When he was on his deathbed in 1066, Edward anointed Harold Godwinson, who was the Earl of Wessex, as his successor. This enraged William, Duke of Normandy, who claimed that Edward had promised him the throne. William mounted a massive invasion from France and on 14 October defeated (and killed) Harold at the Battle of Hastings, before marching on London to claim his prize. William, now dubbed 'the Conqueror', was crowned king of England in Westminster Abbey on 25 December 1066, ensuring the Norman Conquest was complete.

The Best...
Historical Treasures

IN FOCUS HISTORY

Medieval & Tudor London

Successive medieval kings were happy to let the City of London keep its independence as long as its merchants continued to finance their wars and building projects. During the Tudor dynasty, which coincided with the discovery of the Americas and thriving world trade, London became one of the largest and most important cities in Europe.

Henry VIII reigned from 1509 to 1547, built palaces at Whitehall and St James's, and bullied his lord chancellor, Cardinal Thomas Wolsey, into giving him the one at Hampton Court. The most momentous event of his reign, however, was his split with the Catholic Church in 1534 after the Pope refused to annul his marriage to Catherine of Aragon, who had borne him only one surviving daughter after 24 years of marriage.

The 45-year reign (1558–1603) of Henry's daughter Elizabeth I is still regarded as one of the most extraordinary periods in English history. During these four decades

122

Emperor Hadrian pays a visit to Londinium when Roman London is at its pinnacle.

852

Vikings settle in London, having attacked the city a decade previously.

1066

After his victory at the Battle of Hastings, William the Conqueror is crowned king at Westminster Abbey.

English literature reached new heights, and religious tolerance grew gradually. With the defeat of the Spanish Armada in 1588, England became a naval superpower, and London established itself as the premier world trade market with the opening of the Royal Exchange in 1570.

Civil Wars, Plague & Fire

The English Civil War culminated with the execution of Charles I on 30 January 1649 and saw Oliver Cromwell rule the country as a republic for the next 11 years. Under the Commonwealth of England, as the English republic was known, Cromwell banned theatre, dancing, Christmas and just about anything remotely fun. After Cromwell's death, parliament restored the exiled Charles II to the throne in 1660.

Charles II's reign witnessed two great tragedies in London: the Great Plague of 1665, which decimated the population, and the the Great Fire of London, which swept ferociously through the city's densely packed streets the following year.

The wreckage of the inferno at least allowed master architect Christopher Wren to build his 51 magnificent churches. The crowning glory of the 'Great Rebuilding' was his St Paul's Cathedral, which was completed in 1710. A masterpiece of English baroque architecture, it remains one of the city's most prominent and iconic landmarks.

Georgian & Victorian London

While the achievements of the Georgian kings were impressive (though 'mad' George III will forever be remembered as the king who lost the American colonies), they were overshadowed by those of the dazzling Victorian era, dating from Queen Victoria's ascension to the throne in 1837. During the Industrial Revolution London became the nerve centre of the largest and richest empire the world had ever witnessed, in an imperial expansion that covered a quarter of the earth's surface area and ruled over more than 500 million people.

Queen Victoria lived to celebrate her Diamond Jubilee in 1897, but died four years later aged 81 and was laid to rest beside her beloved consort, Prince Albert, at Windsor. Her reign is seen as the climax of Britain's world supremacy, when London was the de facto capital of the world.

The World Wars

What became known as the Great War, WWI broke out in August 1914, and the first German bombs fell from zeppelins near the Guildhall a year later, killing 39 people. Planes were soon dropping bombs on the capital, killing in all some 670 Londoners (half the national total of civilian deaths).

1348
A bubonic plague known as the Black Death wipes out two-thirds of London's population.

1599
The Globe Theatre opens in Southwark; *Macbeth* and *Hamlet* premiere. Shakespeare's Globe (p136)

GRANT FAINT/GETTY IMAGES ©

Great Fire of London

The Great Fire of London broke out in Thomas Farriner's bakery in Pudding Lane on the evening of 2 September 1666. Initially dismissed by London's lord mayor as 'something a woman might pisse out', the fire spread uncontrollably and destroyed 89 churches and more than 13,000 houses, raging for days. Amazingly fewer than a dozen people died.

The fire destroyed medieval London, changing the city forever. Many Londoners left for the countryside or to seek their fortunes in the New World, while the city itself rebuilt its medieval heart with grand buildings such as Wren's St Paul's Cathedral. Wren's magnificent Monument (1677) near London Bridge stands as a memorial to the fire and its victims.

In the 1930s Prime Minister Neville Chamberlain's policy of appeasing Adolf Hitler eventually proved misguided as the German Führer's lust for expansion appeared insatiable. When Nazi Germany invaded Poland on 1 September 1939, Britain declared war, having signed a mutual-assistance pact with that country only a few days before. World War II (1939–45), which would prove to be Europe's darkest hour, had begun.

Winston Churchill, prime minister from 1940, orchestrated much of the nation's war strategy from the Cabinet War Rooms deep below Whitehall, lifting the nation's spirit from here with his stirring wartime speeches. By the time Nazi Germany capitulated in May 1945, up to a third of the East End and the City of London had been flattened, almost 30,000 Londoners had been killed and a further 50,000 seriously wounded.

Postwar London

Once the celebrations of Victory in Europe (VE) day had died down, the nation began to confront the war's appalling toll and to rebuild. The years of austerity had begun, with rationing of essential items and high-rise residences rising up from bombsites. Rationing of most goods ended in 1953, the year Elizabeth II was crowned following the death the year before of her father King George VI.

Immigrants from around the world – particularly the former colonies – flocked to postwar London, where a dwindling population had generated labour shortages, and the city's character changed forever. The place to be during the 1960s, 'Swinging London' became the epicentre of cool in fashion and music, its streets awash with

1666
The Great Fire burns for five days, leaving medieval London in smoking ruins.

1838
Queen Victoria is crowned at Westminster Abbey, ushering in one of the greatest periods of London's history.

1901
Queen Victoria dies after a reign of more than 63 years – the longest (so far) in British history.

The Blitz

The Blitz (from the German *Blitzkrieg*, meaning 'lightning war') struck England between September 1940 and May 1941, when London and other parts of Britain were heavily bombed by the German Luftwaffe. Londoners responded with legendary resilience and stoicism. Underground stations were converted into giant bomb shelters, although this was not always safe – one bomb rolled down the escalator at Bank station and exploded on the platform, killing more than 100 people. Buckingham Palace took a direct hit during a bombing raid early in the campaign, famously prompting Queen Elizabeth (the present monarch's late mother) to announce that 'now we can look the East End in the face'.

colour and vitality. The ensuing 1970s brought glam rock, punk, economic depression and the country's first female prime minister in 1979.

In power for the entire 1980s and pushing an unprecedented program of privatisation, the late Margaret Thatcher is easily the most significant of Britain's postwar leaders. Opinions about 'Maggie' still polarise British opinion today. While poorer Londoners suffered under Thatcher's significant trimming back of the welfare state, things had rarely looked better for the wealthy as London underwent explosive economic growth.

In 1992, much to the astonishment of most Londoners, the Conservative Party was elected for their fourth successive term in government, despite Mrs Thatcher being jettisoned by her party a year and a half before. By 1995 the writing was on the wall for the Conservative Party, as the Labour Party, apparently unelectable for a decade, came back with a new face.

London in the New Century

Invigorated by its sheer desperation to return to power, the Labour Party elected the thoroughly telegenic Tony Blair as its leader, who in turn managed to ditch some of the more socialist-sounding clauses in its party credo and reinvent it as New Labour, leading to a huge landslide win in the May 1997 general election. The Conservatives atomised nationwide; the Blair era had begun in earnest.

Most importantly for London, Labour recognised the demand the city had for local government, and created the London Assembly and the post of mayor. In Ken Livingstone London elected a mayor who introduced a congestion charge and sought to update the ageing public transport network. In 2008, he was defeated by his arch rival, Conservative Boris Johnson.

1940

The Blitz begins, although St Paul's Cathedral, the city's symbol of resistance, largely escapes the bombing.

1953

Queen Elizabeth II's coronation is held, with more than 20 million Britons watching it on television.

1997

Tony Blair rides into office with one of the biggest electoral landslides in British history.

Johnson's second mayoral term coincided with the 2012 Olympic Games, overwhelmingly judged an unqualified success. Britain's 65 medals notwithstanding, perhaps the highlight was that nothing came close to Danny Boyle's Olympics Opening Ceremony in which the world was treated to an extravagant potted history of London, and James Bond (in the form of Daniel Craig) jumped out of a helicopter into the Olympic Stadium accompanied by none other than 'Her Majesty, the Queen'. We Londoners are still laughing.

The Monument (p107), a memorial to the Great Fire of London of 1666

2005
Some 52 people are killed in July by Muslim suicide bombers attacking the London transport network.

2012
London hosts its third Olympic Games, the first city in history to do so.

2013
Prince George, third in line to the throne, is born to the Duke and Duchess of Cambridge.

Family Travel

Ice skating in front of the Natural History Museum (p158)

CULTURA TRAVEL/AXEL BERNSTORFF/GETTY IMAG

London is a fantastic place for children. The city's museums will fascinate all ages, and you'll find theatre, dance and music performances ideal for older kids. Just remember that children are easily exhausted by the crowds and long walks, so don't plan too much, and build in some rest time in London's fantastic public parks, playgrounds and city farms.

Museums

London's museums are particularly child friendly. You'll find storytelling at the National Gallery for children aged three years and over, arts and crafts workshops at the Victoria & Albert Museum, train-making workshops at the Transport Museum, tons of finger-painting opportunities at Tate Modern and Tate Britain, and performance and handicraft workshops at Somerset House. And what's more, they're all free (check websites for details).

Other excellent activities for children include sleepovers at the British, Science and Natural History Museums, though you'll need to book months ahead. The last two are definitive children's museums, with interactive displays and play areas.

Other Attractions

Kids love the London Zoo, London Eye, London Dungeon and Madame Tussauds. Ice rinks glitter around London in winter at the Natural History Museum, Somerset House, Hyde Park and the moat of the Tower of London. There's also a seasonal rink further afield at Hampton Court Palace.

In addition there's the exciting climbs up the dome of St Paul's Cathedral or the Monument, feeding the ducks in St James's Park and watching the performers in Trafalgar Square or Covent Garden Piazza. Many arts and cultural festivals aimed at adults also cater for children. London's parks burst with possibilities: open grass, playgrounds, wildlife, trees and, in the warmer weather, ice-cream trucks.

Most attractions offer family tickets and discounted entry for kids under 15 or 16 years (children under five usually go free).

Eating & Drinking with Kids

Most of London's restaurants and cafes are child-friendly and offer baby-changing facilities and high chairs. Pick your places with a few things in mind: avoid high-end and quiet, small restaurants and cafes if you have toddlers or small babies. Go for noisier restaurants and more relaxed cafes.

The one place that isn't traditionally very welcoming for those with children is the pub. By law, minors aren't allowed into the main bar (though walking through is fine), but many pubs have areas where children are welcome, usually a garden or outdoor space. Things are more relaxed during the day on Sunday.

Getting Around with Kids

When it comes to getting around, buses are better for children than the tube, which is often very crowded and hot in summer. As well as being big, red and iconic, buses in London are usually the famous double-decker ones; kids love to sit on the top deck and get great views of the city. Another excellent way to get around is simply to walk.

Not for Parents

For an insight into London aimed directly at kids, pick up a copy of Lonely Planet's *Not for Parents: London*. Perfect for children aged eight and up, it opens up a world of intriguing stories and fascinating facts about London's people, places, history and culture.

Need to Know

◦ **Public transport** Under-16s travel free on buses, under-11s travel free on the tube, and under-5s ride free on trains.

◦ **Babysitters** Find a babysitter or nanny at **Greatcare** (www.greatcare.co.uk).

◦ **Cots** Available in most hotels, but always request them in advance.

Food & Drink

Cakes and sandwiches at an afternoon tea

MICHAEL BLANN/GETTY IMAG

Once the laughing stock of the cooking world, London has got its culinary act together over the last two decades to become an undisputed dining destination. There are plenty of fine Michelin-starred restaurants, but it is the sheer diversity that is extraordinary: from Afghan to Vietnamese, London is a virtual A to Z of world cuisine.

Food

English & British Food

England may have given the world beans on toast, mushy peas and chip butties (French fries between two slices of buttered, *untoasted* white bread), but that's hardly the whole story. When well prepared – be it a Sunday lunch of roast beef and Yorkshire pudding (light batter baked until fluffy and eaten with gravy) or a cornet of lightly battered fish and chips sprinkled with salt and malt vinegar – English food can have its moments of glory. And nothing beats a fry-up (or full English breakfast) with bacon, sausages, beans, eggs and mushrooms the morning after a big night out.

Modern British food, however, has become a cuisine in its own right, by championing traditional (and sometimes underrated) ingredients such as root vegetables, smoked fish, shellfish, game and prepared meats like sausages and black pudding (a rich kind of sausage stuffed with oatmeal, spices and blood). Dishes can be anything from guinea fowl served with Jerusalem artichoke to seared scallops with orange-scented black pudding, or roast pork with chorizo on rosemary mash.

Food from Everywhere

One of the joys of eating out in London is the profusion of choice. For historical reasons Indian cuisine is widely available (curry is almost the national dish), but Southeast and East Asian cuisines in general are extraordinarily popular: you'll find umpteen Chinese, Thai, Japanese and Korean restaurants, as well as elaborate fusion establishments blending flavours from different parts of Asia. The best Indian – or, more accurately, Bangladeshi and Pakistani – food is found out east around Commercial and Whitechapel Rds.

Food from continental Europe – French, Italian, Spanish, Greek, Scandinavian – is another favourite, with many classy Modern European establishments on offer. Restaurants serving other cuisines tend to congregate where their home community is based; for example Eastern European restaurants are found in Shepherd's Bush, Turkish in Dalston, Vietnamese in Hackney.

You'll find lots of other cuisines – from Eritrean to Burmese – elsewhere in the capital, and part of the joy of London is trying dishes you've never had before.

Seafood

Visitors sometimes point out that, for an island race, Brits seem to make surprisingly little of their seafood, with the exception of the ubiquitous fish and chips. Modern British restaurants have started catching up, however, and many now offer local specialities such as Dover sole, Cornish oysters, Scottish scallops, smoked Norfolk eel, Atlantic herring and mackerel. There are some excellent restaurants specialising in seafood, as well as fish-and-chips counters trading in battered cod, haddock and plaice.

Dining Out

World-Class Restaurants

Food-wise, London has an embarrassment of riches, with 62 Michelin-starred restaurants, including two three-star restaurants, the most famous of which is Gordon Ramsay in Chelsea. The picks in the city today are therefore nothing short of sublime if you want to have a memorable meal (and especially if you don't mind splashing out – as with almost everything in London, you'll get what you pay for). For top tables, you'll always need to reserve in advance, and for the very best you'll need to book several months ahead.

But it's not all about Michelin stars and three-month waiting lists for reservations. Some of London's most glorious treats are both easily accessible and not too expensive.

The Best...
Restaurants

1 Providores & Tapa Room (p85)

2 Gordon Ramsay (p160)

3 Newman Street Tavern (p81)

4 Towpath (p211)

5 Viajante (p191)

Need to Know

- **Most restaurants** open from noon-2.30pm and 6-11pm
- **Chain restaurants** open from noon-11pm
- **Price ranges** The symbols below indicate the average cost per main course at the restaurant in question.
- **£** less than £10
- **££** £10–£20
- **£££** more than £20
- **Reservations** Make reservations for weekends if you're keen on a particular place or if you're in a group of more than four people. Top-end restaurants often run multiple sittings, with allocated time slots (generally two hours); pick a later slot if you don't want to be rushed.

Gastropubs

The culinary revolution in London began with the advent of the so-called 'gastropub' – a smattering of savvy pubs that replaced their stodgy microwave meals with freshly prepared contemporary cuisine, bringing little-known ingredients to the plates of many locals for the first time. The gastropub may now be old hat, but you'll still find them across the city, signposting an area's 'up-and-coming' status and providing meeting places for the young urban professionals slowly colonising London's less expensive boroughs.

Vegetarians & Vegans

London has been one of the best places for vegetarians to dine out since the 1970s, initially due to the many Indian restaurants which, for religious reasons, always cater for people who don't eat meat. A number of dedicated vegetarian restaurants – in fact, some very stylish ones in recent years – have since cropped up, offering imaginative, filling and truly delicious meals. Most non-vegetarian places generally offer a couple of dishes for those who don't eat meat; vegans, however, will find it harder outside Indian or dedicated restaurants.

Supper Clubs

Supper clubs are half-restaurant, half-dinner party. They're run by regular people with a love and talent for cooking and generally cater for 10 to 20 people. Meals are set three- or four-course affairs (£20 to £40), and the clientele couldn't be more eclectic.

The difficulty is that these underground restaurants are rarely permanent and so recommending a supper club can be tricky. The following will help:

Ms Marmite (www.supperclubfangroup.ning. com) An excellent directory of London supper clubs set up by a supper club host.

London Foodie (www.thelondonfoodie.co.uk) This food blog features regular supper club reviews.

Facebook Hosts post details of forthcoming events on their pages.

Food Markets

The boom in London's eating scene has extended to its markets. As well as being found at farmers markets – check out www.lfm.org.uk for a selection of the best, such as Broadway and Marylebone – food stalls are now a part of broader markets (eg Spitalfields, Borough or Camden) and appeal to visitors keen to soak up the atmosphere.

Pubs & Bars

At the heart of London social life, the public house – universally known as the pub – is one of the capital's great social levellers.

You can order almost anything you like, but beer is the staple. Some specialise, offering drinks from local microbreweries, fruit beers, organic ciders and other rarer beverages; others proffer inspired wine lists, especially gastropubs. Some pubs have delightful gardens – crucial in summer.

Unless otherwise stated all pubs and bars reviewed in this guide open at 11am and close at 11pm from Monday to Saturday and close at 10.30pm on Sunday. Some pubs and bars stay open longer, but all close at 2am or 3am at the latest.

Generally open later than pubs, but closing earlier than clubs, bars tempt those keen to skip bedtime at 11pm but not up for clubbing. They may have DJs and a small dance floor and door charges after 11pm.

Architecture

Millennium Bridge (p129) and St Paul's Cathedral (p104)

JOHN HARPER/GETTY IMAG

London has never been planned. Rather, it has developed in a haphazard fashion. London retains architectural reminders from every period, but they are often hidden: part of a Roman wall enclosed in the lobby of a modern building near St Paul's Cathedral, say, or a galleried Restoration coaching inn in a courtyard. This is a city for explorers. Bear that in mind and you'll make discoveries at virtually every turn.

Ancient London Architecture

Traces of medieval London are hard to find thanks to the devastating Great Fire of 1666, but several works by the architect Inigo Jones (1573–1652) have endured, including Covent Garden Piazza in the West End, Banqueting House and the gorgeous Queen's House in Greenwich.

There are a few even older treasures scattered around – including the mighty Tower of London in the City, parts of which date back to the late 11th century. Westminster Abbey and Temple Church are 12th- to 13th-century creations. Few Roman traces survive outside museums, though the Temple of Mithras, built in AD 240, will be relocated to the eastern end of Queen Victoria St in the City when the Bloomberg headquarters is completed at Walbrook Sq. Stretches of the Roman wall remain as foundations to a medieval wall outside Tower

Hill tube station and in a few sections below Bastion highwalk, next to the Museum of London, all in the City.

The Saxons, who moved into the area after the decline of the Roman Empire, found Londinium too small, ignored what the Romans had left behind and built their communities farther up the Thames. The best place to see *in situ* what the Saxons left behind is the church of All Hallows-by-the-Tower, northwest of the Tower of London, which boasts an important archway, the walls of a 7th-century Saxon church and fragments from a Roman pavement.

Noteworthy medieval secular structures include the 1365 Jewel Tower, opposite the Houses of Parliament, and Westminster Hall, both surviving chunks of the medieval Palace of Westminster.

After the Great Fire

After the 1666 fire, Sir Christopher Wren was commissioned to oversee reconstruction, but his vision of a new city layout of broad, symmetrical avenues never made it past the planners. His legacy lives on, however, in St Paul's Cathedral (1710), the maritime precincts at Greenwich and City churches.

Nicholas Hawksmoor joined contemporary James Gibb in taking Wren's English baroque style further; two of the best examples are Spitalfields' Christ Church and St Martin-in-the-Fields in Trafalgar Square.

Like Wren before him, Georgian architect John Nash aimed to impose some symmetry on unruly London and was slightly more successful in achieving this through grand creations such as Trafalgar Square and the elegantly curving arcade of Regent St. Built in similar style, the surrounding squares of St James's remain some of the finest public spaces in London – little wonder then that Queen Victoria decided to move into the recently vacated Buckingham Palace in 1837.

Towards Modernity

Pragmatism replaced grand vision with the Victorians, who desired ornate civic buildings that reflected the glory of empire but were open to the masses too. The decorative neo-Gothic style found champions in George Gilbert Scott (1811–78), Alfred Waterhouse (1830–1905), Augustus Pugin (1812–52) and Charles Barry (1795–1860). The style's turrets, towers and arches are best exemplified by the flamboyant Natural History Museum (Waterhouse), St Pancras Chambers (Scott) and the Houses of Parliament (Pugin and Barry), the latter replacing the Palace of Westminster that had largely burned down in 1834. The Victorians and Edwardians were also ardent builders of functional and cheap terraced houses, many of which became slums but today house London's urban middle classes.

A flirtation with art deco and the great suburban residential building boom of the 1930s was followed by a utilitarian modernism after WWII, as the city rushed to build new housing to replace terraces lost in the Blitz. Low-cost developments and unattractive high-rise housing were thrown up on bomb sites; many of these blocks still fragment the London horizon today. Brutalism – a hard-edged and uncompromising architectural style that flourished from the 1950s to the 1970s,

The Best...
Modern Architecture

1 30 St Mary Axe (p109)

2 Lloyd's of London (p109)

3 Shard (p133)

4 Tate Modern (p124)

5 Millennium Bridge (p129)

Open House London

If you want to see the inside of buildings you wouldn't normally be admitted to, the third weekend in September is the time to visit London. That's when the charity **Open House London** (☎ 020-3006 7008; www.londonopenhouse.org) arranges for owners of some 800 private buildings to throw open their front doors and let in the public free of charge. Major buildings, including 30 St Mary Axe and Lloyd's of London, have already participated. The full program becomes available in August. An architectural London Night Hike winds its way through the city during the same period, and its tours branch **Open City** (☎ 020-7383 2131; www.open-city.org.uk; tours £14.50-35.50) offers architect-led tours year-round.

favouring concrete and reflecting socialist utopian principles – worked better on paper than in real life but made significant contributions to London's architectural melange. Denys Lasdun's National Theatre, begun in 1966, is representative of the style.

Postmodernism & Beyond

The next big wave of development arrived in the derelict wasteland of the former London docks, which were emptied of their terraces and warehouses and rebuilt as towering skyscrapers and 'loft' apartments. Taking pride of place in the Docklands was Cesar Pelli's 244m-high 1 Canada Square (1991), commonly known as Canary Wharf and easily visible from central London. The City was also the site of architectural innovation, including the centrepiece 1986 Lloyd's of London, Sir Richard Rogers' 'inside-out' masterpiece of ducts, pipes, glass and stainless steel. A masterpiece of postmodernist architecture is James Stirling's No 1 Poultry (1997).

Contemporary Architecture

There followed a lull in new construction until around 2000, when a glut of millennium projects unveiled new structures and rejuvenated others: the London Eye, Tate Modern and the Millennium Bridge all spiced up the South Bank, while Norman Foster's iconic 30 St Mary Axe, better known as the Gherkin, started a new wave of skyscraper construction in the City. Even once-mocked Millennium Dome won a new lease of life as the 02 concert and sports hall.

By the middle of the decade London's biggest urban development project ever was under way, the 200-hectare Queen Elizabeth Olympic Park in the Lea River Valley near Stratford in East London, where most of the events of the 2012 Summer Olympics and Paralympics took place. But the park would offer few architectural surprises – except for Zaha Hadid's stunning Aquatics Centre, a breathtaking structure suitably inspired by the fluid geometry of water; and the ArcelorMittal Orbit, a zany public work of art with viewing platforms designed by the sculptor Anish Kapoor.

The spotlight may have been shining on East London, but parts of South London have undergone energetic and even visionary renewal. The centrepiece is the so-called Shard, at 310m the EU's tallest building, completed in 2012. The glass-clad upturned icicle, dramatically poking into the skies, houses offices, residences, a five-star hotel, restaurants and, on the 72nd floor, London's highest public viewing gallery.

Literary London

Charles Dickens Museum (p63)

Ever changing, yet somehow eerily consistent, London has left its mark on some of the most influential writing in the English language. The capital has been the inspiration for the masterful imaginations of such eminent wordsmiths as Shakespeare, Defoe, Dickens, Thackeray, Wells, Orwell, Conrad, Eliot, Greene and Woolf, to name but a few.

Old Literary London

It's hard to reconcile the bawdy portrayal of London in Geoffrey Chaucer's *Canterbury Tales* with Charles Dickens' bleak hellhole in *Oliver Twist*, let alone Daniel Defoe's plague-ravaged metropolis in *A Journal of the Plague Year* with Zadie Smith's multi-ethnic romp *White Teeth*. The first literary reference to London is indeed in Chaucer's *Canterbury Tales*, written between 1387 and 1400, in which pilgrims gather for their trip at the Tabard Inn in Southwark and promise to tell one another stories along the way.

Shakespeare to Defoe

William Shakespeare spent most of his life as an actor and playwright in London around the turn of the 17th century. He trod the boards of Southwark's theatres, writing

The Best...
Literary Sites

his greatest tragedies, including *Hamlet, Othello, Macbeth* and *King Lear,* for the Globe theatre.

Living in and writing about the city during the early 18th century, Daniel Defoe is most famous for *Robinson Crusoe* (1720) and *Moll Flanders* (1722), which he wrote while living in Church St in north London's Stoke Newington. Defoe's *A Journal of the Plague Year* documents the horrors of the Great Plague in London during the summer and autumn of 1665, when the author was a young child.

Dickensian & 19th-Century London

Two early 19th-century Romantic poets drew inspiration from London: John Keats, born above a Moorgate public house in 1795, wrote 'Ode to a Nightingale' while living near Hampstead Heath in 1819 and 'Ode on a Grecian Urn' after inspecting the Parthenon frieze in the British Museum. William Wordsworth visited in 1802, discovering inspiration for the poem 'Upon Westminster Bridge'.

Charles Dickens (1812–70) is the definitive London author. When his father and family were jailed at Marshalsea Prison in Southwark for not paying their debts, the 12-year-old Charles was forced to fend for himself on the streets. His family was released three months later, but that grim period provided a font of experiences on which he would later draw. His novels most closely associated with London are *Oliver Twist, Little Dorrit,* and *Our Mutual Friend*.

Sir Arthur Conan Doyle (1858–1930) portrayed a very different London, with his pipe-smoking, cocaine-snorting sleuth, Sherlock Holmes, coming to exemplify the cool and unflappable Englishman.

London at the end of the 19th century appears in numerous books including HG Wells' *The War of the Worlds,* W Somerset Maugham's first novel, *Liza of Lambeth* and his *Of Human Bondage,* an engaging portrait of late-Victorian London.

20th-Century Writing

American Writers & London

Of Americans writing about London at the turn of the century, Henry James, who settled and died here, stands supreme with *Daisy Miller* and *The Europeans. The People of the Abyss,* by socialist writer Jack London, is a sensitive portrait of poverty and despair in the Whitechapel area of the East End. St Louis–born TS Eliot settled in London in 1915, where he published his poem 'The Love Song of J Alfred Prufrock' almost immediately and moved on to his seminal epic 'The Waste Land'.

Interwar Developments

Between the wars, PG Wodehouse (1881–1975) depicted London high life with his hilarious lampooning of the English upper classes in the Jeeves stories. George Orwell's experience of living as a beggar in London's East End coloured his book *Down and Out in Paris and London*, while the sternly modernist Senate House on Malet St in Bloomsbury was the inspiration for the Ministry of Truth in Orwell's classic dystopian 1949 novel *Nineteen Eighty-Four.*

The Modern Age

The End of the Affair, Graham Greene's novel chronicling a passionate and doomed romance, takes place in and around Clapham Common just after WWII.

Colin MacInnes described the bohemian, multicultural world of 1950s Notting Hill in *Absolute Beginners,* while Doris Lessing captured the political mood of 1960s London in *The Four-Gated City.* Nick Hornby, nostalgic about his days as a young football fan in *Fever Pitch* and vinyl-obsessive in *High Fidelity,* found himself the voice of a generation.

Hanif Kureishi explored London from the perspective of ethnic minorities, specifically young Pakistanis, in *The Black Album* and *The Buddha of Suburbia,* while Timothy Mo's *Sour Sweet* is a poignant and funny account of a Chinese family in the 1960s trying to adjust to English life.

The late 1970s and 1980s were strong for British literature, introducing a dazzling new generation of writers, including Martin Amis *(Money, London Fields),* Julian Barnes *(Metroland, Talking It Over),* Ian McEwan *(Enduring Love, Atonement),* Salman Rushdie *(Midnight's Children, The Satanic Verses),* AS Byatt *(Possession, Angels & Insects)* and Alan Hollinghurst *(The Swimming Pool Library, The Line of Beauty).*

Millennium London & the Current Scene

Helen Fielding's *Bridget Jones's Diary* and and its sequel, *Bridget Jones: The Edge of Reason,* launched the 'chick lit' genre. Will Self has long been the toast of London. His *Grey Area* is a superb collection of short stories, while *The Book of Dave* is both hilarious and surreal.

Literary Readings, Talks & Events

A host of literary events are regularly held across London, ranging from book and poetry readings to talks, open-mic performances, writing workshops and other occasions celebrating the written word.

To catch established and budding authors, attend the monthly **Book Slam** (www.bookslam.com) usually held from 6.30pm on the last Thursday of the month at various clubs around London. Check the website for dates and venues.

Covent Garden's **Poetry Café** (Map p76; ☏ 020-7420 9888; www.poetrysociety.org. uk; 22 Betterton St, WC2; ⏰ 11am-11pm Mon-Fri, from 6.30pm Sat; ⊖ Covent Garden) is a favourite for lovers of verse, with almost daily readings and performances by established poets, open-mic evenings and writing workshops.

The Institute of Contemporary Arts (p66) has excellent talks every month, with well-known writers from all spectrums from the hip to the seriously academic.

Bookshops, particularly **Waterstone's** (Map p72; www.waterstones.com; 203-206 Piccadilly, W1; ⏰ 9am-10pm Mon-Sat, noon-6pm Sun; ⊖ Piccadilly Circus), Foyle's (p93) and the London Review Bookshop (p93), often stage readings. Some major authors also now appear at the Southbank Centre (p139). Many such events are organised on an ad-hoc basis, so keep an eye on the listings in the freebie *Time Out* or the *Guardian Guide* distributed with Saturday's paper.

Held over two weeks in late May/early June, the **London Literature Festival** (www.londonlitfest.com) at the Southbank Centre holds talks and events featuring writers and the literati.

Peter Ackroyd's *London: The Biography* is his inexhaustible paean to the capital, while *Thames: Sacred River* stands as his fine monument to the muck, magic and mystery of the river through history, displaying an ambitious sense of exploration further revealed in his *London Under,* in which the subterranean city comes to life.

Iain Sinclair's acclaimed and ambitious *London Orbital,* a journey on foot around the M25, is required London reading; *Hackney, That Rose Red Empire,* is an exploration of London's most notorious borough, one that underwent enormous changes in the approach to 2012, a subject Sinclair revisited in *Ghost Milk*.

Other new London talent in recent years ranges from Monica Ali, who brought the East End to life in *Brick Lane*, and Zadie Smith, whose *NW* was shortlisted for the Women's Prize for Fiction in 2013, to Jake Arnott's intelligent Soho-based gangster yarn *The Long Firm* and Gautam Malkani's much-hyped *Londonstani*. 'Rediscovered' is Howard Jacobson, who won the Man Booker Prize in 2010 for his comic novel *The Finkler Question*.

The Arts

Street art created by Banksy

DAVID BUKACH/GETTY IMAGES ©

The cultural life in London is the richest and most varied in the English-speaking world. The theatre scene is also the world's most diverse, while dance in London executes some gorgeous moves. Music and London are almost synonymous, and you'll find much to applaud, whatever your genre. Film is celebrated in a host of festivals and cutting-edge cinemas.

Fine Art

London today is the art capital of Europe, with a vibrant gallery scene and some of the world's leading modern art collections. Many of the world's greatest artists have spent time here, including Monet and Van Gogh. Although Britain's artists have historically been eclipsed by their European counterparts, some distinctly innovative artists have emerged from London.

An impressive list of artists have been associated with the city, including the German Hans Holbein the Younger (1497–1543), landscape painter Thomas Gainsborough (1727–88), printmaker and satirist William Hogarth (1697–1764), poet, engraver and watercolourist William Blake (1757–1827) and the eminent Romantic John Constable (1776–1837). JMW Turner (1775–1851) embodied the pinnacle of early 19th-century British art, while the brief but

The Best... London Artworks

1 *The Fighting Temeraire* by JMW Turner (National Gallery)

2 *Ophelia* by Sir John Everett Millais (Tate Britain)

3 *Three Studies for Figures at the Base of a Crucifixion* by Francis Bacon (Tate Britain)

4 *The Light of the World* by William Holman Hunt (St Paul's Cathedral)

5 *Forms in Echelon* by Barbara Hepworth (Tate Modern)

splendid flowering of the pre-Raphaelite Brotherhood (1848–54) took its inspiration from the Romantic poets.

Sculptors Henry Moore and Barbara Hepworth both typified the modernist movement in British sculpture, and Irish-born painter Francis Bacon (1909–92) shook the art world with his repulsive yet mesmerising visions. Other big names include Lucian Freud (1922–2011), David Hockney (1937-) and the nattily dressed duo Gilbert and George.

In more recent years, Brit Art has become a dominant and highly marketable aesthetic, launching such names as Damien Hirst and Tracey Emin. Among the biggest-name artists working in contemporary London today are Banksy (the anonymous street artist whose work has become a worldwide phenomenon), Antony Gormley (best known for the 22m-high sculpture, *Angel of the North*), Anish Kapoor (an Indian sculptor working in London since the 1970s), Sarah Lucas (*Self-Portrait with Fried Eggs*), and Marc Quinn (whose work includes *Self,* a sculpture of his head made from the artist's own frozen blood, at the National Portrait Gallery).

Theatre

London has more theatrical history than almost any-where else on the globe, and it's still being made nightly on the stages of the West End, the South Bank and the epic London fringe. No visit to the city is complete without taking in a show, and just an evening walk through 'theatreland' in the West End is an electrifying experience.

There's something for all dramatic tastes here, from contemporary political satire to creative reworking of old classics and all shades in between. In recent years the mainstream West End has re-established its credentials, with extraordinary hits, while the smarter end of the fringe continues to shine with risky and controversially newsworthy productions. The hottest tickets are still for the National Theatre, which has gone from strength to strength under Nicholas Hytner, with productions enjoying both huge box-office success and critical acclaim. If innovation and change are too much for you, drop by St Martin's Theatre, where the same production of *The Mousetrap* has been running since 1952!

Shakespeare's Globe on the South Bank is a magnificent recreation of the Elizabethan theatre experience. The current artistic director, Dominic Dromgoole, has ensured that Shakespeare's plays remain at the core of the theatre's program, but at the same time has produced a wider range of European and British classics, as well as new material.

Dance

As one of the world's great dance capitals, London's artistic habitat has long created and attracted talented choreographers with both the inspiration and aspiration to fashion innovative dance.

The Place in Euston was the original birthplace of modern British dance, and the training school Laban in Deptford has emerged strongly for cutting-edge performances. Sadler's Wells – the birthplace of English classical ballet in the 19th century – continues to stage an exciting program of various styles from leading national ballets and international troupes.

Covent Garden's Royal Opera House is the stunning home of London's leading classical-dance troupe, the Royal Ballet. The company largely sticks to the traditional, but more-contemporary influences occasionally seep into productions. The Royal Ballet has also made itself more accessible by dropping some ticket prices to as little as £6.

For more cutting-edge work, the innovative Rambert Dance Company (www.rambert.org.uk), now in its own premises behind the National Theatre on the South Bank, is the UK's foremost and most creative contemporary dance troupe.

Also a leading UK dance company and one of the world's best, the English National Ballet (www.ballet.org.uk) is a touring company that can often be seen at various venues in London, but usually at the London Coliseum.

Another important venue for experimental dance is the Barbican; for the latest of what's on, check www.londondance.com. The annual contemporary dance event in London is Dance Umbrella (www.danceumbrella.co.uk) from early October.

The Best...
Theatres

1 National Theatre (p138)

2 Shakespeare's Globe (p139)

3 Old Vic (p139)

4 Royal Court Theatre (p162)

5 Barbican (p117)

Music

The modern music scene is one of London's greatest sources of artistic energy and a magnet for bands and hopefuls from all musical hemispheres. Periodically a world-leader in musical fashion and innovative soundscapes, London blends its home-grown talent with a continuous influx of styles and cultures, keeping currents flowing and inspiration percolating upwards. Classical music at the very highest level can also be heard here.

The freebie weekly listings magazine *Time Out* lists dozens of gigs in a range of genres playing each night across the capital.

Classical

The modern-day London classical calendar peaks with the annual Proms, which has expanded its repertoire in recent years to appeal to a broader audience; the festival mainly takes place in the grand Royal Albert Hall in Kensington. Beyond this, classical music and opera are celebrated and performed within a host of world-class venues across town, notably the Royal Festival Hall.

Opera

With one of the world's leading opera companies at the Royal Opera House in Covent Garden, and impressive direction from Edward Gardner at the Coliseum's English National Opera, London has more than enough for opera goers. It's not just the classics that are produced, as innovative productions bring operatic expression to a host of modern-day subjects. Holland Park in Kensington is the venue for operatic productions in summer.

Film Festivals

A host of London festivals celebrating cinema and ranging across the film spectrum entertains film enthusiasts from the popcorn crowd to art-house intelligentsia.

○ **London Film Festival** (www.bfi.org.uk/lff) Held in October, this is the highlight of London's many festivals celebrating cinema.

○ **Raindance Festival** (www.raindance.co.uk) Europe's leading independent film-making festival. It's a terrific celebration of independent, non-mainstream cinema from across the globe, screening just before the London Film Festival.

○ **Portobello Film Festival** (www.portobellofilmfestival.com) Held in September, it features largely independent works by London filmmakers and international directors. It's free to attend.

○ **London Lesbian & Gay Film Festival** (www.bfi.org.uk/llgff) One of the best of its kind with hundreds of independent films from around the world shown over a fun, party-intensive fortnight at BFI Southbank.

Rock

From the Kinks, the Rolling Stones, the Who, T Rex and David Bowie to Coldplay, Gold-frapp, Lily Allen, Adele, Mumford and Sons, Tinie Tempah and the late Amy Winehouse, London is an unimpeachable roll-call of musical talent. London is virtually synony-mous with indie rock. Find gigs at thumping venues in the West End, Shoreditch and Camden.

Jazz

Jazz aficionados will want to visit the iconic Ronnie Scott's, the 606 Club and other great jazz venues in the West End and central London.

Film

Londoners have a passion for all things celluloid and digital, and frequent every place from the vast BFI IMAX in Waterloo and the huge Empire Leicester Square to a host of art-house and independent cinemas. For back-catalogue classics, turn to the BFI at South Bank, but keep an eye out for film festivals at independent cinemas, which bring in reels of foreign movies. For further eclectic tastes, shorts, foreign cinema as well as mainstream films, London's independent cinemas allow you to put your feet up, sip a glass of wine and feel right at home. You can catch monthly seasons and premieres, as well as actors and directors chatting about their work and answering questions. Cinemas such as the Prince Charles (www.princecharlescinema.com) in Soho have cheap tickets, run minifestivals and screen popular sing-along classics. Many major premieres are held in Leicester Square, the priciest part of London for cinema tickets. Outdoor cinema is rolled out in London in the warmer months at Somerset House's Film4 Summer Screen (www.somersethouse.org.uk/film).

Shopping

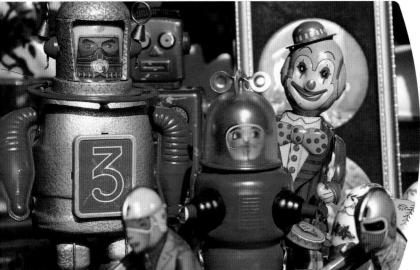

Vintage tin toys at Covent Garden market (p69)

DAVE ELDERFIELD/GETTY IIMAGES ©

London's sights are the main draws, but visitors are also in town to shop. As everywhere, chain stores and global brands dominate, but London has legendary department stores and inspiring independent shops too. Even world-famous designers such as Stella McCartney and Matthew Williamson have one-off boutiques where ordinary mortals can browse the latest in high fashion away from the snobbery of the big couture houses.

Shopping in London

From charity-shop finds to designer bags, there are thousands of ways to part with your cash in London. Fashion may be the city's biggest retail commodity and London has been setting trends ever since Mary Quant created the miniskirt. Mayfair may cater to the high end of the market, but low-priced high street outlets such as Primark and Topshop offer catwalk style on a budget.

For street fashion and London's famous cutting edge, head to the Shoreditch/ Hoxton/Spitalfields areas of East London. Wander past the the boutiques along Brick Lane, Cheshire St, Rivington St and surrounding areas to discover the looks that will soon be heading worldwide.

High Fashion

High fashion is squarely located between Oxford Circus and Knightsbridge. The two big designer streets are Bond St in Mayfair and Sloane St in Knightsbridge, where you'll find nothing but big international names with prices to match.

An alternative place to shop for top brands is in one of London's world-famous department stores. Harrods, Harvey Nichols, Selfridges and Liberty are the top four to choose from. If you're planning a splurge, aim for the sales in June/July or January.

Markets

One of the biggest shopping attractions for visitors is the capital's famed markets. A treasure trove of small designers, unique jewellery pieces, original framed photographs and posters, colourful vintage pieces and bric-a-brac, they are the antidote to impersonal, carbon-copy high-street shopping.

The most popular markets are Camden, Spitalfields and Portobello Rd, all of which are in full swing at the weekend. Although they're all more or less outdoors (Spitalfields is now covered, as are the Stables in Camden), they are always busy, rain or shine.

London also has some excellent food markets – Borough Market, in particular – and dozens of smaller local farmers markets and delicatessens stocked with fine cheeses, charcuterie and artisanal ingredients.

Other Treats

The West End offers plenty of nonsartorial choice, from the electronics shops of Tottenham Court Rd to the small independent bookshops of Charing Cross Rd. For exotic flavours head to Ridley Rd in Hackney or Whitechapel High St in the East End, while for antiques and art, Mayfair and St James's are your best bets.

Don't miss splendid Fortnum & Mason on Piccadilly, the city's 400-year-old grocery store, for all your Anglophile comestibles, and – whether you are with kids or not – make a visit to Hamleys, London's famous toy store.

Charity shops in areas such as Chelsea, Notting Hill and Kensington often have cheap designer wear (usually, the posher the area, the better the second-hand shops).

Survival
Guide

Tower Bridge (p106), the Shard (p133) and City Hall (p123)

PHOTOGRAPHER: ALAN COPSON/GETTY IMAGES ©

Sleeping

Landing the right accommodation is integral to your London experience, and there's no shortage of choice. But just because London is a city that never sleeps doesn't mean it doesn't go to bed: rooms in sought-after hotels can be booked solid. There are some fantastic hotels about, whatever the price tag, but plan ahead.

Accommodation Types

HOTELS

London has a grand roll-call of stately hotels, and many are experiences in their own right. Standards across the top end and much of the boutique bracket are high, but so are the prices. A wealth of budget boutique hotels has exploited a lucrative niche, while a rung or two down in overall quality and charm, midrange chain hotels generally offer good locations and dependable comfort. Demand can often outstrip supply – especially on the bottom step of the market – so book ahead, particularly during holiday periods and in summer.

B&BS

Usually housed in good-looking old properties, bed and breakfasts come in a tier below hotels, often promising boutique-style charm plus a level of service that is more personal. You will find handy clusters of B&Bs appearing through Bloomsbury, South Kensington as well as in Victoria.

HOSTELS

After B&Bs the cheapest forms of accommodation available are hostels, both the official Youth Hostel Association (YHA) ones and the (usually) hipper, more party-orientated independent ones. Hostels vary in quality so be sure to select your accommodation carefully; most offer twin rooms as well as dormitories.

APARTMENTS

If you are staying in London for a week or more, a short-term or serviced apartment, such as **196 Bishopsgate** (☎020-7621 8788; www.196bishopsgate.com; 196 Bishopsgate , EC2; studio/1-bed apt £242/270; ✳ ☏; ⊖Liverpool St), **Number 5 Maddox Street** (☎020-7647 0200; www.5maddoxstreet.com; 5 Maddox St, W1; ste £290-800; ✳ ☏; ⊖Oxford Circus) or **Beaufort House** (☎020-7584 2600; www.beauforthouse.co.uk; 45 Beaufort Gardens SW3; 1-4 bed apt £306-1176; ☏; ⊖Knightsbridge) may prove a sensible choice; rates at the bottom end are comparable to that of B&B accommodation.

Need to Know

PRICE RANGES

In our listings we've used the following codes to represent the price of an en-suite double room in high season:

○ £ under £90

○ ££ £90–180

○ £££ over £180

RESERVATIONS

Book as far in advance as possible, especially for weekends and peak periods. **British Hotel Reservation Centre** (☎020-7592 3055; www.bhronline.com) is at airports and main train stations; booking fee £5. **Visit London** (☎0871 222 3118; www.visitlondonoffers.com) has a free booking service and special deals.

TAX

Value-added tax (VAT; 20%) is added to hotel rooms. Prices listed include it.

CHECKING IN & OUT

Check-in is usually 2pm; check out between 10am and noon.

BREAKFAST

Rates might include a continental breakfast; a full English breakfast could cost extra.

Costs

Deluxe hotel rooms will cost from around £350 per double room but there is a good variety at the top end, so you should find a room from about £180 offering superior comfort without the prestige. Some boutique hotels also occupy this bracket. There is a noticeable dip in quality available below around £180 for a double room, but we have listed the best accommodation options in this range. Once your room costs are under £100, you are at the more serviceable, budget end of the market. Look out for weekend deals that can put a better class of hotel within reach. Rates often slide in winter. Book through the hotels' websites for the best online deals or promotional rates. Unless otherwise indicated, accommodation prices quoted in this guide include breakfast. International Youth Hostel Federation (IYHF) members net discounts on YHA accommodation.

Useful Websites

London Town (www.londontown.com) Great deals and special offers.

Lonely Planet Hotels (www.lonelyplanet.com/hotels) Bookings.

YHA Central Reservations System (📞 0800 019 1700; www.yha.org.uk) Hostel bookings.

Where to Stay

NEIGHBOURHOOD	FOR	AGAINST
The West End	Close to main sights; great transport links; wide accommodation range in all budgets; great restaurants	Busy tourist areas; expensive
The City	St Paul's and Tower of London; good transport links; handy central location; quality hotels; some cheaper weekend rates	Very quiet at weekends; a business district so high prices during the week
South Bank	Near Tate Modern, London Eye and Southbank Centre; cheaper than West End; excellent pubs and views	Many chain hotels; choice and transport limited
Kensington & Hyde Park	Excellent for South Kensington museums and shopping; great accommodation range; stylish area; good transport	Quite expensive; drinking and nightlife options limited
Clerkenwell, Hoxton & Spitalfields	Trendy area with great bars and nightlife; good for boutique hotels	Few top sights; transport options limited
The East End & Docklands	Markets, multicultural feel; great budget restaurants and traditional pubs	Rather limited sleeping options; some areas less safe at night
Hampstead & North London	Leafy; vibrant nightlife; pockets of village charm; excellent boutique hotels and hostels; gastropubs; quiet during the week	Non-central and away from main sights
Greenwich	Boutique options; leafy escapes; near top Greenwich sights	Sights spread out beyond Greenwich; transport limited

Best Places to Stay

NAME		REVIEW
GENERATOR £	The West End	Groovy budget place with industrial decor and 850-plus beds, dorms with four to 12 beds, late-night bar with themed parties.
YHA OXFORD ST £	The West End	Centrally located YHA hostel, intimate and attractive with excellent facilities and bright, funky lounge.
HOTEL LA PLACE ££	The West End	Welcoming 18-room traditional place, modern bathrooms, doubles with orthopaedic mattresses, 24-hour wine bar.
FIELDING HOTEL ££	The West End	Pretty, tucked away 24-room Covent Garden hotel refurbished to a very high standard with pleasant air-conditioned rooms. No breakfast.
DEAN STREET TOWNHOUSE ££	The West End	Soho gem with gorgeous boudoir atmosphere, Georgian furniture, retro black-and-white tiled bathroom floors and beautiful lighting.
NO 10 MANCHESTER STREET £££	The West End	Wonderful Edwardian town-house with print wallpaper, high-tech must haves and impeccable service.
AROSFA HOTEL ££	The West End	Renovated 17 smallish rooms in Bloomsbury, with Philippe Starck furniture in the lounge, a couple of family rooms and a small garden.
DORSET SQUARE HOTEL £££	The West End	Two combined Regency town houses with 38 rooms decorated with antiques and sumptuous fabrics and overlooking leafy Dorset Sq.
HAZLITT'S £££	The West End	Three Georgian houses with bedrooms furnished with antiques, mahogany four-poster beds and all modern creature comforts.
BROWN'S HOTEL £££	The West End	London's oldest hostelry (1838) with 117 individually decorated rooms, antiques and original artworks, oak-panelled English Tea Room and Donovan Bar with stunning stained glass.
HAYMARKET HOTEL £££	The West End	Opulently beautiful with hand-painted Gournay wallpaper, signature fuchsia and green designs, sensational 18m pool, and exquisite library lounge.
LONDON ST PAUL'S YHA £	The City	YHA hostel with 213 beds in a heritage-listed building in the very shadow of St Paul's, dorms with three to 11 beds, and twins and doubles are available.
THREADNEEDLES ££	The City	Wonderfully anonymous with grand circular lobby, and 69 pleasantly attired rooms with dark, sleek furnishings.
WALRUS £	South Bank	This welcoming little hostel is a little shabby but excellent value; dorms (four to 18 beds) and bathrooms are well kept and homely.

PRACTICALITIES	BEST FOR
📞020-7388 7666; www.generatorhostels.com/london; 37 Tavistock Pl, WC1; dm/r from £12/50; @ 🛜; ⊖Russell Sq	Hip, affordable, meeting place.
📞020-7734 1618; www.yha.org.uk; 14 Noel St, W1; dm/tw from £18/46; @ 🛜; ⊖Oxford Circus	Central, budget, very dependable.
📞020-7486 2323; www.hotellaplace.com; 17 Nottingham Pl, W1; s/d from £105/152; ✳ @ 🛜; ⊖Baker St	Family run, welcoming, good for families.
📞020-7836 8305; www.the-fielding-hotel.co.uk; 4 Broad Ct, Bow St, WC2; s/d from £90/140; ✳ 🛜; ⊖Covent Garden	Great value, super central.
📞020-7434 1775; www.deanstreettownhouse.com; 69-71 Dean St, W1; r £180-440; ✳ 🛜; ⊖Tottenham Court Rd	Style and romance.
📞020-7317 5900; www.tenmanchesterstreethotel.com; 10 Manchester St, W1; r £175-245; 🛜; ⊖Baker St	Top-notch elegance.
📞020-7636 2115; www.arosfalondon.com; 83 Gower St, WC1; s/d/tr/q £72/107/130/160; ⊖Goodge St	Affordable style, garden.
📞020-7723 7874; www.firmdalehotels.com; 39 Dorset Sq, NW1; d from £260, ste from £350; ✳ 🛜; ⊖Baker St	Stylish antiques, quiet but central location.
📞020-7434 1771; www.hazlittshotel.com; 6 Frith St, W1; s £222, d/ste from £288/660; ✳ 🛜; ⊖Tottenham Court Rd	Old-school charm with modern comfort.
📞020-7493 6020; www.brownshotel.com; 30 Albemarle St, W1; r/ste from £335/1100; ✳ 🛜; ⊖Green Park	History, classical yet personal style.
📞020-7470 4000; www.haymarkethotel.com; 1 Suffolk Pl, off Haymarket, SW1; r £325-425, ste from £505; ✳ 🛜 ⊠; ⊖Piccadilly Circus	A special treat.
📞020-7236 4965; www.yha.org.uk; 36 Carter Lane , EC4; dm £17-25, d £40-50; @ 🛜; ⊖St Paul's	Excellent location and value.
📞020-7657 8080; www.hotelthreadneedles.co.uk; 5 Threadneedle St, EC2; r weekend/weekday from £150/250; ✳ 🛜; ⊖Bank	Smart boutique elegance.
📞07545 589214; www.walrussocial.com; 172 Westminster Bridge Rd, SE1; dm £18.50-25.50; 🛜; ⊖Waterloo	Individual, friendly, cosy.

NAME		REVIEW
BERMONDSEY SQUARE HOTEL ££	South Bank	Hip, purpose-built, 80-room boutique hotel with smallish rooms but very stylish suites, each unique and named after iconic '60s songs.
CHERRY COURT HOTEL £	Kensington & Hyde Park.	Clean and tidy little 12-room hotel with affordable rates in a five-floor Victorian house near Victoria station.
YHA EARL'S COURT £	Kensington & Hyde Park	On a quiet street in Earl's Court, this is a cheerful, recently upgraded place with clean, airy dormitories.
MEININGER £	Kensington & Hyde Park	Efficient German-run 'city hostel and hotel' opposite the Natural History Museum, with clean rooms, dorms and private rooms. Roof terrace.
ASTER HOUSE ££	Kensington & Hyde Park	Award-winning, lovely house with welcoming staff, comfortable rooms, sparkling bathrooms, delightful orangery and charming garden.
B+B BELGRAVIA ££	Kensington & Hyde Park	Spiffing six-floor Georgian B&B, remodelled with contemporary flair. Rooms aren't huge but there are studio rooms nearby. Pleasant courtyard garden.
NUMBER SIXTEEN ££	Kensington & Hyde Park	Stunning, with 42 individually designed rooms, cosy drawing room and idyllic garden.
LIME TREE HOTEL ££	Kensington & Hyde Park	Smart family-run Georgian town-house hotel with pleasant back garden, contemporary renovations and polite staff.
BLAKES £££	Kensington & Hyde Park	Five Victorian houses cobbled into one hotel, incomparably designed. Each room is distinctive: four-poster beds, rich fabrics and antiques.
GORE £££	Kensington & Hyde Park	Charismatically kooky palace of polished mahogany, oriental carpets, antique-style bathrooms, potted aspidistras, and portraits and prints.
PORTOBELLO HOTEL £££	Kensington & Hyde Park	Beautifully appointed boutique hotel has been a favourite with rock-and-rollers and movie stars.
HOXTON HOTEL ££	Clerkenwell, Hoxton & Spitalfields	Sleek Shoreditch hotel aiming for continually full occupancy with loads of freebies and excellent deals. Small but stylish rooms.
ROOKERY £££	Clerkenwell, Hoxton & Spitalfields	Absolute charmer within a row of 18th-century Georgian houses; antique furniture, original wood panelling and much whimsy.
ZETTER HOTEL & TOWNHOUSE £££	Clerkenwell, Hoxton & Spitalfields	A temple of cool with an overlay of kitsch, small but perfectly formed rooms and lovely rooftop studios with commanding views.
40 WINKS ££	The East End & Docklands	Short on space, not on style; a two-room boutique guesthouse in an old townhouse oozing charm.
TOWN HALL HOTEL & APARTMENTS £££	The East End & Docklands	An erstwhile Edwardian town hall, updated with art deco fea-tures and cutting-edge art. No rooms are identical; apartments are well equipped.

PRACTICALITIES	BEST FOR
☏ 020-7378 2450; www.bermondseysquarehotel.co.uk; Bermondsey Sq, Tower Bridge Rd, SE1; r £99-250, ste £300-500; ❄ @ 🛜; ⊖ Borough	Swinging '60s escapism.
☏ 020-7828 2840; www.cherrycourthotel.co.uk; 23 Hugh St, SW1; s/d/tr £60/68/105; ❄ 🛜; ⊖ Victoria	Great value, central location.
☏ 020-7373 7083; www.yha.org.uk; 38 Bolton Gardens, SW5; dm from £20, tw/d from £48.50/50.50; @ 🛜; ⊖ Earl's Court	Great location, budget bracket.
☏ 020-3318 1407; www.meininger-hostels.com; Baden Powell House, 65-67 Queen's Gate, SW7; dm £16-22, s/tw from £75/90; ❄ @ 🛜; ⊖ Gloucester Rd or South Kensington	Kensington location, non-central prices.
☏ 020-7581 5888; www.asterhouse.com; 3 Sumner Pl, SW7; s £150, d £228-324; ❄ @ 🛜; ⊖ South Kensington	Traditional English charm.
☏ 020-7259 8570; www.bb-belgravia.com; 64-66 Ebury St, SW1; d/apt from £84/225, studio £89-140; @ 🛜; ⊖ Victoria	A snappy, stylish stay.
☏ 020-7589 5232; www.numbersixteenhotel.co.uk; 16 Sumner Pl, SW7; s from £168, d £222-360; ❄ @ 🛜; ⊖ South Kensington	Gorgeous boutique getaway.
☏ 020-7730 8191; www.limetreehotel.co.uk; 135-137 Ebury St, SW1; s £99, d £150-175; @ 🛜; ⊖ Victoria	Great welcome, affordable style.
☏ 020-7370 6701; www.blakeshotels.com; 33 Roland Gardens, SW7; s £195, d £295-395, ste from £695, breakfast £12.50-19.50; ❄ @ 🛜; ⊖ Gloucester Rd	Classic style.
☏ 020-7584 6601; www.gorehotel.com; 190 Queen's Gate, SW7; r from £205; @ 🛜; ⊖ Gloucester Rd	Gorgeous indulgence.
☏ 020-7727 2777; www.portobello-hotel.co.uk; 22 Stanley Gardens, W11; s/d/feature r from £174/234/276; @ 🛜; ⊖ Notting Hill Gate	Exclusive boutique charm.
☏ 020-7550 1000; www.hoxtonhotels.com; 81 Great Eastern St, EC2; d & tw £59-199; @ 🛜; ⊖ Old St	Fine value and stylish stay.
☏ 020-7336 0931; www.rookeryhotel.com; 12 Peter's Lane, Cowcross St, EC1; s £235, d £238-625; ❄ 🛜; ⊖ Farringdon	Mellow elegance.
☏ 020-7324 4444; www.thezetter.com; 86-88 Clerkenwell Rd, EC1M; d from £235, studio £300-450; ❄ 🛜; ⊖ Farringdon	Neat, nifty, exemplary.
☏ 020-7790 0259; www.40winks.org; 109 Mile End Rd, E1; s/d £105/175; 🛜; ⊖ Stepney Green	Exquisite, delicious fun.
☏ 020-7871 0460; www.townhallhotel.com; Patriot Square, E2; d £355-389, apt £410-554, breakfast £17; ❄ 🛜 🏊; ⊖ Bethnal Green	Period style and vintage charm.

NAME		REVIEW
CLINK78 £	Hampstead & North London	Fab hostel with 500 beds in a 19th-century courthouse with heritage features, pod beds (including storage space) and superb kitchen.
CLINK261 £	Hampstead & North London	Refurbished in 2010; a top-notch hostel with bright, funky dorms, a brilliant kitchen and TV lounge.
YORK & ALBANY £££	Hampstead & North London	Luxurious yet cosy, this place oozes Georgian charm with feature fireplaces, antique furniture plus all mod-cons. Five minutes' walk from Camden.
ST PANCRAS RENAISSANCE LONDON HOTEL £££	Hampstead & North London	Gothic, red-brick stunner with a fully-restored interior from grand staircase to Victorian-tiled pool (most rooms not in the original building, though).
ROUGH LUXE £££	Hampstead & North London	Half rough, half luxury, all unique: scraps of old newspaper adorn the walls along with works of art.
ST CHRISTOPHER'S INN GREENWICH £	Greenwich	Hostel-chain branch with 55 beds in quiet and central location next to Greenwich train station, dorms with six to eight beds, lively pub,
CHURCH STREET HOTEL ££	Greenwich	Stylishly individual boutique hotel with colourful and vibrant Mexican theme, cheaper rooms share bathrooms. Sensational breakfast included.
NUMBER 16 ST ALFEGE'S ££	Greenwich	B&B with just two well-appointed doubles and a single, individually decorated in shades of blue, green or yellow and all with bathrooms. Enter from Roan St.

PRACTICALITIES	BEST FOR
☏ 020-7183 9400; www.clinkhostels.com; 78 King's Cross Rd, WC1; dm/r from £9/40; @ 📶; ⊖ King's Cross/St Pancras	History, heritage and budget value.
☏ 020-7833 9400; www.clinkhostels.com; 261-265 Grays Inn Rd, WC1X; dm/r from £9/50; @ 📶; ⊖ King's Cross St Pancras	Great value, perky and popular.
☏ 020-7388 3344; www.gordonramsay.com/yorkandalbany; 127-129 Parkway, NW1; r from £205; ❄ 📶; ⊖ Camden Town	Gorgeously charming with modern touches.
☏ 020-7841 3540; www.marriott.co.uk; Euston Rd, NW1; d from £230; ❄ 📶 ⊠; ⊖ King's Cross St Pancras	Sumptuous magnificence.
☏ 020-7837 5338; www.roughluxe.co.uk; 1 Birkenhead St, WC1H; r £229-289; ❄ 📶; ⊖ King's Cross St Pancras	Trendily different.
☏ 020-8858 3591; www.st-christophers.co.uk; 189 Greenwich High Rd, SE10; dm £10-25, tw £40-55; 📶; �🚆 Greenwich, ⊖ Greenwich	Relative quiet in central location
☏ 020-7703 5984; www.churchstreethotel.com; 29-33 Camberwell Church St, SE5; s £60-90, d £90-170, f £190; ❄ 📶; �🚆 Denmark Hill	Colourful and spicy Greenwich choice
☏ 020-8853 4337; www.st-alfeges.co.uk; 16 St Alfege Passage, SE10; s/d £75/125; 📶; �🚆 DLR Greenwich	Individual, subdued style

Transport

●●●●
Getting to London

Most people arrive in London by air. The city has five airports: Heathrow, which is the largest, to the west; Gatwick to the south; Stansted to the northeast; Luton to the northwest; and London City in the Docklands.

Most trans-Atlantic flights land at Heathrow (average flight time from the US East Coast is between 6½ and 7½ hours, 10 to 11 hours from the West Coast; slightly more on the return).

Visitors from Europe are more likely to arrive at Gatwick, Stansted or Luton (the latter two are used exclusively by low-cost airlines such as easyJet and Ryanair). Most flights to continental Europe last from one to three hours.

An increasingly popular form of transport is the Eurostar – the Channel Tunnel train – between London and Paris or Brussels. The journey lasts 2¼ hours to Paris and less than two hours to Brussels. Travellers depart from and arrive in the centre of each city.

Flights and tours can be booked online at lonelyplanet.com/bookings.

Air

Heathrow Airport
Some 15 miles west of central London, **Heathrow** (LHR; www.heathrowairport.com) is the world's busiest international airport and has five terminals, including the totally revamped Terminal 2.

Train
Underground (www.tfl.gov.uk) Three stations on the Piccadilly Line serve Heathrow: one for Terminals 1, 2 and 3, another for Terminal 4, and the terminus for Terminal 5. The Underground, commonly referred to as 'the tube' (one way £5, from central London one hour, every three to nine minutes) is the cheapest way of getting to Heathrow.

....

Heathrow Express (www.heathrowexpress.com; one way/return £20/34, 15 minutes, every 15 minutes) This high-speed train whisks passengers from Heathrow Central station (serving Terminals 1, 2 and 3) and Terminal 5 to Paddington. Terminal 4 passengers should take the free inter-terminal shuttle train available to Heathrow Central and board there.

....

Heathrow Connect (www.heathrowconnect.com; one way £9.50, 25 minutes, every half hour) Travelling between Heathrow and Paddington station, this modern passenger train service departs every 25 minutes and makes five stops en route at places like Southall and Ealing Broadway.

Bus
National Express (www.nationalexpress.com; one way from £5.50, 45 minutes to 90 minutes, every 30 minutes to one hour) services link the Heathrow Central Bus Station with Victoria coach station about 45 times per day. At night the **N9 bus** (£1.40, 1¼ hours, every 20 minutes) connects Heathrow with central London.

Taxi
A metered black cab trip to/from central London will cost between £45 and £65 (£60 from Oxford St) and take 45 minutes to an hour.

Gatwick Airport
Located some 30 miles south of central London, **Gatwick** (LGW; www.gatwickairport.com) is smaller than Heathrow. The North and South Terminals are linked by a 24-hour shuttle train, with the journey time about three minutes.

Train
National Rail (☎ 0845 7484950; www.nationalrail.co.uk) There are regular train services to/from London Bridge (30 minutes, every 15 to 30 minutes), King's Cross (55 minutes, every 15 to 30 minutes) and London Victoria (30 minutes, every 10 to 15 minutes). Fares are £8 to £10 for a single.

....

Gatwick Express (www.gatwickexpress.com; one way/return £19.90/34.90, 30 minutes, every 15 minutes) This dedicated train service links the station near the South Terminal with Victoria station in central London.

Bus

National Express (www.nationalexpress.com; one way from £7, 65 minutes to 90 minutes) coach services run throughout the day from Gatwick airport to Victoria coach station. Services to and from the airport run at least once an hour.

easyBus (www.easybus.co.uk; one way £10, return from £12) This budget outfit runs 19-seater minibuses every 10 to 20 minutes from Earl's Court/West Brompton to Gatwick from 3am to 12.30am daily. Journey time averages 75 minutes.

Taxi

A metered black cab trip to/from central London costs about £90 and takes just over an hour.

Stansted Airport

Stansted (STN; www.stanstedairport.com) is 35 miles north-east of central London.

Train

Stansted Express (📞 0845 8500150; www.stanstedexpress.com) rail service (one way/return £23.40/32.80, 45 minutes, every 15 to 30 minutes) links the airport and Liverpool St station.

Bus

National Express (www.nationalexpress.com) coaches run around the clock, offering well over 100 services per day. The A6 runs to Victoria coach station (one way from £10, 85 to 110 minutes, every 10 to 20 minutes) via north London.

The A9 runs to Liverpool St Station (one way from £8, 70 minutes, every 30 minutes).

Terravision (www.terravision.eu) These coaches link Stansted to both Liverpool St train station (bus A51, one way/return from £9/15, 55 minutes) and Victoria coach station (bus A50, one way/return from £8/14, 75 minutes) every 20 to 40 minutes between 6am and 1am.

Taxi

A metered black cab trip to/from central London costs around £90.

Luton Airport

A smallish airport 32 miles northwest of London, **Luton** (LTN; www.london-luton.co.uk) generally caters for cheap charter flights and discount airlines.

Train

National Rail services (www.nationalexpress.com; one way from £15, 30 to 40 minutes, every six to 15 minutes, from 7am to 10pm) run from London Bridge and King's Cross St Pancras stations to Luton Airport Parkway station, from where an airport shuttle bus will take you to the airport in eight minutes.

Bus

easyBus (www.easybus.co.uk; one way £10, from £12 return, one hour, every 30 minutes) minibuses run from Victoria coach station to/from Luton via Marble Arch, Baker St and Finchley Rd tube stations

Climate Change & Travel

Every form of transport that relies on carbon-based fuel generates CO_2, the main cause of human-induced climate change. Modern travel is dependent on aeroplanes, which might use less fuel per kilometre per person than most cars but travel much greater distances. The altitude at which aircraft emit gases (including CO_2) and particles also contributes to their climate change impact. Many websites offer 'carbon calculators' that allow people to estimate the carbon emissions generated by their journey and, for those who wish to do so, to offset the impact of the greenhouse gases emitted with contributions to portfolios of climate-friendly initiatives throughout the world. Lonely Planet offsets the carbon footprint of all staff and author travel.

every half-hour round the clock.

Green Line Bus 757 (www.greenline.co.uk) Buses from/to Luton (one way/return £17/25, tickets valid three months, 75 to 90 minutes) run to/from Buckingham Palace Rd just south of Victoria station, leaving approximately every half-hour round the clock.

Taxi

A metered black cab trip to/from central London costs about £75.

Oyster Card

The Oyster card is a smart card on which you can store credit towards so-called 'prepay' fares, as well as Travelcards. Oyster cards are valid across the entire public transport network in London. All you need to do when passing through the turnstile is to touch your card on a reader (which has a yellow circle with the image of an Oyster card on it) and then touch again on your way out. For bus journeys, you only need to touch when you are boarding.

The benefit lies in the fact that fares for Oyster-users are lower than standard ones.

Oyster cards can be bought (£5 refundable deposit) and topped up at any Underground station, travel info centre or shop displaying the Oyster logo.

Getting Around London

Public transport in London is extensive, often excellent and always pricey. It is managed by **Transport for London** (www.tfl.gov.uk), which has a user-friendly, multilingual website with a journey planner, maps, detailed information on every mode of transport in the capital and live updates on traffic.

The tube, DLR and Overground network are ideal for zooming across different parts of the city; buses and the new Barclays bikes are great for shorter journeys. Use an Oyster card for the cheapest fares.

London City Airport

Its proximity to central London, which is just 6 miles to the west, and to the commercial district of Canary Wharf means **London City Airport** (LCY; www.londoncityairport.com) is predominantly a gateway airport for business travellers, although it does also serve holidaymakers with its 40-odd continental European and half-dozen national destinations. You can also now fly to New York from here.

Train

Docklands Light Railway (DLR; www.tfl.gov.uk/dlr) stops at the London City Airport station (one way £4.50, with an Oyster card £2.10 to £3.90). The journey to Bank usually takes just over 20 minutes.

Taxi

A metered black cab trip to or from the City/Oxford St costs about £30.

Train

Main national rail routes are served by InterCity trains, which are neither cheap nor punctual. Check **National Rail Enquiries** (0845 748 4950; www.nationalrail.co.uk) for timetables and fares.

....

Eurostar (www.eurostar.com) The high-speed rail service links St Pancras International Station with Gare du Nord in Paris (or Bruxelles Midi in Brussels), with between 14 and 16 daily departures. Fares vary enormously, from £69 for the cheapest return to almost £310 for a fully flexible return at busy periods.

Bus

....

National Express (www.nationalexpress.com) This is the main coach operator in the UK, with generally comfortable and reliable services to/from Victoria Coach Station (Map p152; 164 Buckingham Palace Rd, SW1; Victoria).

Underground, DLR & Overground

The London Underground ('the tube'; 11 colour-coded lines), is part of an integrated transport system that also includes the Docklands Light Railway (DLR; a driverless overhead train operating in the eastern part of the city) and Overground network (mostly outside of Zone 1 and sometimes underground). Despite the never-ending upgrades and 'engineering works' requiring weekend closures, it is overall the quickest and easiest way of getting around the city, if not the cheapest.

The first trains operate from around 5.30am Monday to Saturday and 6.45am Sunday. The last trains leave around 12.30am Monday to Saturday and 11.30pm Sunday.

Fares

London is divided into nine concentric fare zones.

It will always be cheaper to travel with an Oyster card than a paper ticket.

Children aged 10 and under travel free.

Bus

There are excellent bus maps at every stop detailing all routes and destinations served from that particular area. Bus services normally operate from 5am to 11.30pm.

Night Bus

More than 50 night bus routes (prefixed with the letter 'N') run from around 11.30pm to 5am.

There are also another 60 bus routes operating 24 hours; the frequency decreases between 11pm and 5am.

Fares

Oyster cards are valid on all bus services, including night buses, and are cheaper than cash fares. Bus journeys cost a flat fare (non-Oyster/Oyster £2.40/1.40) regardless of how far you go.

At bus stops with a yellow background, if you don't have an Oyster card, you must buy your ticket *before* boarding the bus at the stop's ticket machine (exact change only).

Children under 11 travel for free.

Taxi

The London **black cab** (www.londonblackcabs.co.uk) is as much a feature of the cityscape as the red bus double-decker bus.

Cabs are available for hire when the yellow sign above the windscreen is lit; just stick your arm out to signal one.

Fares are metered, with the flag-fall charge of £2.20 (covering the first 336m during a weekday), rising by increments of 20p for each subsequent 168m.

Fares are more expensive in the evenings and overnight. To tip just round up to the nearest pound.

Boat

There are a number of companies operating along the River Thames. Only **Thames Clippers** (www.thamesclippers. com; adult/child £6.50/3.25) really offers commuter services, however.

Boats run every 20 to 30 minutes from 6am to between 10pm and midnight. The route goes from London Eye Millennium Pier to Woolwich Arsenal Piers, serving London Eye, Tate Modern, Shakespeare's Globe, Borough Market, Tower Bridge, Canary Wharf, Greenwich and the O2.

Car & Motorcycle

As a visitor, it's very unlikely you'll need to drive in London. If the traffic jams don't dis-

Barclays Cycle Hire Scheme

London has its own cycling-hire scheme called **Barclays bikes** (☎ 0845 026 3630; www.tfl.gov.uk.) but universally known as 'Boris bikes' after Mayor Boris Johnson, who launched the initiative.

The idea is simple: pick up a bike from one of the 570 docking stations dotted around the capital. Cycle. Drop it off at another docking station.

The access fee costs £2 for 24 hours, £10 for a week. All you need is a credit or debit card.

Hire rates:

Up to 30min	free
Up to 1hr	£1
Up to 1½hrs	£4
Up to 3hrs	£15
Up to 24hrs (maximum)	£50

You can take as many bikes as you like during your access period (24 hours or one week), leaving five minutes between each trip.

You must be 18 to buy access to a bike and at least 14 to ride.

courage you, the congestion charge, extortionate parking fees, high price of petrol, fiendishly efficient traffic wardens and wheel clamps/boots will!

Congestion Charge

London followed Singapore's lead in 2003 and introduced a congestion charge to reduce the flow of traffic into its centre. For full details log on to www.tfl.gov.uk/roadusers/congestioncharging.

Hire

There's no shortage of car hire agencies in London. The following rental agencies have branches across the capital:

easyCar (www.easycar.com)

Avis (www.avis.com)

Hertz (www.hertz.com)

Tours

🚢 Boat

Circular Cruise (📞 020-7936 2033; www.crownriver.

com; adult/child/family one way £9.50/4.75/28.50, return £12.30/6.15/36.90; 🕙 11am-6.30pm late May-early Sep, to 5pm early Apr-late May & early Sep-Oct) Vessels travel east from Westminster Pier to St Katharine's Pier near the Tower of London and back, calling at Embankment, Festival and Bankside Piers.

Thames River Services (www.thamesriverservices.co.uk; adult/child single £12/6, return £15.50/7.75) These cruise boats leave Westminster Pier for Greenwich, stopping at the Tower of London.

🚌 Bus

Big Bus Tours (www.bigbustours.com; adult/child/family £29/12/70; 🕙 every 20min 8.30am-6pm Apr-Sep, to 5pm Oct & Mar, to 4.30pm Nov-Feb) Informative commentaries in eight languages.

Specialist Tours

Guide London (Association of Professional Tourist Guides; 📞 020-7611 2545; www.

guidelondon.org.uk; half-/full day £140/225) Hire a prestigious Blue Badge Tourist Guide, know-it-all guides who have studied for two years and passed a dozen written and practical exams to do their job. Go by car, public transport, bike or on foot.

Directory

Customs Regulations

The UK distinguishes between goods bought duty-free outside the EU and those bought in another EU country, where taxes and duties will have already been paid.

For European goods, there is officially no limit to how much you can bring but customs use certain guidelines to distinguish between personal and commercial use.

Discount Cards

Of interest to visitors who want to take in lots of paid sights in a short time is

Import Restrictions

ITEM	DUTY-FREE	TAX & DUTY PAID
Tobacco	200 cigarettes, 100 cigarillos, 50 cigars or 250g tobacco	800 cigarettes, 400 cigarillos, 200 cigars, 1kg tobacco
Spirits & liqueurs	1L spirit or 2L of fortified wine (eg sherry or port)	10L spirit, 20L fortified wine
Beer & wine	16L beer and 4L still wine	110L beer, 90L still wine
Other goods	Up to a value of £390	n/a

the **London Pass** (www.
londonpass.com; per 1/2/3/6
days £47/64/77/102). It offers
free entry and queue-jumping
to all major attractions and
can also include travel on the
Underground and buses for an
extra fee. Check the website
for details.

Electricity

230V/50Hz

Emergency

Dial 999 to call the police, fire
brigade or ambulance in the
event of an emergency.

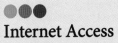

Internet Access

Almost all hotels in London
now provide wi-fi, although
a few, particularly top-end
places, continue to charge for
the service.

A huge number of cafes
offer free wi-fi to customers,
including chains such as
Starbucks, Cafe Nero, Costa
and Pret a Manger as well as
McDonalds.

Open-air and street wi-fi
access is available in areas
across London, including
Oxford St, Trafalgar Sq,
Piccadilly Circus, the City of
London and Islington's Upper
St. Users have to register but
there is no charge.

Most major train stations,
airport terminals and even
certain Underground stations
also have wi-fi access, but it
can be quite pricey.

Medical Services

EU nationals can obtain free
emergency treatment (and,
in some cases, reduced-cost
healthcare) on presenta-
tion of a **European Health
Insurance Card** (www.ehic.
org.uk).

Reciprocal arrangements
with the UK allow Australians,
New Zealanders and residents
and nationals of several other
countries to receive free
emergency medical treatment
and subsidised dental care
through the **National
Health Service** (NHS;
☎ 0845 4647; www.nhs.uk).

Dental Services

For emergency dental care,
visit the NHS website or call
into **University College
London Hospital** (☎ 020-
3447 0083; www.uclh.org; 235
Euston Rd, NW1; ⊖ Euston Sq
or Warren St).

Hospitals

The following hospitals
have 24-hour accident and
emergency departments.
However, in an emer-
gency just call 999 and an
ambulance will normally be
dispatched from the hospital
nearest to you.

Charing Cross Hospital
(☎ 020-3311 1234; www.
imperial.nhs.uk/charingcross;
Fulham Palace Rd, W6;
⊖ Hammersmith)

**Chelsea & Westminster
Hospital** (☎ 020-8746 8000;
www.chelwest.nhs.uk; 369
Fulham Rd, SW10; 🚌 then 14
or 414, ⊖ South Kensington or
Fulham Broadway)

Guy's Hospital (☎ 020-7188
7188; www.guysandstthomas.
nhs.uk; Great Maze Pond, SE1;
⊖ London Bridge)

Money

Although it is a member of the
EU, the UK has not adopted
the euro and has retained the
pound sterling (£) as its unit
of currency.

One pound sterling is made
up of 100 pence (called 'pee'
colloquially).

Notes come in
denominations of £5, £10,
£20 and £50, while coins are
1p ('penny'), 2p, 5p, 10p, 20p,
50p, £1 and £2.

Unless otherwise noted,
all prices in this guide are in
pounds sterling.

ATMs

ATMs are located everywhere
and will generally accept
Visa, MasterCard, Cirrus or

Practicalities

o **Weights & Measures** The UK uses a confusing mix of metric and imperial systems.

o **Smoking** Forbidden in all enclosed public places nationwide. Most pubs have some sort of smoking area outside.

Maestro cards, as well as more obscure ones. There is almost always a transaction surcharge for cash withdrawals with foreign cards. There are nonbank-run ATMs that charge £1.50 to £2 per transaction (usually inside shops).

Changing Money

The best place to change money is in any local post office branch, where no commission is charged.

You can also change money in most high-street banks and some travel agencies, as well as at the numerous bureaux de change throughout the city.

Credit & Debit Cards

Credit and debit cards are accepted almost universally in London, from restaurants and bars to shops and even by some taxis.

American Express and Diners Club are far less widely used than Visa and MasterCard.

Tipping

Many restaurants add a 'discretionary' service charge to your bill. In places that don't, you are expected to leave 10% extra unless the service was unsatisfactory.

Opening Hours

The following table summarises standard opening hours. Reviews will list exact times for each venue.

Sights	10am-6pm
Banks	9am-5pm Mon-Fri
Shops	9am-7pm Mon-Sat, noon-6pm Sun
Restaurants	noon-2.30pm & 6-11pm
Pubs & bars	11am-11pm

Post

The **Royal Mail** (www.royal-mail.co.uk) is no longer the humdinger it once was but is generally reliable.

Postal Rates

Domestic 1st-class mail is quicker (next working day) but more expensive (60p per letter under 100g) than 2nd class (50p), which takes three working days.

Postcards and letters up to 40g cost £1.28 to anywhere in Europe; to everywhere else it's £1.88.

Airmail letters to the USA or Canada generally take three to five days; to Australia or New Zealand, allow five days to a week.

Public Holidays

Most attractions and businesses close for a couple of days over the Christmas period and sometimes Easter as well.

New Year's Day 1 January

Good Friday Late March/April

Easter Monday Late March/April

May Day Holiday First Monday in May

Spring Bank Holiday Last Monday in May

Summer Bank Holiday Last Monday in August

Christmas Day 25 December

Boxing Day 26 December

Taxes & Refunds

Value-added tax (VAT) is a sales tax of up to 20% levied on most goods and services except food, books and children's clothing. Restaurants must, by law, include VAT in their menu prices, although VAT is not always included in hotel room prices so always ask when booking.

It's sometimes possible for visitors to claim a refund

of VAT paid on goods. You're eligible if you have spent fewer than 365 days out of the two years prior to making the purchase living in the UK, and if you're leaving the EU within three months of making the purchase.

Not all shops participate in what is called either the VAT Retail Export Scheme or Tax Free Shopping, and different shops will have different minimum purchase conditions (normally around £75 in any one shop). On request, participating shops will give you a special form (VAT 407). This must be presented with the goods and receipts to customs when you depart the country. (VAT-free goods can't be posted or shipped home.)

●●●●
Telephone

British Telecom's famous red phone boxes survive in conservation areas only (notably the Westminster area).

Some BT phones still accept coins, but most will take phonecards (these are available from retailers, including most post offices and some newsagents) or credit cards.

Useful phone numbers (charged calls) include:

Directory enquiries, international (☎118 505, ☎118 102)

Directory enquiries, local & national (☎118 118, ☎118 500)

Operator, international (☎155)

Phone codes worth knowing:

International dialling code (☎00)

Local call rate applies (☎08457)

National call rate applies (☎0870 & ☎0871)

Premium rate applies (☎09) From 65p per minute

Toll-free (☎0800)

Calling London

London's area code is 020, which is followed by an eight-digit number beginning with 7 (central London), 8 (Greater London) or 3 (non-geographic).

You only need to dial the 020 when you are calling London from elsewhere in the UK or if you're dialling from a mobile.

To call London from abroad, dial your country's international access code (usually 00 but 011 in Canada and the USA), then 44 (the UK's country code), then 20 (dropping the initial 0), followed by the eight-digit phone number.

International Calls & Rates

International direct dialling (IDD) calls to almost anywhere can be made from nearly all public telephones. Direct dialling is cheaper than making a reverse-charge (collect) call through the international operator (155).

Many private firms offer cheaper international calls than BT. In such places you phone from a metered booth and then pay the bill. Some

cybercafes and internet shops also offer cheap rates for international calls.

International calling cards with stored value (usually £5, £10 or £20) and a PIN, which you can use from any phone by dialling a special access number, are usually the cheapest way to call abroad. These cards are available for purchase at most corner shops.

Skype may be restricted in some hostels and internet cafes because of noise and/or band-width issues.

Local & National Call Rates

Local calls are charged by time alone; regional and national calls are charged by both time and distance.

Daytime calling rates apply from 7am to 7pm Monday to Friday.

The cheap rate applies from 7pm to 7am Monday to Friday and again over the weekend from 7pm Friday to 7am Monday.

Mobile Phones

The UK uses the GSM 900 network, which covers Europe, Australia and New Zealand, but is not compatible with the North American GSM 1900 or Japanese mobile technology.

If you have a GSM phone, check with your service provider about using it in the UK and enquire about roaming charges.

It's usually better to buy a local SIM card from any mobile-phone shop, though in order to do that you must ensure your handset from home is unlocked before leaving home.

●●● Time

Wherever you are in the world, the time on your watch is measured in relation to the time at Greenwich in London – Greenwich Mean Time (GMT). British Summer Time, the UK's form of daylight-savings time, muddies the water so that even London is ahead of GMT from late March to late October.

Paris	GMT +1
New York	GMT -5
San Francisco	GMT -8
Sydney	GMT +10

●●● Tourist Information

Visit London (☎ 0870 156 6366; www.visitlondon.com) Can fill you in on everything from tourist attractions, festivals and events (such as the Changing of the Guard and Chinese New Year parade) to river trips and city tours, accommodation options, theatre, shopping, children's London, as well as gay and lesbian venues.

Heathrow Airport (Terminal 1, 2 & 3 Underground station; ⏰ 7.15am-8pm Mon-Sat, 8.15am-8pm Sun)

King's Cross St Pancras Station (⏰ 7.15am-9.15pm Mon-Sat, 8.15am-8.15pm Sun)

Liverpool Street Station (⏰ 7.15am-7pm Mon-Sat, 8.15am-7pm Sun)

Piccadilly Circus Underground Station (⏰ 9.15am-7pm)

Victoria Station (⏰ 7.15am-9.15pm Mon-Sat, 8.15am-7pm Sun)

●●● Travellers with Disabilities

For travellers with disabilities, London is an odd mix of user-friendliness and downright disinterest. New hotels and modern tourist attractions are legally required to be accessible to people in wheelchairs, but many historic buildings, B&Bs and guesthouses are in older buildings, which are hard to adapt.

Transport is equally hit and miss, but slowly improving: Only 66 of London's 270 tube stations have step-free access; the rest have escalators or stairs.

The DLR is entirely accessible for people using wheelchairs.

All buses can be lowered to street level when they stop; wheelchair users travel free.

Guide dogs are universally welcome on public transport and in hotels, restaurants, attractions etc.

Transport for London (p284) publishes the *Getting Around London* guide, which contains the latest information on accessibility for passengers with disabilities. Download it from the website.

●●● Visas

The table below indicates who will need a visa for what, but make sure you check the website of the **UK Border Agency** (www.ukba.homeoffice.gov.uk) or with your local British embassy or consulate for the most up-to-date information.

Visa Extensions

Tourist visas can only be extended in clear emergencies (eg an accident, death of a relative). Otherwise you'll have to leave the UK (perhaps going to Ireland or France) and apply for a fresh one. To extend (or attempt to extend) your stay in the UK, ring the **Visa & Passport Information Line** (☎ 0870 606 7766; 40 Wellesley Rd, Home Office's Immigration & Nationality Directorate, Lunar House, Croydon, CR9 2BY; ⏰ 8am-4pm Mon-Fri; 🚉 East Croydon) before your current visa expires.

Visa Requirements

COUNTRY	TOURISM	WORK	STUDY
European Economic Area	X	X	X
Australia, Canada, New Zealand, South Africa, USA	X (for stay of up to 6 months)	√	√
Other nationalities	√	√	√

Women Travellers

Female visitors to London are unlikely to have many problems provided they take the usual big-city precautions. **Lady Mini Cabs** (📞020-7272 3300; www.ladyminicabs. co.uk) based in Archway in north London has women drivers.

Apart from the occasional wolf whistle and unwelcome body contact on the tube, women will find male Londoners reasonably enlightened. Going into pubs alone may not always be a comfortable experience, though it is in no way out of the ordinary.

Marie Stopes International (📞0845 300 8090; www.mariestopes. org.uk; 108 Whitfield St, W1; ⊙8.30am-5pm Mon, Wed & Fri, 9.30am-6pm Tue & Thu; ⊖Warren St) provides contraception, sexual health checks and abortions.

Behind the Scenes

Author Thanks

STEVE FALLON

A million thanks for all the help, advice and suggestions from Lonely Planet authors Emilie Filou, Damian Harper and Vesna Maric. Fellow Blue Badge Tourist Guide Lia Lalli was a gold mine for eating ideas; Stephen Unwin went beyond the call of duty with help on the gay and lesbian sections. As always, I'd like to state my admiration, gratitude and great love for my partner Michael Rothschild.

Acknowledgments

Cover photographs: Front: Tower Bridge, Maurizio Rellini/4Corners; Back: St Paul's Cathedral seen from One New Change, David Bank/AWL

Illustrations pp102-3, pp126-7 byJavier Zarracina.

This Book

This 3rd edition of Lonely Planet's *Discover London* guidebook was coordinated by Steve Fallon, and researched and written by Steve, Emilie Filou, Damian Harper and Vesna Maric. The previous edition was written by Damian Harper, Emilie Filou, Sally Schafer, Vesna Maric and Steve Fallon. This guidebook was commissioned in Lonely Planet's London office, and produced by the following:

Commissioning Editor James Smart
Coordinating Editors Alison Ridgway, Fionnuala Twomey
Senior Cartographer Jennifer Johnston
Book Designer Lauren Egan
Managing Editors Martine Power, Angela Tinson
Senior Editors Karyn Noble, Catherine Naghten
Assisting Editors Paul Harding, Jeanette Wall
Assisting Cartographer Mick Garrett
Assisting Book Designer Wibowo Rusli
Cover Research Naomi Parker
Thanks to Anita Banh, Ryan Evans, Larissa Frost, Briohny Hooper, Genesys India, Jouve India, Asha Ioculari, Wayne Murphy, Chad Parkhill, Trent Paton, Dianne Schallmeiner, Saralinda Turner, Gerard Walker

Index

See also separate subindexes for:

- 🍴 Eating p297
- 🍷 Drinking & Nightlife p298
- ⭐ Entertainment p299
- 🛍 Shopping p300

Sights 000
Map pages 000

Sights 000
Map pages 000

Drinking & Nightlife

Sights 000
Map pages 000

How to Use This Book

These symbols give you the vital information for each listing:

☏	Telephone Numbers	🛜	Wi-Fi Access	🚍	Bus
⊙	Opening Hours	☒	Swimming Pool	⛴	Ferry
P	Parking	✎	Vegetarian Selection	Ⓜ	Metro
⊖	Nonsmoking	🗐	English-Language Menu	Ⓢ	Subway
✳	Air-Conditioning	✚	Family-Friendly	⊖	London Tube
@	Internet Access	✿	Pet-Friendly	🚋	Tram

Look out for these icons:

FREE No payment required

🍃 A green or sustainable option

Our authors have nominated these places as demonstrating a strong commitment to sustainability – for example by supporting local communities and producers, operating in an environmentally friendly way, or supporting conservation projects.

All reviews are ordered in our authors' preference, starting with their most preferred option. Additionally:

Sights are arranged in the geographic order that we suggest you visit them, and within this order, by author preference.

Eating and Sleeping reviews are ordered by price range (budget, mid-range, top end) and within these ranges, by author preference.

Map Legend

Sights
- 🏖 Beach
- ☸ Buddhist
- 🏰 Castle
- ✚ Christian
- 🕉 Hindu
- ☪ Islamic
- ✡ Jewish
- ❶ Monument
- 🏛 Museum/Gallery
- ⊗ Ruin
- 🍷 Winery/Vineyard
- 🐾 Zoo
- ◎ Other Sight

Sports & Activities
- 🤿 Diving/Snorkelling
- 🛶 Canoeing/Kayaking
- ⛷ Skiing
- 🏄 Surfing
- 🏊 Swimming/Pool
- 🚶 Walking
- 🏄 Windsurfing
- ✚ Other Sports & Activities

Eating
- 🍴 Eating

Drinking & Nightlife
- ☕ Drinking
- ☕ Cafe

Entertainment
- 🎭 Entertainment

Shopping
- 🛍 Shopping

Sleeping
- 🛏 Sleeping
- ⛺ Camping

Information
- Post Office
- ❶ Tourist Information

Transport
- ✈ Airport
- ⊗ Border Crossing
- 🚍 Bus
- +⊕+ Cable Car/Funicular
- ⊶ Cycling
- 🚢 Ferry
- 🚝 Monorail
- P Parking
- Ⓢ S-Bahn
- 🚕 Taxi
- +Ⓡ+ Train/Railway
- 🚋 Tram
- ⊖ Tube Station
- Ⓤ U-Bahn
- Ⓜ Underground Train Station
- • Other Transport

Routes
- Tollway
- Freeway
- Primary
- Secondary
- Tertiary
- Lane
- Unsealed Road
- Plaza/Mall
- Steps
-)=(Tunnel
- Pedestrian Overpass
- Walking Tour
- Walking Tour Detour
- Path

Boundaries
- – – – International
- – – – – State/Province
- – – – Disputed
- – – – Regional/Suburb
- Marine Park
- Cliff
- Wall

Geographic
- ❶ Hut/Shelter
- 🚩 Lighthouse
- ⊙ Lookout
- ▲ Mountain/Volcano
- 🌴 Oasis
- ❶ Park
-)(Pass
- 🍴 Picnic Area
- ◎ Waterfall

Hydrography
- River/Creek
- Intermittent River
- Swamp/Mangrove
- Reef
- Canal
- Water
- Dry/Salt/Intermittent Lake
- Glacier

Areas
- Beach/Desert
- Cemetery (Christian)
- Cemetery (Other)
- Park/Forest
- Sportsground
- Sight (Building)
- Top Sight (Building)

Our Story

A beat-up old car, a few dollars in the pocket and a sense of adventure. In 1972 that's all Tony and Maureen Wheeler needed for the trip of a lifetime – across Europe and Asia overland to Australia. It took several months, and at the end – broke but inspired – they sat at their kitchen table writing and stapling together their first travel guide, *Across Asia on the Cheap*. Within a week they'd sold 1500 copies. Lonely Planet was born.

Today, Lonely Planet has offices in Melbourne, London and Oakland, with more than 600 staff and writers. We share Tony's belief that 'a great guidebook should do three things: inform, educate and amuse'.

Our Writers

STEVE FALLON

Coordinating Author, The West End, The City After a dozen years living in the centre of the known universe – East London – Steve cockney-rhymes in his sleep, eats jellied eel for brekkie, drinks lager by the bucketful and dances round the occasional handbag. As always, for this edition of *Discover London* he did everything the hard/fun way: walking the walks, seeing the sights, taking (some) advice from friends, colleagues and the odd taxi driver and digesting everything in sight. Steve is a qualified London Blue Badge Tourist Guide (www.steveslondon.com).

Read more about Steve at:
lonelyplanet.com/members/stevefallon

EMILIE FILOU

The South Bank, Hampstead & North London, Greenwich Emilie was born in Paris, where she lived until she was 18. Following her three-year degree and three gap years, she found herself in London, fell in love with the place and never really left. She now works as a journalist, specialising in Africa, and makes regular trips to the region from her home in North London. For this book, Emilie had the enviable task of researching both North and South London and concluded – controversially – that south of the river is just as lovely as north! You can see her work on www.emiliefilou.com; she tweets at @EmilieFilou.

Read more about Emilie at:
lonelyplanet.com/members/emiliefilou

DAMIAN HARPER

Kensington & Hyde Park, Day Trips Born off the Strand within earshot of Bow Bells (favourable-wind permitting), Damian grew up in Notting Hill way before it was discovered by Hollywood. A onetime Shakespeare and Company bookseller and radio presenter, Damian has been authoring guidebooks for Lonely Planet since the late 1990s. He lives in South London with his wife and two kids, frequently returning to China (his second home).

Read more about Damian at:
lonelyplanet.com/members/damianharper

VESNA MARIC

Clerkenwell, Hoxton & Spitalfields; The East End & Docklands Vesna has lived in London for nearly two decades and still considers this to be the best of all cities. Researching the East End and Spitalfields and Shoreditch areas for this edition has been a treat.

Published by Lonely Planet Publications Pty Ltd
ABN 36 005 607 983
3rd edition – May 2014
ISBN 978 1 74220 880 0
© Lonely Planet 2014   Photographs © as indicated 2014
10 9 8 7 6 5 4 3 2 1
Printed in China

Although the authors and Lonely Planet have taken all reasonable care in preparing this book, we make no warranty about the accuracy or completeness of its content and, to the maximum extent permitted, disclaim all liability arising from its use.